TO BE A SOLDIER

TO BE A SOLDIER

by

Tom McCourt

Southpaw Publications

ISBN: 0-9741568-2-5
Library of Congress Control Number: 2004098417

To Be A Soldier was created and published by:

Southpaw Publications
400 East 3000 South
Price, Utah 84501
(435) 637-4544
www.southpawpublications.net
tom@southpawpublications.net

SOUTHPAW PUBLICATIONS

About the cover:
    The cover photo is the author, Army Lieutenant Tom McCourt. The
picture was taken in early 1968 near Loch Ninh in South Vietnam. The
white shirt is a non-regulation "Love and Peace," hippy-type T-shirt. It
was a borrowed shirt, and the author wore it just long enough to have
his picture taken, as a joke.

Printed By:
Peczuh Printing Co.
P.O. Box 1024 · Price, UT 84501

To all the men
who served with honor
on the battlefields of Vietnam.

TABLE OF CONTENTS

ACKNOWLEDGMENTS

I could never have written this book without Jeannie, the angel who lived this experience with me. She is the girl I left behind when I went to be a soldier, and the beautiful young wife who held my hand across an ocean as I served my country in Vietnam. It was Jeannie who waited faithfully, and sent her love by mail and through the firmament of the heavens to touch my heart.

It was Jeannie who saved all my letters from Vietnam. From that tattered box of memories, intentionally buried for more that thirty years, I have been able to reconstruct a good deal of what went into these pages.

Jeannie is still my sweetheart, my best friend and loving wife of thirty-seven years. She has given me four handsome sons and a lifetime of love and support. Every man should have such a woman.

Author's Introduction

I suppose I could have disguised myself in the pages of a novel, but I have chosen not to do that. This book is written in the first person singular. I use the pronouns "I" and "me" throughout. Vietnam was like that.

Vietnam was a very personal, individual experience for most of us who served there. We went there alone, as battle-field replacements, and joined a unit of strangers. If we were lucky, and not wounded or killed, we did make a few friends, had some adventures, and grew up fast. And then, for those of us who were lucky, came a time to go home again. Once more we traveled alone, and never again heard from those friends we left behind in the jungle. Forty years after the war, some of us still wonder if buddies ever made it home.

Almost three million American soldiers served in Vietnam. Each one has a unique and different story to tell. This is just one of those three million stories.

THE BIG ONE

The bomber came low over the water, alone but charging bravely. The morning sun was at her back as she raced her shadow over the waves. A Japanese fireball dotted each wing, bold and bright in the early morning sunshine. Her propeller slashed through the air like a great Samurai blade. She came low from out of the morning mist, wrapped in a shroud of stealth and strategy. The eyes and the guns of the fleet were turned upward, to the air battles raging high overhead.

Klaxons sounded and hearts stood still as gun turrets spun to meet her. She was closing fast and the scream of her engine threw shockwaves across the ocean. Her deadly intent was obvious and her fate already sealed. The whole craft was a projectile, as sure as a cannon shell.

She came as the Divine Wind of legend and hope, a sacrifice on the Altar of the Rising Sun. Her very presence on the field of battle the gift of a young life, delivered with honor and all earnestness to a lost cause.

Shell bursts splattered against the sky like bugs hitting a windshield, and the bomber came right through them, unflinching, unhurt, and filled with a terrible resolve. She came on madly, wild and reckless, boring headlong into the storm of flak and tracer bullets.

The ship's guns were barking viciously and the noise was deafening. The guns punched at the bomber frantically, desperately reaching out to fend her off, slapping wildly in fear as she bore down on them. Long ribbons of tracer bullets crisscrossed over the water and raked through the ocean waves throwing spouts of water high in the air. Glowing metal slugs skipped along the ocean surface and then bounced away at crazy angles. The air was completely filled with bullets, shell bursts, and waterspouts - and still the bomber came. She was charging desperately and without hope, throwing herself at the guns like a screaming Banshee, bravely plunging into a fiery death.

Tracers thudded into her engine cowling and flecks of metal skin ripped away and fluttered back in the bomber's wake. Her belly exploded in a flash of fire and smoke and she staggered through the air as the bullets took her apart. She was now a mindless burning missile, engineless and pilotless and carried on only by the weight of her own inertia, finally exploding in a shower of burning parts and fluttering wings. She died in a hundred pieces, splashing down over the water like a handful of burning chaff while tracer bullets fought for the scraps.

I sat transfixed as I watched that bomber go down. My emotions were in a tangle. I was fascinated by the loud and riotous spectacle of the guns, the flames, and the skyrocket explosions, and yet, at the same time, I was strangely humbled by what I had just witnessed. There was a man in that airplane ... and I had watched him die. I had never known such violence.

That brave Japanese pilot died in the auditorium of my elementary school. It was a film, a newsreel-type documentary about the not-so-long-ago global war that my father and my uncles had fought in. It was an educational piece, meant to enlighten the children of the World War II generation about the trials and the sacrifices of their fathers. It was about fighting and winning the war in the Pacific. The year was 1955 and the war was ten years over. I was a little boy and in the third grade.

That old wartime newsreel changed my life. As a child, I had heard rumors about the big war that ended just before I was born, but it was never real to me until I saw that bomber hit the water. I was suddenly awakened to the fact that my father had been there when that brave Kamikaze went down. Dad had fought at Leyte Gulf in the Philippines, and from a distance he had watched General McArthur stomp ashore through the surf. I had heard him tell about it many times. Men on dad's little ship shot down two Japanese bombers, just like the one in the newsreel, and some of the men on dad's boat were wounded when a Zero fighter strafed them with machine-gun fire.

After watching that film, dad became more of a hero to me than he had been. He had always been my hero: tall, brave, handsome and strong, but now he was my war hero too. For the first time, I began to understand what had happened when my father went to war.

Dad and his brother Pat had joined the navy at the beginning of World War II, and sailed out into that lake of fire to mete vengeance on the Japanese Empire. They were righteous warriors, brave soldiers who put their lives on the line for freedom, justice, and the American way. They were avenging a great wrong, and they saved the world from tyranny and made it a safe place for peace and democracy. The newsreel used those very words set to a background of fluttering flags and quickstep martial music. At the age of nine, I was charmed. I wanted to be a brave soldier too.

I never forgot the graphic visuals of that documentary film. They were etched into my young mind like acid on glass. Over the next few years I shot down the whole Japanese Air Force. Walking across the farm fields on my way to and from school, I shot down hundreds and hundreds of suicide bombers. In my mind, I could see the enemy on the attack, coming at me from out of the clouds, and I could see my tracer bullets reaching out to club him from the sky. I could see the red dot of the Japanese flag on the wings as the plane heeled over and arched into the hay stubble that was the ocean, long streamers of flame and smoke tracing his path through the sky.

I shot down Zero fighters by the score, sometimes through the gun sights of a fighter plane and sometimes while looking down the long barrels of a make-believe forty-millimeter pom-pom gun. I won my father's war over and over again, and saved the world from tyranny – whatever that was.

At the movie hall, I watched spellbound as John Wayne led Marines across "The Sands of Iwo Jima," and I went "To Hell and Back" with Audie Murphy. I fought with Davy Crockett at the Alamo and killed hundreds of painted savages along the Oregon Trail. I fought Arabs with Beau Geste and Pirates with Errol Flynn. I spent many long and restless hours in a seventh grade English class watching Civil War battles play out on a hill near the school. Cannon smoke, battle flags, bayonets, and cavalry charges blunted the raw edge of those unbearably boring lectures about prepositional phrases and dangling participles. Old Mrs. Holbrook never suspected that the Battle of Gettysburg was happening just out the window and on the other side of the softball field.

As I grew older, I became aware that many of the men in my life had been soldiers. I learned that my neighbor, Mr. Petersen, had been a soldier during the First World War. His good wife kept an old brown and white photograph of him in his soldier's uniform. He was a handsome and vibrant young man in a uniform, and not the weather-beaten old farmer that I knew. There was something magic about uniforms that transformed people.

I discovered that my uncle Glen, my mother's older brother, had served as an Officer and a Gentleman during the war. He was a Captain in the Army Medical Corps and was badly wounded by Japanese shell fragments while rescuing wounded men on one of the Pacific Islands. He had spent a long time in the hospital and had been awarded a Purple Heart. My Grandparents and my family were all so very proud of him. Uncle Glen served in the National Guard after the war, and his unit was activated and sent to Florida during the Cuban Missile Crisis in 1962. Uncle Glen was a warrior of the Cold War when I knew him, and I worried and prayed for him. I always hoped that he wouldn't have to be wounded again, by the Russians.

Glen's father, my maternal grandfather, was a major influence in my young life. He was a patriot, a man proud of America and all she stood for. He was born in 1900 and was a member of that in-between generation, too young to serve in World War I, and too old to serve in World War II ... and he mourned.

Grandpa was an armchair historian, and he knew all about soldiers and soldiering, even though he had never been one. He taught me all about Spartans, Crusaders and Spanish Conquistadors. He could tell the whole story of Napoleon and the Battle of Waterloo, about Robert E. Lee, and about Cortez who conquered the Aztecs. He took me up San Juan Hill with Teddy Roosevelt, and he could talk about Alexander the Great and Richard the Lionhearted. But then of course, his own personal favorite was the rotund and more recent war hero, Sir Winston Churchill. Grandpa would quote Churchill with a big smile on his face and a twinkle in his eye: "We shall fight them on the beaches! We shall fight them in the streets! We will Neva Surrenda!"

My grandfather was a poet at heart, and he made up silly little ditties and memorized serious works from the literary masters. One of his favorite poems to recite was "The Charge of the Light Brigade" by Alfred, Lord Tennyson. "The Charge of the Light Brigade" is the true story of a unit of English cavalry who, by mistake, were ordered to charge Russian cannons during the Crimean War in 1854.

I can still see my grandfather sitting at his kitchen table, elbows on the tablecloth, leaning forward over a steaming cup of coffee as he recited that poem over and over again as I requested it, and struggled to absorb it:

5

To Be A Soldier

Half a league, half a league,
    Half a league onward,
All in the Valley of Death
    Rode the six hundred.
"Forward the Light Brigade!"
"Charge for the guns!" he said:
Into the Valley of Death
    Rode the six hundred.

"Forward the Light Brigade!"
Was there a man dismayed?
Not tho' every soldier knew
    Someone had blundered.
Their's not to make reply,
Their's not to reason why,
Their's but to do and die:
Into the Valley of Death
    Rode the six hundred.

Cannons to the right of them,
Cannons to the left of them,
Cannons in front of them
    Volleyed and thundered:
Stormed at by shot and shell,
Boldly they rode and well,
Into the jaws of Death,
Into the mouth of Hell
    Rode the six hundred.

I saw it happen. As my grandfather recited the lines of that old poem with his eyes shining brightly, I saw those brave cavalry soldiers sweep across that valley, sabers flashing in the sun, as they died a gallant death. I mourned at the senseless waste of such a noble sacrifice, but at the same time, I was captivated by the glory of it all. As a boy, I wanted to brandish a gleaming saber and make the charge with them. I wanted to spur a great, thundering warhorse into the enemy ranks and take those smoking cannons. I wanted to return with my head held high and with my saber dripping blood, to take my place in the ranks of honor. I wanted to ride home at the head of the column and carry the tattered battle flag of the Regiment to be presented to the King. I wanted people to notice when I walked past them, and to hear them whisper one to another, "There goes a brave and noble soldier, home from the wars."

My resolve to be a warrior grew with my body and my years. As I reached my early teenage years, I was more and more determined to be a soldier. I watched in awe as American Legion members in our little town marched in parades and carried rifles and flags. Many of them were veterans of the First World War. The men and the uniforms were old and tattered, but the pride was born anew with each holiday and each new parade. The old soldiers marched proudly for their families and their loved ones. As those gallant old warriors paraded past in the shadow of the flags, we all cheered and took our hats off in reverent respect. I was enthralled.

While still in junior high school, I played "Taps" on my trumpet at the cemetery on Memorial Day, as the Veterans of Foreign Wars fired a rifle salute to fallen comrades. I was deeply touched to be a part of the ceremony. The VFW men were dressed in old uniforms bedecked with ribbons, stripes, and polished brass. They were brave old soldiers, but I saw that some had tears in their eyes when that Honor Guard was dismissed. At the age of fourteen, I knew that my life would never be complete until I was an honored member of that brotherhood of soldiers.

WARS AND RUMORS OF WARS

America has always been a nation of warriors. Only the boldest and the bravest of the blood of Europe made the perilous Atlantic crossing to settle the new world in the early years of the Age of Discovery. And then, it took brave hearts to venture into the vast, interior wilderness. There, our forefathers fought men, animals, and the raw forces of the natural world. It was a great winnowing process, and the weak links in the genetic chain were purged. Only the strong survived. Early America became a land of warrior farmers, always pressing the frontier, ever willing to fight.

Our country has a long history of conflict and war. The earliest settlers built stockaded towns and had frequent conflicts with the indigenous peoples of the Atlantic coast. At the same time, they dealt with pirates and privateers on the high seas. Supply lines from Mother England were long and thin. The pilgrims fought storms, severe winters, and looming starvation as bravely as they fought other men. They fought four French and Indian Wars in the forests of the old Northwest between 1689 and 1763.

Our nation was born from the ashes of a War of Independence that began in 1776. It was a family quarrel, and we drove our brothers, the Englishmen, out of the family circle. And then, soldiers from the newly formed United States of America fought their English brothers, cousins, and best friends again in 1812. They beat up their neighbors the Mexicans in 1845, and then fought each other through the 1860s (the American Civil War). Our soldiers then spent the next thirty years sending Native Americans to reservations and the Happy Hunting Grounds in what would be known as the Indian Wars of the American West. In 1898 we took on Spain, and in 1916 we sent troops against Poncho Villa inside old Mexico. We fought Germans in 1918, and went back to do it again in 1942. We whipped the Italians and rescued the French. We fought the Japanese for four long years in the 1940s, and then the North Koreans and Chinese communists beginning in 1950. In the second half of the twentieth century, American troops fought in Vietnam, Cambodia, Laos, Haiti, Grenada, Panama, Somalia, Bosnia, and Afghanistan. We went all out against the Iraqi Army in "The Mother of all Battles" in 1991, and we did it again in 2003. September 11, 2001, made us all participants in a worldwide guerrilla war that has yet to be resolved.

Precious few Americans have known the peace and contentment that our Constitution and Declaration of Independence promise. Every ten or twenty years since the birth of our nation, our citizens have been called to man the guns. My generation was no exception.

My generation received our call to arms in the mid-1960s. It was to become the longest and most controversial war in our nation's history. Our war was different from the wars our fathers had known. It was an unconventional war, a civil war, a guerrilla war, an ideological war, a political war, a war of aggression, a war of attrition, and a war of dissention, all rolled into one. And ... it had been a long time in the making. America's involvement in Vietnam began in 1954, when most of the soldiers who would fight there were in the early grades of elementary school.

In a nutshell, here is how it happened:

At the end of the Second World War, the French Army, recently rescued from Nazi tyranny, marched back into "French

Indochina" to reclaim and re-tyrannize their old colonies there. The French colonial empire dated back to the 1850s, and for almost a hundred years France had dominated the area. Five generations of Frenchmen had skimmed the cream of Southeast Asian produce and resources. Originally, French Indochina included all of Vietnam, Laos and Cambodia.

At the beginning of World War II, the Japanese kicked the Frenchmen out and held the ground during the war. The century-old iron grip of French colonialism was broken. Unfortunately, once the war was over and the Japanese were defeated, the Frenchmen expected things to return to "normal" again. After all, "French Indochina" belonged to France. The French were soon to learn that times had changed. Their former subjects would have none of it.

A man named Ho Chi Minh became the leader of the anti-French rebels. He was a remarkable man: an intellectual, a world traveler, and a warrior of the first order. He was a communist by inclination, but a true nationalist at heart. He first came to prominence during the Second World War.

When Japan invaded Vietnam in 1940, many Vietnamese expected the Imperial Japanese Army to be their saviors. Surely, their Asian cousins would rescue them from French bondage and they could all live in peace and harmony ever after. Sadly, it was not to be. The Japanese brutalized the Vietnamese as they did all other conquered peoples. The Japanese were indifferent to race, national origin and religious preference. They were equal opportunity oppressors. The Vietnamese learned to hate them.

Ho Chi Minh was living in Russia when the war started, studying communism first-hand. When the Japanese invaded his French-dominated homeland, he went back to be a freedom fighter and the Marxist Father of his Country. To counter the Japanese, Ho Chi Minh organized a resistance group known as the Vietminh. Uncle Ho, as his devoted followers sometimes called him, led a guerilla war against the Japanese occupation. His Vietminh soldiers learned lessons and tactics that would be invaluable to them in the horrors to come.

In September 1945, as the tattered remnants of the Japanese Army retreated to the confines of their defeated island nation, Ho Chi Minh declared Vietnam an Independent Nation. He put the French government on notice that things would not return to the pre-World War II status quo. It is said that the American Declaration of Independence might have been his inspiration.

Sadly, by standing up to the Frenchmen, Ho Chi Minh found himself to be an enemy of the Americans. France was an "ally" of the Americans in the Post World War II era and Washington (President Harry Truman) turned a blind eye to the attempted re-subjugation of the former French Colonies. After all, the French had ruled Vietnam for 100 years and had a "right" to reinstate their claim. And besides, French colonialism was the lesser of two evils. Better to have the people of Southeast Asia under the thumb of the capitalist Frenchmen than in the sphere of the evil communists. The will of the weak and humble Vietnamese people didn't seem to matter in the big scheme of things.

The Frenchmen carried their tri-colored flag back to the old colonies in 1946, and true to Ho Chi Minh's warnings, they were greeted by bullets instead of cheers. Rebellion was in the wind. Vietnamese farmers took up arms. Between 1946 and 1954, war raged in French Indochina.

The war waxed and waned for eight long years, slowly eating away at French resources and French resolve. The French people grew tired of the constant flow of casualties and the constant drain on the national treasury. The war became a political liability in Paris. The Americans tried to help by sending supplies and materiel to the beleaguered French Army, but the French were outgeneraled and unable to make headway against a determined foe.

And then, when the Frenchmen were tired, discouraged, low on morale and home-front support, Ho Chi Minh's guerilla army overran the French garrison at Dien Bien Phu and helped the Frenchmen take down their flag. An estimated 2,200 French defenders were killed during the fight and more than 10,000 were taken prisoner. The number of Vietnamese casualties is not known, but is thought to be much higher. Shock waves from the battle sent ripples all around the world.

The defeat of the French Army set a precedent. Ho Chi Minh had shown the world a blueprint for successful guerilla war. An army of peasant farmers could beat a superpower if the formula was followed. Hitler had given the world Blitzkrieg - Lightening War. Ho Chi Minh offered the humble doctrine of attrition.

To win by attrition takes a few years, but patience is one of the virtues of the meek who shall inherit the earth. Little pigmies eat big elephants one bite at a time. Ho Chi Minh showed the world that when you don't have the resources to blow your opponent away, the next best thing is to wear him down like sand paper. If you cut him just a little, but cut him often, over the long haul he will die from blood loss and internal infections. It happened to the French and the Americans in Vietnam, and it happened to the Russians in Afghanistan.

In 1954, Ho Chi Minh and the retreating Frenchmen signed a peace agreement in Geneva Switzerland that temporarily divided Vietnam in half. The communists got the Northern half. The French-leaning factions got the Southern half. Ho Chi Minh assumed control in the North. The French-supported Bao Dai Government kept control in the South.

The Geneva Accords called for a nationwide election in 1956 to reunify the country and settle the issue of sovereignty once and for all. The fate of the whole nation, North and South, would be determined by the will of the people. It was a good plan, and both sides agreed to those terms.

Posturing and campaigning began in earnest. The communists consolidated their gains in North Vietnam and the Chinese communists were eager to help. In South Vietnam, Americans took over for the war-weary Frenchmen and stepped in to support the fledgling "Republic of South Vietnam." With no hope of ever getting their colonies back, the Frenchmen lost interest in the fate of their former subjects and went home.

It is ironic that America supported the French in their war to re-colonize Vietnam, and then, when the Frenchmen were defeated, we sought to stand with the South Vietnamese and help protect them from communist "aggression." It is obvious that the ultimate goal of the American government was to keep the country free of communism, no matter how it happened. The humanitarian element was a secondary concern.

We were looking after our own interests in Vietnam, but that's not always a bad thing. Communism is an enemy of freedom and democracy. The communist political and economic system is incompatible with individual freedoms, basic human rights, self-determination, free travel and trade. Communism dooms whole cultures to economic serfdom and political slavery. And, it is a godless system. The State becomes the national deity. The moral underpinnings that guide most other economic and political systems are destroyed under a communist regime.

The spread of world communism was accelerating in the early 1950s, and it was alarming. The communists had vowed to "bury" capitalism and democracy everywhere. The Cold War between the two great political philosophies was in full swing worldwide. Armies on both sides were stockpiling nuclear weapons for the final big showdown. It was scary as hell. Both sides were consolidating power and recruiting friends. The whole world was being divided into two camps. And, in Eastern Europe, Asia, Africa, and Latin America, the communists seemed to be making inroads everywhere.

Each small country that slipped behind the Iron Curtain became a potential enemy whose people and resources might be used against us one day. Better to make friends and keep them on our side. Also, when countries went communist, we lost them as prospective markets and trading partners. Capitalism requires customers, consumers, free trade, open borders, individual and social freedoms, the free flow of currency, and lots of raw materials. Communism is against all of those things.

In 1954, we went to Vietnam to make a stand against world communism. We were there to introduce American influence in the region, show support for democracy, curb communist expansion, and make friends and potential trading partners. Our interest was self-serving, but honorable.

In the late 1950s, some brilliant mind who helped to grease the machinery of American foreign policy come up with the idea that the conflict with the communists in Asia was like a game of dominos. If one small country "fell" to the other side, it would topple the one next to it, and so on, until all of the nations in the region had "fallen" into the Communist realm. It was a brilliant piece of propaganda, simple in theory and rich with symbolism. Everyone could visualize the concept. We had to do whatever it took to keep those little dominos from falling.

But, American influence in the region was overshadowed by the strong communist presence of Red China. Chairman Mao was consolidating power and the stain of Chinese communism was seeping across his borders. Ho Chi Minh sought help from his powerful ally to the North, and got it.

The French-appointed leader of South Vietnam was the "Emperor" Bao Dai, a member of the old Vietnamese monarchy.

Through him and his fathers, the Frenchmen had ruled Vietnam for 100 years. Unfortunately, Bao Dai was a man of royal lineage and French cultural assimilation who lacked substance. He had proven himself to be a self-serving collaborator of both the French and the Japanese. He was a worthy nominee to preside over the end of the family dynasty.

In 1955, Bao Dai appointed a man named Ngo Dinh Diem as Prime Minister of South Vietnam. Ngo Dinh Diem was also a Vietnamese Frenchman by education and inclination. As a young man, Diem had adopted French dress, deportment, and the Roman Catholic religion. Diem too was a self-serving individual, and soon after assuming his duties as Prime Minister, he ousted his boss Bao Dai in a rigged national referendum. Diem got more votes in some precincts than the number of registered voters. When the dust settled, the Vietnamese Monarchy was no more. Diem proudly stepped up to the podium as the new "President" of the Republic of South Vietnam.

When the time came for the 1956 elections to decide the fate of the Vietnamese nation, South Vietnamese President Diem refused to allow it. He did so with the blessing and the backing of American President Dwight D. Eisenhower. Things didn't look good for the South in the coming election. Ho Chi Minh and his Vietnamese communists were winning more hearts and minds than the self-serving minions of the Diem regime. The Americans and President Diem decided that half a country in the sphere of democracy was better than no country at all. A precedent for dividing a country between communism and capitalism had recently been set in Korea.

As a reason for violating the Geneva Accords and not allowing the promised elections, Diem told the world that the communists could not be trusted to participate in fair elections. He didn't even blush at the blatant hypocrisy.

The Communists rightfully cried "foul," and beat their swords upon their shields. Eisenhower sent several hundred American civilian and military advisors to South Vietnam to underscore his commitment and give courage and comfort to the Diem regime. The "temporary" dividing line along the seventeenth parallel was drawn on American maps in indelible ink. The idea that there would be two Vietnams forever soaked into the Western consciousness.

President Diem of South Vietnam, emboldened by his chummy relationship with the United States - his big brother protector - then turned his back on his own people. He arrogantly proceeded to dismantle the promised freedoms inherent in a democracy. In 1956, he discontinued all local elections and began to appoint government officials by himself. The appointment system was rife with corruption and stinky nepotism. Diem was setting himself up as a dictator. Of course, this was contrary to what the Republic of South Vietnam was supposed to be all about, and it sowed the seeds of rebellion. North Vietnam was quick to supply aid to the malcontents, and Diem himself gave the rebels a name when he branded them the Viet Cong, an acronym that stood for "Vietnamese Communists."

The ranks of the rebels grew as hatred for the Diem regime spread, and by 1960 there were an estimated 10,000 Viet Cong operatives causing trouble in South Vietnam. The Viet Cong harassed government workers and disrupted travel and commerce. They intimidated village officials and traded bullets with the South Vietnamese military and police. By 1961, the rebellion was strong enough to threaten the overthrow of the government of South Vietnam.

President Kennedy intervened, and America had more than 16,000 military advisors in South Vietnam by early 1963. There was a sort of stalemate until May of that year, and then the excesses of the Diem government provoked an uprising of religious leaders. President Diem and his family were members of a Roman Catholic minority, and the much larger congregation of Buddhists accused them of religious persecutions. The Buddhists were powerful in Vietnam, and they could sway a lot of people. There were riots in the streets. The rioters were violently suppressed by Diem's troops and people were killed.

And then, the magic of television brought gasoline-soaked and self-ignited Buddhist Monks into American living rooms. The stench was awful. The holy men were killing themselves to protest the excesses of the Diem government.

Monks as votive candles was the end of the line for the Kennedy administration. Enough was enough. The shaky Diem government was infested with corruption, rotten with incompetence, seething in civil discontent, encircled by communist guerillas, and now broiling on the flames of a religious uprising. President Kennedy secretly supported a group of South Vietnamese Army Generals in a coup to oust the unpopular leader. Against Kennedy's wishes, Diem and his brother were brutally murdered.

The fall of the Diem government set off a period of turmoil in South Vietnam. The South struggled to put together a viable government while the Communists took full advantage of the chaos. By 1964, the Communists were in control of an estimated 75% of the population of South Vietnam. The North Vietnamese were consolidating their gains and the whole country was marching into Communism. The Vietnamese were voting.

Things looked bad for the Republic of South Vietnam. The weight of the communist leanings was threatening to crush America's little buddy in Southeast Asia. A new American president took notice, and resolved that the United States would not loose face or influence under his watch. Lyndon Johnson, and his global strategist, the Ford Motor Company's whiz kid, Robert McNamara, decided that there was only one sure way to rescue South Vietnam, and that was to commit American troops.

In early 1964, shortly after taking office, Johnson and Secretary of Defense McNamara authorized the use of clandestine "special operations" in both Laos and North Vietnam. The goal was to put "pressure" on the North Vietnamese and to signal American support for the South. American pilots began to fly bombing raids in unmarked or South Vietnamese marked aircraft, and Army Special Forces and Navy Seal Teams began sneaking into "enemy" territory to sabotage, take prisoners, and gather information.

Johnson knew that he was taking the tiger by the tail with his secret military support, but even the mighty Russians had backed down during the Cuban Missile Crisis of only two years before. Surely, subtle reminders of American power and resolve would scare the hell out of the lowly North Vietnamese and keep them in line.

True to his nature, the new president kept his meddling with the communist nation a secret. Congress and the American people had no idea that American soldiers were flying combat missions and cutting throats in the jungles of Vietnam. From the very beginning, Johnson used deceit to cover his tracks from those who might have held him accountable.

It is ironic that during the presidential campaign of 1964, Johnson ran as the "peace candidate." He opposed Senator Barry Goldwater, whom he vilified as a "warmonger" and "dangerous" to the future of the country. The Johnson campaign's TV commercial of the little girl counting daisy pedals while the nuclear countdown progresses in the background has come down to us as the all-time champion of dirty campaign ads. And sadly, while he touted peace from the pulpit, it was Johnson himself with his finger on the trigger and counting down to war. His "special operations" people were

already secretly engaged. The American people, in their innocence, were duped into electing the "peace candidate" by a
landslide. They surely didn't want another war.

In August 1964, during the height of the presidential
campaign, the headlines began screaming about something
called "The Gulf of Tonkin Incident." We were told that evil and
arrogant communists had fired on innocent American warships
cruising in international waters off the coast of Vietnam. It was
an insult to our flag, a challenge to our national will, and an
affront to peace-loving people everywhere. Americans were
outraged. Who did those nasty Asian Communists think they
were dealing with?

Within seventy-two hours, an indignant congress gave
Lyndon Johnson the power to take "all necessary measures to
repel an armed attack against the forces of the United States
and to prevent further aggression." Johnson ordered an immediate bombing campaign against North Vietnam. There was no
formal Declaration Of War.

Years later, we were to learn that covert American military
operations had provoked the Gulf of Tonkin Incident. Navy Seals
had been operating out of Danang, South Vietnam, in PT boats.
They were performing acts of sabotage and actually shelling North
Vietnamese port and shore facilities with rockets and mortars. The
covert actions were codenamed Operations Plan 34A by the
Johnson administration. Only a few of the president's closest advisors were aware. Secretary of Defense Robert McNamara was in
charge of the operations. The American destroyers were standing
by in international waters during the actions to monitor the situation and to be close at hand if needed to support or rescue the
special operations people. Even the sailors on the ships had no
idea about the real purpose for their patrols.

When North Vietnamese gunboats attacked the Destroyers
Maddox and Turner Joy on the night of August 2, 1964, they

were rightfully defending their national sovereignty. They knew the navy ships were somehow involved with the boats that had just attacked North Vietnam. Any nation would have been justified in responding the way they did.

Johnson and McNamara, of course, knew the cause and effect of the incident, but remained silent as congress and the American press rattled the sabers of war. In briefings with top congressional leaders, the President and his Secretary of Defense failed to reveal America's role in provoking the incident. Johnson assumed the demeanor of a reluctant warrior chieftain as he dutifully accepted the congressional mandate that gave him a free hand to defend American honor and conduct combat operations against North Vietnam any way he saw fit. What really happened in the Gulf of Tonkin would remain his little secret for a time.

By orders of the President, American jets with American bombs went winging over North Vietnam to "avenge" the "unprovoked" attack on our Navy ships. The lid to Pandora's box had been opened.

Called to Serve

In May 1965, the newest batch of High School Graduates marched across the stage to receive our diplomas. As we did, Americans everywhere were celebrating the twentieth anniversary of the end of World War II in Europe. There were speeches, parades, and special Memorial Day services. Flags were displayed everywhere, and our fathers and Uncles were proud.

But, as we celebrated the end of the Second World War, a new storm was gathering on the horizon. For the third time in twenty years, war clouds were casting a dark shadow along the far rim of the blue Pacific. Just two months earlier, in March, Lyndon Johnson had committed the first ground forces to combat in Vietnam.

America had air bases in Vietnam by early 1965, and they needed protecting. Marines were sent to do the job. It made for great television. Handsome young Marines stormed ashore and planted the flag like conquering heroes. They were there to make a stand against world communism and to rescue the poor and downtrodden. Seven months had passed since the Gulf of Tonkin Incident in August, 1964.

In retrospect, it seems odd that Marines were Lyndon Johnson's first choice to "defend" the airfields. Something bigger must have been in the works from the very beginning. The US Marine Corps has never been a military force best suited for static defense. Young Marines have always played on America's offensive team.

Soon, on the six o'clock evening news, we were watching black and white television images of firefights, pitched battles, and American casualties. Those handsome young Marines were bleeding and dying as they defended freedom in far-off Southeast Asia. American honor and American pride were on the line and under fire. Most of us didn't know what it was all about, but we were assured the cause was just. Americans were always the good guys in the battle between good and evil.

It was all very exciting to an eighteen-year-old boy like me. It looked like a grand adventure. I longed to wear the uniform and join the fight. My friend, Chester Housekeeper and I, decided to join the Marine Corps right out of high school. Unfortunately (or fortunately, depending on your point of view), our parents talked us out of it. Our fathers had both served in World War II and neither was excited about having a son in the Marine Corps, especially with a new war starting up. Chester and I were disappointed, but we honored our parents and gave up the idea ... for now. Even at the wild and rebellious age of eighteen, we were faithful and obedient sons. Our fathers were happy. The Marines were short a few good men.

We didn't sign up, but Chester and I both knew that we would soon be in uniform. We were single and healthy young men, just out of high school, and the cold-eyed old woman who ran the local draft board would surely have our names on her list. There was no lottery for the draft in those days. Inductees were selected at the discretion of the local draft board.

The shadow of the draft hung heavy over my generation, and it was frustrating. With a new war starting, it was impossible for a young man to plan a future. Kids my age were hesitant to embark on any grand adventures because we knew that any far-reaching, ambitious, and expensive plans might be foiled. Any day, a letter from Uncle Sam might be in the mailbox and our world and our options would change forever. Our government, and especially the local draft board, had control of our destiny, like it or not.

Of course, it wasn't supposed to happen, but local politics, race, family name, pedigree, and social standing were factors that sometimes influenced the decisions about who was drafted and who was not. It was to become a point of contention all across the country. A few years later, a lottery system was implemented to limit the "discretions" of the local draft officials.

As in all wars, there were young men who sought exclusions from military service ... some by creative means. Some of our friends were able to secure draft deferments by getting married as teenagers, or by becoming perpetual college students. Some set out into the wilds of the world as Peace Corps volunteers or church missionaries, while others worked hard at developing a paper trail of medical problems like asthma or bad feet. Some, who could, used political connections or the shield of wealth and privilege to stay out of the military. In the coming years, some would flee to Canada.

Chester and I wanted to be soldiers, and so we just waited for it to happen. I did complete one semester at the local junior college (college was not a draft exemption in 1966), but my grades were atrocious. I couldn't concentrate on schoolwork. I was far too anxious about the war. My heart and mind were with the soldiers. I longed to get on with it. Every morning I checked the mail, waiting for the letter that would allow me to be a soldier without my father's permission.

I truly believe that the draft is a good thing. Citizen soldiers have always been the best kind of soldiers, from the days of the Greek City States and the early Roman Legions to the present time. Citizen soldiers bring the morals, ideals, and civilizing traditions of the national culture into the armed forces. They are temporary soldiers, and they are often immune, or at least insulated, from the politics of rank and power in the military. They are not career people, and they seldom owe allegiance to Generals or politicians. They remain civilians at heart, ever loyal to home and family. They generally have a strong sense of community, nationality, and morality. Usually, they are less corruptible. And, when presented with a worthy cause to fight for, like the defense of home and family, draftees do a good job. Some of our nation's greatest military heroes have been draftees, including Medal of Honor winner, Sergeant Alvin York, whom General "Blackjack" Pershing called, "The greatest citizen soldier of the [First] World War."

And, for the most part, the draft was as fair as our politicians could make it; especially after the lottery system was introduced in 1969. In theory, any young man might be called to serve his country and put his life at risk. Even Elvis was drafted – and served. Like jury duty, being drafted was a civic duty that most people grudgingly accepted. Someone had to do it.

The draft was also a great social equalizer. Rich kids and poor kids were all in the mix together – or were supposed to be. And, better than that, the draft put a price on citizenship. Living in this free country wasn't free. We were expected to serve and defend the nation if needed. We might even be called to give our lives if necessary. We all understood that. Many of our fathers, uncles, and older brothers had made that ultimate sacrifice in the wars before Vietnam.

For young men, the possibility of compulsory military service was an obligation that came with citizenship. No one was required to join the military, but if needed, and if called, we were damn well expected to show up and shoulder a portion of the load. We accepted that, and most of us did our duty. There were severe social and legal penalties for "draft dodgers."

I fear that the sense of ownership in the defense of the country is lost to the modern generation. With a "professional" Army like we have today, too many of America's young people are detached. There is no price to pay for the blessings of citizenship ... and that cheapens the value. Many young people of today see the sacrifices of military service as someone else's problem. It is up to "them" to fight and die, those "professionals" who "volunteered" to do it. In my humble opinion, the all-volunteer Army builds a firewall between citizens and their military.

The all-volunteer Army also has the detrimental effect of skewing the military ranks toward the poor and disadvantaged among us. Many young people, especially minorities, join the military to escape poverty and to take advantage of college and career benefits denied them in other venues. If the children of wealth and privilege are not compelled to sign on, or at least subjected to social, legal, and political pressures, they seldom do. This has the effect of creating a culture within the military where not all elements of the general population are fully represented. In the long haul, history has shown that this can be a dangerous thing.

When we had an Army of citizen soldiers, we all had a stake in the military adventures of our country. We shared the risks and the burdens. The possibility of being called to give two years of your life to the armed forces made politics and foreign policy very personal. Young people were more in tune with world affairs back then, and that is one of the reasons there were riots in the streets. People were demanding accountability from their politicians. Riots and civil discontent are not always bad things. After all, that is how we began as a nation.

I do believe that being a professional soldier is noble service to our country, and I'm grateful to all who have served in the all-volunteer Army, including my oldest son. I truly appreciate their sacrifices. But, being drafted was a different kind of sacrifice. I submit that a man who gives two years of life as a draftee, and who does so to fulfill an obligation as a citizen, is different from the man who serves and counts the time as part of a professional career. The taste and the realities are different. To answer a draft call is to put your future, your plans, and your life on hold involuntarily. To serve as a draftee is to lay a real sacrifice on the altar of patriotism. I salute all who have served America as draftees.

My draft notice came in May 1966. It said something like: "Greetings, your friends and neighbors have selected you, to represent them, in the Armed Forces of the United States." It then went on to give all the details about where and when I was to report for active duty in the Army. At the end of the letter was a friendly reminder that I would be put in jail if I failed to show up. I was given six weeks to put my affairs in order.

I was told to report to the Continental Trailways bus terminal on the fifth day of July. Several young men from the nearby towns were being drafted with me, and we would all report together. At the bus terminal, a government official would meet us and check our papers. He would then escort us to Fort Douglas in Salt Lake City for induction into the Army.

I had mixed feelings about being drafted. On the one hand, I was relieved. It had finally happened. The suspense was over. The frustrations, turmoil, and uncertainties of my young life were being resolved for me. I would finally have direction and purpose in my life. Now, I could be the soldier of my daydreams, and maybe travel and see the world. I could meet my destiny head-on and see where my bright star might take me.

On the other hand, I was apprehensive. The war in Vietnam was heating up, and I realized that I was being sucked into the vortex of a storm by forces that were beyond my control. I was facing an uncertain journey into darkness, and I didn't know where this new road might take me.

And then, there was a third side to the equation. Entering military service was a right of passage. Finally, I would be a man. I would be leaving boyhood behind me forever. From this point into forever, I would be the Captain of my destiny. It would be a clean break from the shelter of my father's home and family. From this day onward, I would set my own sails on the oceans of life. I was ready to make the transition. I welcomed both the challenge and the opportunity.

And then of course, I would be proud to be a soldier. There had always been that young boy's daydream: flags, sabers, rifle salutes, polished brass, and thundering warhorses. I had always wanted to be in uniform. I would never have admitted it to anyone, but deep down in the bottom of my naïve country boy's heart, I really wanted to charge those cannons. I wanted to win a medal and come home with lots of stripes on my shirtsleeves. I wanted to make my grandpa proud. And then, when I had conquered, like my old farmer neighbor, Lorenzo Petersen, I wanted to have my picture taken in a uniform, so that years into the future, a pretty woman could remember who I was when I was young, handsome, and brave.

But, as I packed my bags to leave, I realized that I was being asked to make sacrifices that many of my teenaged friends would not be burdened with. My government, my "friends and neighbors," were ordering me to put aside my youth, my innocence, my formative years, and the promise of a bright future, to face whatever demons awaited me in the jungles of Vietnam. My small portion of the American dream, my birthright to be a happy kid, was being taken from me. The sand remaining in the hourglass of my youth would be poured out on the dust of a battlefield. I was being ordered to give my body and soul to a far-off Asian war. I might never be back.

My friend, Chester Housekeeper, was drafted into the Army a month later. He was sent to Fort Lewis, Washington for Basic

Training. Our paths wouldn't cross again until we were both home from Vietnam, almost three years later.

Chester served his country faithfully and with honor. He would serve with the Ninth Infantry Division on a river patrol boat in the Mekong Delta, operating out of Duong Tam. He would fight through the 1968 Tet Offensive and win the Army Commendation Medal. He was destined to meet the devil many times, on the water and in the dark. God was good to him, and he came home unhurt.

Most people would never notice, or care, that we were serving in the Army. Life in our little town would go on without us. The sacrifices of the young soldiers of my generation went largely ignored. Our parents, the World War II generation, were busy making a living. Public prayers and tributes to those in uniform were almost non-existent. There were very few stars in the windows of the homes of servicemen like those seen in the 1940s. There were precious few monuments or memorials erected in public places with public funds. There were no yellow ribbons or homecoming parades.

Vietnam was controversial. And, like Korea, Vietnam was no big deal. There had been no Pearl Harbor. Our freedoms and way of life were not in jeopardy. There had been no great, unifying cause to rally around. It was all so very far away. And besides, Vietnam was not a real war anyway. World War II had been a real war.

There were no flags, marching bands, parades, speeches or pats on the back from church and civic leaders as the latest batch of Vietnam-bound draftees boarded the bus for Fort Douglas on that bright, summer morning in 1966. There was only a small group of parents, teary-eyed girlfriends, and sad little brothers to see us off.

THE WALKING WOUNDED

As the bus took us out of town and toward an uncertain future, I wore a brave and happy face, but deep in my heart I was very much afraid. I didn't want to die, and more than that, I didn't want to be crippled or maimed. In my young life I had known a couple of wounded old war veterans. I didn't want to come home like them.

There was a man named Leonard Allred who lived in my little town. Leonard had served in World War I. He lived by himself in a tarpaper shack down by the river. He never had a job, and I was told that he lived on a small government pension. He was a simple old man, childlike in his thoughts and actions. He was often dirty, ragged and unshaven. When I was a little boy, my friends and I stopped to visit with Leonard often. Mentally and emotionally he was our age, and most of the adults in town would have nothing to do with him.

Leonard didn't own a car or have a driver's license. He rode a fancy bicycle all weighted down with chrome, bells, and bright streamers of naugahide. He had a little red wagon with wooden side-racks that he attached to his bicycle, and he would ride along the highway and pick up pop bottles to redeem for a penny or two. He liked to be around kids, and he would go on long bike rides with us.

People in town laughed at Leonard. He was clumsy and simple-minded. Occasionally, he did things that seemed outrageous. Sometimes he would take a handful of pennies and nickels and buy a loaf of bread at Grundvig's store. He would then go across the street to the café and sit in one of the booths and eat bread and catsup. He would never order anything, just sit there and put free catsup on slices of bread and eat them. It was a great joke, and people in town would laugh and laugh.

One day my friends and I stopped to see Leonard and found him in terrible distress. He asked us to help him find his money. He told us that he hid his money in a coffee can that he buried on a sandbar along the river behind his house. A big flood had come down the river and washed the sandbar away. All of Leonard's money was gone. We helped him look for his money for a couple of days, and then we boys lost interest. For several weeks thereafter, we saw Leonard often, down along the river-bank, walking slowly with his eyes to the ground while wringing his hands in hopeless distress. He never did find his money.

I don't know what ever happened to Leonard. As I got older, I outgrew him. By the time I was a teenager he wasn't my age anymore. A younger generation of little boys was stopping by to see his nifty bicycle. One day his old shack wasn't there anymore, and I never saw him again.

People in town said that Leonard had been "shell shocked" in the trenches of the First World War. The bombs and shells had "rattled his brains." They said he was like everyone else when he went away to war, but he came home a mental and emotional cripple.

There was another man with war wounds who was a friend of my grandfathers. I don't remember his name, but he would stop and see grandpa once in a while and he had wooden legs. He walked with a cane in each hand. That man too, had been in World War I.

One day while he and grandpa were having coffee, I noticed that there were only wooden pegs coming out of his socks instead of legs. I was probably seven or eight years old, and I just couldn't stop staring. The man saw what I was looking at, and so he called me over to him and then pulled up his pant legs to show me his prosthesis. His lower legs were made of polished wood, and his knee joints were mechanical hinges with screws, pins, and metal plates. I was shocked.

Grandpa then explained to me that the man had lost his legs in the war. Grandpa's friend had been one of those brave soldiers who had charged the German machine-guns.

The man laughed nervously and patted me on the head. He told me that he sure hoped I didn't have to charge any German machine-guns when I grew up. I told him I sure hoped so too. I didn't want to have wooden legs.

A QUESTION OF CLASS

Just a few days into it, I found myself at Fort Bliss Texas, out on the bleak and wind-swept sands of a desert wasteland. Fort Bliss is near El Paso, and just across the Rio Grande from Juarez, Mexico. It is the sunburnt and sand-filled belly button (wink) of the whole world. Mid-July temperatures languish in the 100 to 110-degree range. Davy Crockett, Merle Travis, and Jim Bowie had always been my heroes, but now, I was beginning to have second thoughts. Why would anyone fight for Texas?

I spent my first few days standing in long lines in my new G.I. haircut, getting sunburned and "accustomatized" to the climate – to quote one of my drill sergeants. In the coming year, I would spend several months in Texas, and I actually learned to like the place. I dusted Davy Crockett off and put him back on his pedestal. Maybe it was okay to fight for Texas after all.

The clerk gave me a contemptuous look over the top of his typewriter. He was a surly and sarcastic individual, five or six years older than me, but with no stripes on his sleeves. His lack of insignia told me that he was a new guy too. He was a draftee no doubt, and a young man who felt that his current job and situation were far below his deserved station in life. He was obviously a well-educated young fellow who didn't want to be there.

The snooty clerk was adapting well to the dog-eat-dog world of rank and station in the Army. As a Private E-2, he didn't rate any stripes, but there was still one whole class of soldiers below him in rank, and that was the brand-new recruits like me. I was a Private E-1, and at the very bottom of the military food chain. The snooty clerk reveled in his superior rank and position.

"Name, rank, and service number," the clerk demanded. I gave them to him, proud that I had already memorized the eight-digit service number embossed on my dog tags. He shot several other questions at me in rapid-fire as his fingers stomped my answers on the typewriter keys.

He asked for my hometown and home state, and I told him I was from Wellington, Utah.

The snooty clerk just couldn't restrain himself. "Does Welling-town, Utah have electric lights and flush toilets?" He asked sarcastically.

"Yes," I assured him.

He didn't write it down.

"Are you one of those Mormon boys from Utah?" he asked with a patronizing smirk.

"Yes," I said again.

"Spell it," he said with a sneer, but then he typed my religious preference before I could answer.

He then asked for my highest level of education. I told him I had completed one semester of college.

"Working on a PhD?" he quipped.

"Yes," I said without blushing.

My goal in life was to be an archaeologist, and most archaeologists have PhDs. Getting a PhD is a long process. It made perfect sense to me that one semester at a junior college was the first step.

The clerk sat and looked at me for a moment, and then an amused grin crept across his snooty face. He rolled his eyes and went back to his typewriter. He wasn't quite sure if I was digging back at him of if I was just a stupid hillbilly.

His questions went on for several more minutes, and then he came to a section about background information.

"Is your background upper middle class or lower middle class?" he snapped.

The question made me think. I had never considered such a question before. I knew nothing about social class. I was an American, and I thought all Americans were equal. I thought about it for a while before I answered. Where did I fit? Was I upper class or lower class?

I decided that all of my family members were good and honorable people. None of the family had ever been in jail. There were no drug addicts, prostitutes, petty thieves, or moonshiners in the family that I knew about. My extended family all had jobs, they worked hard, they went to church and were well-respected members of the community. Personally, I had never been in any kind of trouble. I was a High School Graduate and a good person.

"Upper middle class," I said, and the typewriter hammered it home.

The clerk looked at me without his smirk, and he raised an eyebrow thoughtfully.

"What does your old man do for a living?" was the next question.

"He's a deputy sheriff for Carbon County," I said proudly. "He used to be a coalminer."

There was silence for a moment. I looked at the clerk and met a cold, hate-filled and contemptuous stare coming back at me from over the typewriter.

"You stupid (expletive deleted)," the clerk hissed as he ripped the page out of his typewriter, crumpled it, and threw it at a distant wastepaper basket.

"You're lower class like all the rest of the livestock in this shipment," he sneered.

He then turned to another clerk at a nearby desk and called out, "Hey Frank, you wanna trade Gomers? I got a real live wire over here." The other clerk shot me an amused and haughty glance. They both laughed.

I was embarrassed and angry at the same time. I fought to control my emotions.

"So who is upper class?" I asked in a quiet voice, struggling to control my temper and trying not to blush. I hated to expose myself to further ridicule, but I desperately wanted to know the answer.

"Doctors, lawyers and Indian chiefs," the snooty clerk responded. "People with money; people with big houses and big cars and big appetites. Deputy sheriffs and coalminers need not apply." And then he giggled wickedly at his own cleverness.

I was crushed.

I couldn't believe it. Was that really what it meant to be upper class? Was money the only measuring rod? It seemed so vile and so shallow to me. I had been taught that the measure of a good man was virtue, honesty, and honor. That's what upper class meant to me. Lower class people were trashy and immoral. Lower class people were jailbirds and welfare cheats. If what this sneering clerk had just told me was true, then my whole world had just been turned upside down. If money was the only unit of measure, then everything I had been taught as a child was a lie.

I was very confused by it all too. Even by using money as the yardstick, my family would still qualify as upper class by the standards of my hometown. My family lived in one of the nicest houses in our little community. Dad owned a car that was only a couple of years old, and we all wore good clothes. There were lots of people in our little town who had less than we did. But then, it was true that there weren't any doctors, lawyers, or Indian chiefs in our little community of farmers and coalminers. I thought about it for a few days, and decided that maybe I didn't know anyone who was truly upper class.

The consequences of my conclusions were disheartening. If I didn't know anyone who was upper class, that meant that everyone I knew and loved were lower class people - myself included. It was depressing.

But, all was not lost. I soon discovered that the Army had a certain measure of institutionalized compensation when it came to social class. Standing in the ranks in a GI haircut and a uniform, I was the equal of anyone, and I knew it. We were all the same in the ranks. The playing field was level. The sons of wealth and privilege stood shoulder to shoulder with the sons of coalminers and farmers, and no one could tell the difference. Money didn't matter. It all came down to what you were made of. The Army fulfills the American ideal of equal opportunity.

I decided that there were those who might look down their privileged noses and call me lower class, but no one would ever call me anything but a first-class soldier. I set my sails in that direction, and resolved to make it happen.

THE LAND OF OPPORTUNITY

The First Sergeant snorted as I saluted in a very unpracticed and civilian sort-of-way. "Private McCourt reporting as ordered, First Sergeant," I said.

"Damn it, McCourt, you don't salute First Sergeants," he said as he picked through a stack of papers.

"At ease," he said dryly.

I spread my feet slightly, crossed my hands behind my back, and stood at parade rest, just as I'd been taught.

"Sit down a minute ... we've got to talk," the First Sergeant said impatiently as he looked over a particular piece of paper with a wrinkled brow.

I sat down in the chair next to his desk, suddenly afraid and wondering who had died back home.

He laid the piece of paper on his desk and looked at me for a moment, and then he said, "Private McCourt, you have qualified for Officer Candidate School."

It bounced off.

In my mind, I was planning an emergency trip home. I completely didn't understand what he said to me. I just sat there stupidly.

"We just got the results of your induction examinations, aptitude testing, psychological profile and I.Q. test. You are one of a handful of recruits in this training battalion to qualify for Officer Candidate School."

It started to sink in, slowly.

"Do you want to be an Officer in the Army?" The First Sergeant asked from behind a wry and almost painful smile.

I could see that my First Sergeant was struggling with the irony of it all. He was a military professional, a man who had devoted his whole life to military service. He had worked hard to earn his coveted rank and station over a period of many long years. He was knowledgeable, capable, and mature. He had proven himself to be a leader of men in the crucible of combat. He had served with distinction in Korea. With all of that, he was not an officer.

His face was filled with a quiet, almost hurtful resignation, as our eyes met and we each knew what the other was thinking. We both knew who we were, and we both knew that I was unworthy. I was nineteen years old, barely a year out of high school and green as grass. I was a kid who hadn't paid my dues yet. I had been in the Army for only a couple of weeks. We both knew that I was being offered something that was still denied him after all those years of work and sacrifice. It made me feel very humble. I wished at that moment that I could have passed that opportunity on to that man who had earned it.

The First Sergeant's eyes snapped back to a cold professionalism, and he said, "I know you are a draftee. And, if you make a formal application and they accept you, you will need to make a new commitment that will keep you in the Army for a few more years. But, let me tell you that it's one hell of an opportunity. I know people who would do anything to be offered a chance like this. This sort of thing doesn't happen very often. The Army is expanding rapidly right now. We are going on a full war footing. We need junior officers very badly – lots of them."

Then he said, "I don't want an answer today. You think it over for a few days and let me know what you want to do. You will have to make a formal application and pass a board of review to be accepted, and even then, the washout rate for OCS is very high. Don't go out and buy any Lieutenant's bars yet. You are still a long ways from being an Officer. All we are offering you today is a chance to make a formal application. You think about it, and let me know what you want to do in a couple of days. And, let me congratulate you ... most people never make it this far."

It was something totally unexpected. Uncle Glen had been a Captain during World War II, but I had never dreamed of being an officer myself. Officers were mystical beings to basic trainees. Officers were the swashbuckling Knights of the Realm. Even the all-powerful drill Sergeants snapped to attention, saluted, and showed humble deference in the presence of an Officer.

All around the military base, brash young Lieutenants strutted like peacocks and enjoyed privileges undreamed of by lowly recruits. Officers never pulled KP or Latrine duty. Officers lived off-post in civilian housing and never stayed in the crowded barracks. Officers were rich and they drove fancy new cars. They always had pretty girls on their arms. Everyone saluted and obeyed them. And, the Officer's Clubs were always bigger, better, and happier places than the grubby beer halls of the enlisted men.

I had never dreamed of being an officer, and I was at once flattered to be considered, and yet hesitant to rise to the challenge. I was afraid I could never measure up. I knew next to nothing about the Army, and I just couldn't imagine myself as a cocky and confident young Lieutenant. I was still getting used to being that lower classed person the snooty personnel clerk had assured me that I was.

I chewed on the First Sergeant's offer for a while. I couldn't swallow it all at once. I had to savor it slowly and get used to the taste. I did think about it deeply, and decided that I had nothing to loose and everything to gain. I was on my way to Vietnam anyway, and probably as a combat medic. I had followed Uncle Glen's lead and told the Army that I wanted to be a medic. I hated blood and guts, but being a medic seemed to be a noble way to serve. Uncle Glen had served in the Medical Corps, and it had won him a great deal of respect. I admired Uncle Glen and I wanted to be like him. I had never dreamed that I might be given a chance to be an officer ... like him.

I decided that I might as well go for broke. It was a great opportunity and, even if I failed, the worst that could happen would be to end up back where I already was. Hell yes, what did I have to loose? I went back to the First Sergeant and asked to fill out the papers. He assured me that I was doing the right thing.

Within just a week or so, I was summoned to appear before a Board of Review for OCS. I was one of several applicants being screened that day from all over the post. I sat on a tin chair in the lobby for what seemed like a long time before an orderly finally came and ushered me into a big room where the Review Board was convened.

I was taken into the presence of three Army officers, two First Lieutenants and a Major, veritable Gods in the Pantheon of humble recruits. They were seated on soft chairs behind a long, elevated podium. It was like going to court.

My future and my fate rested with this much-decorated military tribunal, and in the face of the pressure, I fumbled the ball. I gave a too-eager and completely awkward salute, and then stammered my introduction in a broken and squeaky voice. I knew instantly that I had screwed it up, and I compounded the damage when I winced, blushed like a school-girl, and ducked my head slightly before regaining some small measure of military decorum.

An old man with shining gold leaves on his shoulders frowned and told me to take a seat. His hair was gray and he looked too old and too stern to be a Major. He should have been a General. The chair he offered stood all-alone in the middle of the floor. There was no place to hide.

The panel members were experienced, and they immediately started asking me a series of well-prepared and well-rehearsed questions. It was not at all what I had expected. I was amazed at some of the trivial things they asked me. How much does a pound of butter cost? What's the speed limit on the interstate? What city is the Capitol of New York State? Who was Mark Twain? Have you ever stopped to help anyone involved in an accident? Tell us about it.

And then they slipped into military questions. Who was the first Commander-in-Chief of the Army? What's the cyclic rate of fire for the M14 rifle? Which of your drill sergeants do you like best, and why? The questions went on and on.

And then came a big question. "Private McCourt, if you were Chief of Staff of the Army today, what would you do to win the war in Vietnam?"

Bingo! I had anticipated just such a question. I answered with confidence and without hesitation.

"I would mine and blockade the port of Haiphong. I would begin an unrestricted bombing campaign over all of North Vietnam. I would curtail defensive operations in the South, move across the demilitarized zone, and take the fight to the North Vietnamese."

There was silence from the officers for a few moments, and then the Major, who should have been a General, smiled and told me that I had advocates of just such actions right there in the room.

Yes! I had scored a basket.

And then came a very big question. One of the officers set up a hypothetical military scenario for me. He said: "Suppose that you are a platoon leader and you have been ordered to retreat. You must leave someone behind to cover your retreat, knowing that the man you leave behind is sure to be killed. You cannot stay yourself. You must choose a man to stay and die for the rest of you. What will you do?"

I thought about it for a moment, and then I said, "I would ask for volunteers."

"Very good," the officer said.

And then he said, "Unfortunately, no one volunteered to stay and die. What do you do now?

I thought about it again for a moment, and then I said, "We draw lots."

"Very good," the officer said again.

And then he said, "Unfortunately, the man who drew the lot to stay and fight tells you to go to hell. He's not going to stay. What do you do now?"

I thought about it for a while. What were the options? Shoot the man who refused to stay? What then? Shoot each of the men in turn as they refuse to die for me? What would that accomplish? And, does an officer really have the authority to order a man to die in the first place? It didn't sound right to me.

And then, I wondered if it might be a trick question. Was there some other way to get out of the situation without someone having to make that ultimate sacrifice? I brooded over it, but I couldn't find an answer. I couldn't guess what those military guys were looking for. I squirmed on the hook.

"Do I really have to leave a man behind to die?" I asked the officer.

"Yes," came the reply.

"And there's no way that I can stay and fight while my men retreat?"

"No," the officer said, "That's a noble gesture, but you absolutely must retreat with the group. You cannot stay and sacrifice yourself for your men."

I didn't know what to say. I was cornered. I was checkmated.

I was dead. I couldn't find the answer. I sat stupidly in silence for a few moments while my mind raced. The Major frowned and looked at his watch.

I took a deep breath and let it out very slowly. My goose was cooked. I had failed. My place in OCS would go to some other guy who was smarter than me. I looked up at the all-knowing and all-powerful judges of my inquisition, and then sadly, I said, "I don't know what I would do, Sir."

There was silence for a few moments, and then the Major smiled and said, "By God ... that's the best answer I've heard in here today!"

There was a collective sigh as the tension of the moment was broken. The officers began to smile and nod at one another as they scribbled notes on their clipboards. I didn't know if that was a good sign or a bad sign.

"Private McCourt," the Major said, with just a small measure of fatherly kindness in his tone, "This will conclude your interview. You have a long way to go in developing a proper military bearing suitable for an officer, but we realize that you are young and in your first weeks of basic training. Work hard Private. This will not be an easy road for you if you are to succeed. There is a great deal for you to learn in a very short period of time if you are to become an officer. You will be notified of our decision in a week or two. We do wish you luck."

Then, the Major called for an orderly to escort me outside. I saluted in parting much better than I had done during the greeting. As the orderly walked me to the door, we passed another Private who was sweating anxiously in the lobby, waiting to take his turn on the hot seat.

The First Sergeant called me to his office a week or so later and congratulated me for being accepted to OCS. I was shocked. It had happened! The Review Board had accepted me after all. I was going to be given a chance to be an Officer and a Gentleman like Uncle Glen. I walked out of the First Sergeant's office without touching the ground. I was floating on air. I stopped and borrowed a handful of dimes from the company clerk. Happiness isn't complete until it's shared. I had some phone calls to make.

A few days later, I filled out the necessary papers. The First Sergeant explained that I would temporarily be promoted to E-5 (sergeant) before reporting for OCS, even though I would not be allowed to wear the stripes. The Army did this to make it possible for me to buy the necessary uniforms and supplies I would need for Officer Candidate School. I also got to fill out a "dream sheet" and request the branch of service I would serve in and where I would attend OCS. The First Sergeant explained to me that because of my tender age and lack of formal education, I had virtually no chance of getting into one of the more prestigious and less threatening branches of the Army, like Engineers, Signal Corps, or Quartermaster. No matter what I put on the dream sheet, I would likely be relegated to one of the combat arms: Infantry, Artillery, or Armor. He didn't say it, but what the Army needed most right then was young officers who could fight. There were plenty of older, better-educated, career people standing by to staff the safer and more genteel positions.

I chose infantry. I don't know why. It must have been that deep down in the corners of my innocent teenager's heart, I wanted to be Audie Murphy or Alvin York. I asked to be sent to Fort Benning, Georgia, to be trained as an Infantry Platoon Leader.

Officer Candidate School is an opportunity always available to a select few in the Army, but it is only in times of war and extreme need when raw recruits are given a chance to attend. In the normal course of things, the Military Academy at West Point supplies the top crop of junior officers while ROTC programs from colleges and universities take up the slack. This system keeps the Army supplied with a steady flow of well educated, highly motivated, and more mature (early to mid-twenties-aged) young officers.

Officer Candidate Schools are generally reserved for those soldiers from the ranks who truly excel in leadership and command ability, and whose superiors feel they should be offered a chance. It almost never happens that an uneducated, nineteen-year-old draftee in basic training is allowed a chance to reach for the golden ring, or in this case, the gold bars of a Second Lieutenant. I was lucky.

FORT McCLELLAN

I was assigned to Fort McClellan, Alabama, for Advanced Individual Training (AIT) before reporting for Officer Candidate School. At Fort McClellan, the Army had just created a brand-new jungle-training course. I was with the first 200 infantry soldiers to be sent there for training since World War II. There would eventually be an Advanced Infantry Training Brigade there, but I was with the very first infantry company to arrive. The post was a chemical depot, and WAC (Women's Army Corps) Headquarters for Third Army. There were girls in uniform everywhere.

We were a special unit. Every member of our rifle company was waiting for orders to the Infantry Officer Candidate School at Fort Benning. Our training was geared to be a pre-OCS leadership school. It was very much like an NCO (Non Commissioned Officer) Academy, even though we were all just out of basic training. And, since we were such a fine group of potential young officers, our schooling was very intense and very demanding. They took us into the swamps first-thing and taught us all about snakes, mosquitoes, leeches, and mud.

At Fort McClellan, we learned the tactics of close-quarters jungle fighting from experts. Most of our instructors were recently back from Vietnam. One of the Sergeants had an ugly scar on his cheek that was the imprint of a bullet. He told us himself that the sniper's bullet had hit his cheek from behind and exited through his open mouth. War stories with ugly scars as visual aids were very sobering to those of us destined for the jungles. We took our training very seriously.

A few of our instructors were veterans of World War II and Korea. They were the last of the breed. They were old guys, Sergeants of many stripes with long rows of hash marks on their sleeves. They were professional soldiers, "Lifers" in the jargon of the military, who had already given twenty or thirty years to Uncle Sam. It was September 1966, and World War II was only twenty-one years behind them.

When an old Sergeant began his presentation with, "I was in the Brown Boot Army," we knew he was telling us that he was a veteran of World War II and/or Korea. We listened carefully when such men stood before us. They were the very last of that "greatest generation" of soldiers who had served with our fathers. By sharing their knowledge with us, they were passing the torch.

The brown boot veterans taught us small arms and small arms tactics. We trained with every infantry weapon in the arsenal and learned how best to kill people with each of them. My favorite course of instruction was machine-gun school.

When I first fired an M60 machine-gun, it was the end of innocence for me. Back in basic training, my M14 rifle had been a flirtatious little wench who had stolen my heart. At Fort McClellan, the M60 machine-gun was a bold and aggressive Lady of the Evening. At the age of nineteen, I couldn't resist her. To young men of my generation, machine-guns ranked right up there with pretty girls, fast cars, and rock-n-roll music.

The M60 is patterned after the World War II German MG42 machine-gun, and she is truly a work of art. The gun fires long, 200-round belts of 7.62mm (.308) ammo at about 650 rounds pr. minute – almost eleven rounds a second. It was magic. A good machine-gunner can cut down a tree with a steady aim and a smooth trigger finger. I did it more than once. Rifles, grenade launchers, bazookas, claymores and mortars all lost their sparkle. I couldn't get enough of that lovely machine-gun.

Unfortunately, I was born with a sinistral bent. I'm hard-wired to be left-handed. At machine-gun school, I learned big-time that what the drill sergeants in basic training had told me about shooting left-handed was true. The spent shell casings ejected from the right side of the gun and sometimes hit me in the face or went down my neck or down my right shirtsleeve. The hot brass burned tender skin, and I always had burned spots on my chest, neck, and forearm like someone had worked me over with a lit cigarette. I was persistent however, and ever true to my genetic makeup. I simply clenched my teeth, squinted my eyes tight, concentrated on the target, and endured the blistering brass. I stubbornly refused to surrender my inherent portsidedness by putting the gun to my right shoulder. I may well have been the only machine-gunner in the US Army who insisted on shooting left-handed.

The old combat veteran Sergeants never tried to make me change shoulders the way the younger, basic training drill instructors had done. They were realists. They were experienced enough to know that when "the defecation hits the oscillator," as one of them was fond of saying, I would instinctively shoot the way I was genetically programmed. They left me alone, and only smiled as I nursed hot-brass burns on my chest and arm.

After initial familiarization, the Brown Boot Army veterans passed to my generation the dark knowledge of the machine-gunner's craft.

We were told to always remember that tracer bullets work in both directions, and that needlessly wasting ammo and lighting up a night sky is a sure way to bring down the wrath of God. We were assured that a machine-gunner is always a priority target.

We were told to shoot short bursts of fire - three round "taps" on the trigger - to suppress incoming fire without needlessly giving away our position. We were told to hold the trigger down and "fire for effect" only when we had an absolute and high-value target in our sights. We were told to aim low in the dark because a gunner has a natural tendency to shoot high at low-visibility targets.

We were taught to position the gun to shoot flat across the ground to create a zone of enfilading fire. Enfilading fire is when a gunner can send his bullets parallel to the ground to cover a wide expanse of the battlefield. To enfilade, is an old French military term that literally means to shoot along the whole length of a line of soldiers or trenches. If you are in a good enfilading position, you might miss the guy you are shooting at and still hit some of his friends in the background that you hadn't even noticed.

We were also taught that sometimes it's a good idea to leave a wounded enemy soldier out on the field where he can struggle and scream for his companions to come and get him. "Use the wounded guy for bait," one of the old soldiers told us somberly. "There is always someone over there on the other side with more guts than brains who will risk it all to rescue the wounded guy. It happens all the time. It's human nature. Our guys do it too. Use the rescue attempt to your advantage. Bide your time, watch closely, and you will likely get fresh targets. Sometimes you can stack two or three of them up around a wounded guy who is making a lot of noise."

And, "It's usually better to wound an enemy than to kill him anyway. If you wound the guy, you take him out of the fight and it takes two or three of his people to deal with him. If you kill him, he's out of the fight, but the two other guys are still coming at you."

We were told not to follow a man with the gun barrel if he was running parallel to us. It's like shooting ducks. "Swing the gun past him. Position the sights out in front of him somewhere and layback on the trigger. Let him run through the bullets. The bullets are coming at him in a long stream and two or three will surely take him down."

And then, "When a man is running right at you, shoot at his knees. Knock his legs out from under him and he'll likely fall through the stream of bullets. If you hold on his chest, you have a tendency to shoot high as he gets closer and you get more excited, especially when you are confronted with multiple, fast moving targets. And, when you shoot high at close range you loose the effect of enfilading fire. That's how your position might be overrun. Enemy soldiers in the back ranks can get to you while you shoot too high at the front ranks. Keep your fire low at their knees and even the bullets that miss will keep the guys in the rear with their heads down. Enfilading fire is your best friend when the enemy moves on you."

My mind flashed back to that old-man visitor at my grandfather's house when I was a boy, the man with the wooden legs who had charged the German machine-guns. I suddenly felt very sad. Now I knew what that German machine-gunner had been taught. It echoed through my mind again and again ... "Shoot at his knees when he's coming right at you." Remembering those wooden legs with the hinge-pinned knee joints made me shudder. I tried to push it out of my mind. If I was going to do this for real, I had to focus on the mechanics of the thing and not dwell on the consequences of what I was doing. Machine-gunning is a gruesome business, and not a good line of work for a man with a conscience.

As our Pre-OCS, advanced infantry jungle training came to an end at Fort McClellan, we were all waiting for orders to OCS at Fort Benning. One evening the First Sergeant came into the barracks as we were shutting down for the night, and announced that he had just received the first batch of orders. He then read four or five names from a list on his clipboard. My name was among them. He then asked that the men whose names he had read come forward. We did.

The First Sergeant stood and looked at us for a moment with a wry smile, and then he shook his head, shrugged his shoulders helplessly, and said: "Gentlemen, God and the Army sometimes work in mysterious ways. You guys are being sent to the Artillery and Missile School at Fort Sill, Oklahoma."

There was silence for a moment, and then one of the guys whose name had not been called started to laugh. The laugh was followed by hoots of derision and muttered oaths of disbelief from the assembled troops.

"OCS?" one of my flabbergasted companions asked the First Sergeant.

"That's right ... Artillery and Missile OCS," the First Sergeant nodded. "I've got the orders right here."

I was stunned. What was going on? I had volunteered to be an Infantry Platoon Leader. I had just completed eight weeks of the best light weapons infantry training my country had to offer, and now I was being sent to the Mother of all Artillery Schools without a drop of prior training or experience. I had never seen a cannon fired outside a John Wayne movie. Artillery OCS is an advanced course. To go there without the prerequisites would be very difficult. I would have no foundation to build on.

It took a while to soak in. I laid awake most of the night, fretting, cussing, and mourning. It was a bitter pill to swallow. I knew nothing about artillery. I would have to start all over again with my training. I couldn't imagine what the wizards who cut army orders could be thinking. Were they deliberately setting me up to fail? I was among the youngest of OCS applicants and one of the least educated. What I really needed was a boost, not another mountain to climb.

The next morning I asked to speak with the First Sergeant again. I asked him if he had any idea what was going on. He said he had no clue, but orders were orders and I had better get used to it.

I shrugged helplessly, and tried to put a happy face on it. I said something like, "Oh well, I've probably got a better chance of surviving the war with an artillery battery than in a foxhole with a machine-gun." To which the First Sergeant replied, very matter-of-factly, "Not necessarily, they train artillery Lieutenants to be Forward Observers. You'll probably be way out front in Vietnam, and you'll have a map and a radio and only wish you had a machine-gun."

Holy Cow! I hadn't known anything about that. This might be scarier than I thought. I wasn't sure just what a Forward Observer did, but it sounded dangerous.

When I had time to think about it for a while, I was able to reconcile myself to the unexpected change in my destiny. The weighty title, "Forward Artillery Observer," did sound important, and maybe just a tad glamorous too. I rolled it around on my tongue for a while. It had a manly texture and a Hollywood taste. And, it sounded like a job a soldier could be proud to do. What the hell ... artillery school might not be so bad after all. I would give it my best shot. The Army was becoming a grand adventure.

In the years since, I have wondered if I wasn't sent to the artillery school because I had excelled in the map reading and compass courses at Fort McClellan. I was one of a precious few trainees to complete the nighttime compass course through the swamps of Alabama on-target and on time. A compass, map, and radio, are the primary weapons of a Forward Observer. I'll never know for sure, but my basic Boy Scout orienteering skills might have rescued me from the Infantry.

An Officer and a Gentleman

It was a cold and gloomy November day when I reported to Robinson Barracks at Fort Sill, Oklahoma, for Artillery and Missile OCS. I was still nineteen years old. I had been in the Army for just over four months. The upper classmen pounced on me as I reported in, and stripped me of all rank and insignia. They were arrogant, insulting, and even more intimidating than the drill instructors in basic training had been. It was a lot like being taken prisoner.

I had my first lesson in things I didn't know about artillery in the first few minutes of my arrival. As a haughty upper classman stripped my uniform of what meager signs of rank it held, he got right up close in my face and told me there was a lanyard on my uniform and I should remove it immediately. I had no idea what he was talking about. I just stood there, staring straight ahead as I had always done when being dressed-down by the drill sergeants in basic training.

The smug and pompous upper classman became enraged when I failed to respond to his directive, and with a red face and bulging eyeballs he ordered me to drop and give him fifty push-ups. I dutifully complied, there on the asphalt of the parking lot, in my class "A" uniform, jacket, necktie and all. As I stood again, out of breath, sweating, and with dirt stains on my hands and knees, he got in my face again and told me to remove the lanyard. I stared straight ahead again, but this time I told him that I didn't know what a lanyard was.

"You're shitting me!" was his incredulous reply. "What's

your MOS (military occupational specialty), Candidate?"

"Eleven Bravo - light weapons," I stammered. "I'm a machine-gunner."

"You're shitting me!" he said again. "What are you doing here, Mr. Eleven Bravo?"

"I have orders to be here, Sir."

"Let's see your orders," the upper classman snapped. I dug into my folder and produced the official documents. The upper classman looked them over, and then called a couple of his buddies to come and look too. They couldn't believe it. I hadn't made a mistake. I was at the right place.

The upper classman stood before me again, but this time his attitude had softened considerably. "You don't have a snow-ball's chance in hell of graduating from this school, candidate," he said finally. "Do you know that?"

"No Sir," I said defiantly. "They sent me here and I'll graduate ... Sir."

"Sure you will," the upper classman said, almost sadly.

"Well, Candidate McCourt, Mr. Eleven Bravo, let me give you your first lesson in artillery terminology. A lanyard is a short rope that is pulled to fire a cannon. You have a small thread hanging out from the second buttonhole on your uniform. Around here we call that a lanyard. Remove the lanyard on your uniform, Candidate McCourt, or I'll make you drop and give me another fifty."

"Yes Sir," I said, as I fished for the thread.

"And then," the upper classman said, as he smiled wickedly, "Around here, whenever you remove a lanyard, you must yell BOOM. After all, candidate, a lanyard does fire the gun."

"Yes Sir ... BOOM Sir," I said as I pulled the thread, not daring to even smile.

"Very good, candidate," the upper classman purred. "See, you're learning to be an artilleryman already."

In World War II, young Lieutenants were often called "Ninety-day Wonders." It supposedly stems from the fact that during the worst days of the world conflict, Officer Candidate School was cut back to a three-month course of instruction. When I reported for OCS in November 1966, the school lasted twice that long.

The Artillery and Missile Officer Candidate School was divided into three segments. Each segment lasted eight or nine weeks, and each segment had a different goal and course of instruction. There were very few Sergeants as instructors. We were under the tutelage of "TAC (Training and Cadre) Officers." Lieutenants, Captains, and even a few Majors took the place of drill instructors. Upper class OCS candidates took the place of most NCOs at the school.

The first segment was physical and psychological torture. It was geared that way to find out who really wanted to be there, and who could function under stress. A new candidate was called a lower classman, and he wore a blue tab on each epaulet. Lower classmen were treated worse than cattle, and it was part of the plan.

As Lower classmen, we didn't rank high enough to walk on the sidewalks. We had to walk in the gutter. In fact, we couldn't walk at all unless given explicit permission. Most of the time we jogged everywhere we went. Lower classmen were routinely deprived of nourishment and sleep, and they were constantly harassed and belittled. Harsh physical conditioning was endless, and we spent hours and hours marching, running in formation, and doing push-ups and sit-ups. We were often cold, usually hungry, and always exhausted and in need of sleep. I lost ten pounds in the first couple of weeks. It doesn't sound like much, but I weighed less than 140 to begin with.

The hardships and deprivation was a test to see who would fold under pressure. We were constantly reminded that we were suffering at our own request and we could quit at anytime. We had volunteered to be there, and we could volunteer to leave. The choice was ours. Several young candidates took the option and dropped out.

Some of the tortures were creative. They would march us to the mess hall after an all-night field problem and make us stand behind our chairs at attention while the presiding upper classmen took their seats at the head of each table. Then, by command, we were ordered to sit. We could sit at the table, but still in a position of attention, and pity the man who reached out to grab a fork without permission. Reprimands and punishments were severe, and the whole group was punished for the infractions of an individual. We would sit at attention and smell the sausage and eggs, pancakes and coffee, while the upper classman at the head of the table gave us a chatty lesson in proper table etiquette. He would sometimes be eating as he talked to us. We did not have permission to eat yet. When he finished his lecture, the upper classman would give us permission to eat. We would no sooner get a taste of scrambled eggs than a whistle would blow and the upper classman would order us to attention behind our chairs again. Our fifteen minutes for eating had passed. It was time to go on another hike. Our uneaten breakfast was dumped in the trash.

By the second or third week, a lower class candidate was a zombie. The stresses were as close to battlefield trauma as the Army could duplicate without actually shooting at us. They were finding who could function under pressure, and who had the will and intestinal fortitude to tuff it out.

Several of the candidates quit, and that was the plan. The weeks of torture were a great winnowing process. To survive as a lower classman, a person had to have an iron will, be in complete control of his emotions, be willing to suffer to win the prize, and be able to stay focused through weeks and months of unrelenting hardship. Only the strong survive.

And then, one day we were called into formation, congratulated for having passed the first test, and were allowed to don the
green epaulet tabs of a middle classman. Things began to
lighten-up from there on out. A middle classman gets to eat
regular meals, and he gets a few hours of sleep at night.

But, in spite of the hardships, lower class training was not
all torture and tears. I experienced something during my lower
class tenure at Robinson Barracks that has remained one of my
most treasured memories of military service. It was truly
profound, and it happened quite by accident.

We were on a forced march, just a few days before
Christmas, 1966. It was cold, and we were all bundled up in old,
mothball-stinking World War II surplus overcoats that flopped
around our knees as we trudged through the boondocks. We
were all wearing steel helmets, carrying rucksacks and M14
rifles. We looked like a ragged band of survivors from The Battle
of the Bulge. We had been out all day. We were hungry and
tired. My feet hurt.

We were marching back to the Army base after dark,
following an old dirt road that wound its way across the
wilderness. As we approached the lights of Fort Sill, it began
to snow heavily, and soon the ground was covered. The
heavy clomp, clomp, clomp of our marching boots took on
the squeaky crunch, crunch, crunch, of walking on fresh,
new snow.

From deep in the ranks, someone started to hum a
Christmas Carol. To my utter amazement, the song fit our
marching cadence perfectly. We all began to hum, and then to
sing. It was spontaneous, heartfelt, and incredible. "Oh come all
ye faith-ful, joy-ful and tri-um-phant!" The sound of our boots
on the wet, new snow beat a soft and perfect cadence. A surge of
new energy rippled through our weary formation.

As one Christmas Carol faded into the night, another took

its place. Incredibly, we found that we could adapt almost all of them to the rhythm of our marching feet. If we didn't know all the words, we hummed or waited for clues from those singing around us. I would never have guessed, but the songs "Joy to the World," and "Far, Far Away on Judea's Plains," have perfect rhythms for marching that could actually be set to fife and drums. When we discovered that fact, our wet, cold, and hungry formation came alive. Our chorus, and the sound of our marching feet, resonated through the stormy night. "Glory to God" – crunch – "Glory to God" – crunch – "Glory to God in the high-est" - crunch.

Our TAC Officers loved it. Any show of spirit and cama-raderie from the ranks of the starving and oppressed lower classmen was a positive thing. Our superiors altered our route and took us through one of the residential areas of the fort. We marched through the streets of a humble, enlisted man's resi-dential housing unit, and we continued to sing Christmas Carols as we marched.

The streets were deserted and the snow was beautiful. Huge snowflakes filtered down around the streetlights and the ground was blanketed in white. There were sparkling Christmas lights decorating many of the homes, and people peeked out from colored-light-framed windows to watch as we marched past. Our wet boots kept a perfect cadence on the squeaky new snow. "Si-lent night," - crunch, crunch - "Ho-ly night," - crunch, crunch - "All is calm," - crunch, crunch - "all is bright," - crunch, crunch.

Porch lights came on half-a-block ahead of us as the sound of our marching Christmas tribute went before us up the street. People came out on their porches to stand silently and watch as we marched past, singing in cadence. No one cheered, no one waved, and no one sang with us. Families stood with arms around each other, babes wrapped in blankets, and watched reverently, some with bowed heads. Even the children were quiet and respectful. The scene was wondrous and dreamlike against the background of falling snow and the twinkling of colored Christmas lights. The feeling was incredible.

It was a powerful, spiritual moment for me. These were Army families, the people who carried the burdens of the Vietnam War. How many would know the pain of separation in the coming year? How many would know the agony of losing a father or a husband? How many of the brave young voices from within our ranks would forever be silenced before they knew another Christmas? I thought of all of those things as I offered my weak and humble voice to the chorus. I don't know what the other soldiers in that formation were thinking, but I was praising God and offering a gift of hope and love to soldier families everywhere.

Every Christmas since that night, I have remembered the images and the feelings of that special Christmas tribute, and wished that I could do it again.

The eight or nine weeks of middle class training were slanted toward academic endeavors. It was during this time period when we learned the black arts of the artilleryman's craft. A lot of the instruction was live-fire exercises on the guns. We learned to set the fuses, load the guns, and "lay" (orient) the battery. We were also taught the ballistic wizardry that puts a shell on target from ten or twelve miles away. In those days we used slide rules and long division to make the calculations. The Army had no computers. And, I know it sounds unbelievable, but hand-held calculators had not been invented yet.

As middle classmen, we were also taught intensive map reading, proper compass usage, escape and evasion, military protocols, military history, and dozens of other soldierly subjects. An OCS middle classman spends a lot of time in a classroom.

In 1967, the Army still combined Artillery and Missiles into one branch of the service. The two disciplines were separated in 1968. While at OCS, my classmates and I were trained to shoot Honest John and Little John Missiles as well as tube artillery.

The academic courses were tough for a kid like me without any college. I knew little of math, and geometry is the mother's milk of hitting targets over the horizon. Lucky for me, I had innocently and unknowingly made a decision on my first afternoon at OCS that helped to sustain me. It happened when I picked a roommate.

On my first afternoon at Robinson Barracks, I was escorted to a squad bay and told to select a bunk. The bunks were separated into cubicles. Each cubicle had two beds and two desks. Each candidate had a "roommate." About half of the cubicles were filled by the time I reported in, but there were still a few choices available. I walked through the barracks checking out the possibilities.

In one cubicle, a young man was sitting on a bed by himself, and he watched me as I walked through the squad bay. He had sad, but very intelligent eyes, and his face had strength of character. He was obviously of Mexican or Latin American ancestry, and he looked just a little out-of-place in that bowl of white milk. Back home in the coalmine country of Carbon County, some of my best friends were the children of Mexican emigrants. I walked over and asked if the other bunk in his cubicle was taken.

"Be my guest," he said with a smile and an extended hand of friendship. "My name is Felix Martinez."

Felix Martinez proved to be one of the most intriguing people I have ever known. He was older than me, twenty-six, if I remember correctly. He was a bachelor and a draftee who had lived his whole life on the Navajo Reservation in Arizona. His family owned and operated the Chinle Valley Store. He could play guitar and sing like a bird in five languages, including Navajo. Lucky for me, he also had a Master's Degree in mathematics.

Felix became my mentor and my tutor. He was my roommate and my big brother. He was incredulous when he discovered that I had been sent there without any prior artillery training, and he took me on as a project. He did all he could to fill me in on what I had missed. In the evenings, he would sit me down and explain things about ballistics, computations, the mechanics of how cannons work, and the glossary of terms. He checked my homework and helped me cram for weekly exams. He would recap lectures for me and explain in detail any questions I might have. He pointed out things that I had missed, and showed me other and "better" ways to do the math on some of the equations. I don't think I could have made it through without his tutelage. I owe him a great deal.

Many of our classmates were "washed-out" or "set-back" during the academic segment. Washed-out means they were dropped from OCS and sent back to a regular Army unit because of academic, leadership, or personal failures. "Set-Back" means they were sent back to the starting point of the academic section and given a second chance to pass, but with a different group of candidates. And then too, a few more of our "contemporaries" folded under the pressure and resigned.

At the end of eight or nine weeks of middle class academics, we were promoted to upper class. It was then we began our true officer training. Again, OCS is broken down into three parts. The lower class segment is a torture chamber, the middle class segment is an academic boiler, and the upper class segment is true leadership training. By the time a group of Candidates reaches upper class status, most of the dead wood has been culled.

Upperclassmen wore red epaulet tabs, and they were called "Redbirds." Red is the Army's designated color for artillery. An artilleryman wears a red braid on his uniform. The infantry color is blue, and armor (cavalry) is yellow. Redbirds routinely practiced their swagger in the presence of the lower class candidates. It was part of their job and part of their training.

As mentioned earlier, upper classmen were the enforcers and the drill instructors for the outfit. It was in dominating the lower classmen where they practiced giving orders, calling marching cadence, and thinking up creative and sometimes humorous tortures for the new guys. If a candidate had a penchant for sadism, it would show up during his upper class tenure. Even a few upper classmen were washed-out for excessive exuberance in creative disciplining. The TAC Officers kept a close eye on the haughty Redbirds.

Part of our job as upper classmen was to meet and greet the new arrivals at OCS. It was our duty to shock and intimidate the new guys immediately, and to strip them of all rank and insignia. It was just my luck that the first man I confronted as a new upper classman was a Staff Sergeant with Vietnam campaign ribbons, a First Air Cavalry shoulder patch, a Purple Heart, and a Silver Star. The man was everything I ever wanted to be as a soldier.

I stood in front of that man for what seemed like a long time as I thought it over. He was years older than me, and he stood at attention, straight and tall, with eyes to the front, staring straight ahead, very soldierly and completely professional. I took a deep breath and cleared my throat. There was chaos going on all around us as other upper classmen demoralized and yelled at the new guys.

"Sergeant," I said in a still, small voice, hoping that my contemporaries were all busy with other new candidates and not paying attention to what I was doing. "I'm supposed to strip you of all rank and insignia, to include decorations, chevrons, and shoulder patches. But ... I will not remove those decorations or that shoulder patch in such a disrespectful way. Would you please remove those items by yourself, Sergeant, and put them in your pocket?"

The Sergeant turned his stern military gaze to meet my eyes, and then he said very quietly, "Thank you, Sir." It was the first time a Sergeant ever called me "Sir." It was a great way for it to happen.

When the items were safely in his pockets, I told him to drop and give me twenty-five, just for the hell of it. As he did his push-ups in his stripped-down dress uniform, necktie and all, I knelt on one knee next to him on the asphalt and said, "Welcome to OCS Sergeant, and I do wish you the very best."

"Thank you, Sir," he said a second time, as he sweated to complete the push-ups I had ordered.

It was during our upper class training when we received most of our instruction in being Forward Observers. I found the job to be every bit as glamorous as the name sounded. It must have cost hundreds of thousands of dollars to train each new artillery officer. We each expended hundreds of rounds of artillery ammunition on the target ranges.

They would take us out on a hill and point out a distant target through a spotting scope. We would then plot a fire mission for the guns. We had to estimate the range and then give the proper coordinates and the compass bearing to the target. Remember, this was in the days before GPS satellites and laser range-finding systems. We had to shoot by the "best guess" method. It was an inexact science, and some of us were better guessers than others.

We had to properly identify the target, and then choose the type of shell and fuse best suited for that target. We then directed fire on the target, adjusting the exploding shells ever closer in 50 or 100-meter increments (best guess) until we got a hit. We were graded at the end of the exercise on how well we did. The guy who properly identified the target, selected the proper fuse and shell, and hit the target in the fastest time using the fewest number of shells, won the accolades.

Like machine-gun school, artillerymen are taught how best to kill people using the tools at hand. First, there is the selection of caliber. If you have a choice, and want to blow things up from long range, we were taught to use the heavy guns, eight-inch or 175mm. They make a big splash. For intermediate work, and for heavy hitting on fortified positions, a 155mm does a good job. But most often, we were taught to shoot using the smaller, 105mm howitzers. The bursting radius of a 105 is smaller (about 35 yards), which makes them just a little safer for close-in work. And then of course, the smaller caliber ammunition is less expensive for training purposes.

For clarification, I should point out that there is a difference between a howitzer and a gun, even though both might be called cannons. A gun is a direct-fire weapon. It sends a shell on a relatively flat trajectory at a distant target, much like a rifle. Battleships use sixteen-inch guns. A howitzer, on the other hand, can be used like a gun or like a mortar. A howitzer can point its barrel high in the air and lob a shell over an obstacle, like a building or a grove of trees. A howitzer can sit on one side of a hill and put shells on the other side of the same hill on targets that are only a short distance away. Howitzers are more versatile than guns. Most Army cannons are howitzers.

There are several kinds of artillery shells available, and the Forward Observer gets to choose, depending on what he wants to do to the target. He can blow it up, set it on fire, pepper it with fleshettes, hide it with a smoke screen, or light it up in the dark.

After the proper shell has been selected, comes the selection of the fuse. Artillery shells are shipped without a fuse attached. The fuse is screwed into the nose of the shell just before it is fired. Several types of fuses are available. To bust bunkers, collapse trenches, or bring down large buildings, the Forward Observer tells the gun-bunnies to use a delayed fuse so the shell will bury deep into the ground or the target before exploding. For most surface targets, such as vehicles and small buildings, a point-detonating fuse is often best. For troops in the open, or in foxholes, an airburst is the method of choice. The observer calls for VT (variable-timed), "proximity" fuses that detonate the shell above the ground. If you are the bad guy and caught out in the open, it's hard to hide from an airburst.

Sometimes in training, we were given targets that were only a couple of hundred yards away. That's when things got tense. When the fireball of the explosion and the BOOM of the concussion happened at the same time, you knew you had better not screw-up when you made the next adjustment. You were in a zone the artillery calls "danger-close."

There were times when our instructors countermanded a candidate's orders to the guns in the interests of safety. The trainee then got his butt chewed as the TAC Officer explained that the order, as first given, would probably have killed us all. Young soldiers and their instructors do get killed in training sometimes.

A few upper class candidates were washed-out on the gunnery ranges. Some could not learn to judge distance properly (a potentially fatal defect for an FO), and a few others proved to be careless, or to lack good judgment. An FO must keep a level head and focus completely on the job at hand. The middle of a fire mission is not the time to show off for your buddies or loose track of what it was you told six cannons to do a few moments ago (a standard artillery battery has six guns). No one usually cares if a stupid FO kills himself, but the Army really frowns on a sloppy artillery spotter who takes half a rifle company to hell with him. (It happens.)

I was proud to be trained as a Forward Observer. In the world of artillerymen, the FO is King. He is the "eyes" of the artillery battery. All of the critical decisions about target selection, ammunition type, fusing, and the number of shells expended, are decisions made by the FO. All other officers who serve the gun battery, whether they outrank him or not, defer to the FO's decisions. He is the man on the scene. In most instances, the FO is the only man in the artillery who actually gets to see the shells hit the ground. Those who hump the ammo, set the fuses, sight the guns, calculate the angles, and give the commands to fire, are usually too far from the targets to even hear the shells explode.

We would lie on our stomachs on top of a hill (you don't want to create a profile that a sniper might recognize), and use a radio to call a fire mission to a gun battery eight or ten miles away. We then waited to hear the warbling flutter of the shells passing high overhead. We would watch the target through binoculars and howl with delight as the fireballs exploded and the fender of an antique Chevy went spinning off into the stratosphere. It was a feeling of power I can't even describe.

They took us up in fragile little airplanes and taught us to direct artillery from the air. From the air you can see concussion rings from the explosions expanding through the air like ripples in water. It was fascinating.

For a kid like me who always wanted to blow things up, directing artillery was absolute magic. I loved to snuggle up next to a warm and friendly machine-gun, but I had never dreamed of yielding such raw power until I called white-hot and exploding projectiles from out of the clouds like bolts of lightening. I found that with just my voice over the radio, I had the power of Zeus, the strength of Atlas, and the war-making potential of Odin, the father of Thor.

Few young men have ever experienced such a feeling of power. From ten miles away, a hundred artillerymen jumped to obey my every command. A dozen cannons roared when I gave the order. I could plow a field, cut down a grove of trees, or roll an old tank carcass down a hill with the exploding shells. It was magic.

I truly enjoyed Forward Observer training. It was more fun than Disneyland. But then, all too soon, it was over. On the sixteenth day of May 1967, I was awarded my gold bars. I was officially commissioned an Officer and a Gentleman in the Army of the United States. I was twenty years old. I had been in the Army for ten months and ten days.

SIX DAYS IN JUNE

My first duty station as a new Lieutenant was with the Second Armored Division at Fort Hood, Texas. I reported for duty on the first day of June and was assigned to a self-propelled 105mm gun battery.

I was humbled to join that unit as a new officer. I had none of the swagger or exuberant self-confidence common to the species. I was painfully aware that I was not up to the job yet. It was my very first assignment to a regular army unit and I had an awful lot to learn. Everything I had done in the Army to that day had been training. I didn't know the routines or the details of how a non-training unit functioned. It would take a while to catch up.

The battlefields of Vietnam had absorbed almost half-a-million American troops by then, and the soldier ranks at Fort Hood were decimated. The whole division was critically short in the junior officer department. The gun battery I was assigned to had Sergeants doing some of the jobs usually performed by Lieutenants.

As the newest and lowest ranking young officer in the unit, I was assigned to the motor pool, a job that no one else wanted, and a place where I couldn't get into too much trouble. But, the day I reported in, I was overwhelmed to find myself designated as the "acting" Executive Officer – temporarily the second in command. A higher-ranking First Lieutenant had been assigned the job, but he was on leave and wouldn't join the unit for another week or two.

It was highly irregular for someone like me to be put in a situation like that, even on a temporary basis. It was a sign of how difficult things were in the stateside Army of the time. The Captain was improvising, and shuffling his people to best meet the needs of the moment.

There was another, more senior Second Lieutenant at the gun battery who should have had the "acting" Executive Officer assignment, but the Captain preferred to keep him in FDC (Fire Direction Control). FDC is a critical, safety sensitive job, and the battery was scheduled for a series of field problems in the next few days. The Captain didn't want a brand new guy in FDC. The Colonel, and maybe even the General, would be evaluating the unit's performance.

The Captain's plan was to give me a big pile of backlogged paperwork, reports, and housekeeping chores to do until the "real" XO (Executive Officer) reported in. Then, I would be banished to the motor pool. We all knew I would be "acting" as the unit XO in name only, office help really, without any of the real authority of the job. It was okay. I couldn't get into much trouble. The Captain and the First Sergeant had me surrounded.

And then, just four days later, came war in the Middle East. On the fifth day of June 1967, the Israeli Air force hit Egypt hard. Israeli tanks rolled into Gaza, the Sinai, and the Golan Heights. The whole Middle East exploded.

It had been brewing for a long time, and it didn't look like a fair fight to begin with. The Arabs had an overwhelming advantage in men and material. Egypt, Syria, and Jordan had been sounding the trumpets of war and rattling sabers for months, eager for a fight. But, the Jewish David surprised the Arab Goliath with a sucker punch that evened the odds.

The Soviets had trained, supplied, and provided the coaching staff for the Arab Armies, and they were about to be humiliated. Russian equipment, Russian tactics, and Russian friends were going up in flames all across the desert. The angry and embarrassed Soviets mounted their chariots of war and threatened immediate intervention.

The American Army was instantly on red alert. All the klaxons sounded and there was a mad scramble for the guns. Strategic bombers went skyward and nuclear submarines went deep. Deep inside Cheyenne Mountain, seals were broken on contingency plan options. Target grids were plotted and fed to primitive, refrigerator-sized computers.

I knew we were in trouble when I saw the panic in the eyes of the old-time Sergeants. We were going against the Russians … and we were unprepared. We had orders to prepare for immediate overseas deployment.

On paper, the Second Armored Division was a ready reaction force capable of responding to any threat, anywhere in the world, with just a few hours notice. In reality, the Second Armored had been cannibalized like the body of an old automobile to feed the battlefields of Vietnam. We were hopelessly short of everything, men most of all.

Mile-long trains of flatcars were pushed onto railroad sidings at Fort Hood. We hurriedly loaded the howitzers and packed our gear. Locomotives would take us to the gulf coast. At the ports, we would embark on ships for deployment to the deserts of the Middle East.

As an inexperienced new officer with only four days in the unit, I was hopelessly overwhelmed. I didn't know the standard operating procedures for the battery or the division. Lucky for me, the old Sergeants knew what to do. They talked me through the decisions and guided my hand in the signing of orders and requisitions. Some were visibly annoyed by my perfect incompetence, but ever true to military protocol, they still grudgingly called me "Sir." It made me blush. No one knew better than I, that as an officer, I could have been replaced with a rubber stamp. I felt like a pathetic little geek ... with shiny gold bars. But, I tried to be professional and not show how I felt. I did the best I could.

This new change in our fortunes put a frightening new twist on the very idea of my being the "acting" Executive Officer. Something else would have to happen very soon. My temporary assignment was not a big deal when we were inside an office and the Captain was never more than a phone call away. But now, as we prepared to face the Russian Army, the matter of chain-of-command and succession of power became a real issue. If the other, more senior Second Lieutenant at the battery was moved up to Executive Officer, as he surely would be, then I would become the new Fire Direction Officer. Could it be that the first fire mission I would ever calculate in earnest would be aimed at Russian tanks? The very thought filled me with panic.

And then, during the hectic process of loading the big guns on the railcars, I became painfully aware that we had six howitzers but only enough men to man three of them. It was a realization that took the wind out of me. How could this be? We were on our way to fight a war!

At a late-night staff meeting, held after the guns and gear were secured atop the flatcars, I foolishly pointed out to my Captain that his unit was only at half-strength. The Captain gave me a look that would have knocked a pigeon off a post, and then he said thanks, but he already knew about it.

The Captain was haggard and drawn. He looked sick. In a somewhat more tolerant tone of voice, he told me that the whole division was in the same shape. Everyone was in Vietnam, Germany, or Korea. He said the Colonel had promised him that they would send replacements to meet us at sea. I ask how we were supposed to train new gun crews with the cannons stored in the holds of the ships. The Captain didn't answer.

I knew we were dead. To be so completely unprepared and on our way to meet the Russian Army was suicide. Into the mouth of hell and into the jaws of death, indeed.

In true military fashion, we sat on our duffle bags at the railhead and waited, and waited, and waited. And while we waited, we suffered the mental torments of hell. To make matters even worse, we were quarantined. We could not write letters or make phone calls. Our destination was supposed to be top secret. To keep that secret, we would not be allowed to offer our last goodbyes to family, friends, and loved ones. We sat for three or four days and nights in the shadow of the railcars and waited. And while we waited, we stared into the empty, blue sky of Texas and tried to remember the faces of those who meant the most to us.

Some of us worried that we might not live to see the Middle East. Russian submarines or bombers might try to sink our ships in mid-Atlantic. And, we knew that if we went head-to-head with the Russians, it was probably the end of the world anyway. We were not equipped in men, material, or firepower to win the coming contest, and we knew that our side would not accept defeat. We had backed the Russians down in Cuba in 1962, and they had spent the last five years brooding about it. They might not back down this time. This one might go atomic. If it did, nothing would ever matter after that.

For four or five days we were isolated, cut off from everyone and everything, sitting on our duffle bags and waiting for the end of the world. And then came an order we had not expected: "Stand down."

My God ... it was over! We had been granted a reprieve. We might not be killed after all.

That conflict in the desert has since become known as the Six-Day War. It couldn't have been timed better. Had it lasted six months, or even six weeks, I'm sure I would have been dead ... maybe you too.

The General Staff must have shared my fears, because within days of our little adventure, new people began arriving at our unit. Someone in Washington had finally been awakened to the fact that the Ruskies were not going to give us a pass just because we were spending our treasure and our army in Vietnam. We had best keep a few cannons cocked and ready to cover our back while we beat up the Viet Cong.

Within just a week or so, my artillery battery had two new Lieutenants report for duty. One of them was a First Lieutenant just back from Vietnam who shouldered the title and responsibility of Executive Officer. I was relegated to the motor pool where I should have been in the first place. I was happy. It was as if the weight of the world had been lifted from my shoulders. I wallowed in the grease, diesel smoke, and endless paperwork of the motor pool until December, and then I got orders for Vietnam.

The Girl I Left Behind Me

Oh, ne'er shall I forget the night,
The stars were bright above me,
And gently lent their silv'ry light,
When she first vowed she loved me,
But now I'm bound for Brighton Camp,
Kind Heaven may favour find me,
And send me safely back again,
To the girl I left behind me.

The second verse of an old English marching song written by Samuel Lover, 1797-1868. The song was more recently made popular by John Wayne and Glen Ford in cavalry movies like: *She Wore a Yellow Ribbon (1949).*

There was a special young woman in my life when I went away to war. She was a farmer's daughter with laughing eyes who rode horses, milked cows, and wore flowers in her hair. She was a beautiful girl, radiant with health, strength, and the joy of living. We were high school sweethearts and I loved her dearly.

She promised to wait for me when I got my draft notice, but I worried that it wouldn't happen. She was a beautiful girl, and sure to have her pick of the handsome young cowboys. While I was away, she did get several offers. More than a few young men offered to take her dancing, to a show, or out to dinner for the evening. Though sometimes tempted, she did not partake. She remained ever true to her soldier.

In May 1967, after graduating from OCS, I came home on leave as an Officer and a Gentleman, driving a new GTO and wearing my polished gold bars. She was proud of me, and she expected me to sweep her off her feet like Sir Galahad and carry her away. I didn't, and it broke her heart.

Through the turmoil of the months of exhaustive training and my knowing of the dragons I had yet to face, I was convinced that I didn't want to be married yet. I truly loved Jeannie, but I was torn between two loyalties. The Army had become my life.

The Army was the mistress who nurtured and sustained me. I owed the Army everything: my job, my station in life, and my future. As a brand new officer, and still reeling from the many months of selfless commitment to the training, I felt a loyalty to the Army that bordered on worship. The Marine Corps does the same thing to new recruits. After a few months of intensive military indoctrination, a fluttering flag and a muttered Semper Fidelis (always faithful) can bring tears to the eyes of a young Marine Recruit. As a brand new Second Lieutenant, I felt much the same way about the Army. After ten long months of nothing but training, self-sacrifice and indoctrination, I was completely programmed. I was mentally primed, physically conditioned, and spiritually prepared to charge the cannons. A new wife just wouldn't fit into the equation.

Through the depths of her disappointment, I tried to make Jeannie understand how I felt. I counted all the reasons we should wait to be married. In the first place, we were still very young. She was nineteen and I was twenty. And then, I was going back to face my first duty assignment as an officer and I was very apprehensive about it. In fact, I was scared to death. I knew that it would be a real struggle. I would be putting in endless hours catching up on everything I was supposed to know as an officer and didn't. From my point of view, taking a new wife into the turmoil of that situation would only add to the stress in my life. I didn't need any more stress.

And then of course, there was an ethical consideration too. Vietnam was a sure thing for me. In my training I had been given a peek into Dante's hell, and I knew somewhat of the horrors that awaited me. I would likely be a Forward Observer, out in front of the troops and on the razor's edge. The odds were very high that I would be wounded or killed. How could I ask a young wife to wait for me, not knowing if, or how, I would return? I might come home in a body bag, or even worse. Was it right to ask her to marry me, knowing that we might not have a future together?

Jeannie didn't see things my way. She was convinced that she would be a solid rock of support for me. She would be my companion and my helpmate. She was willing to get a job and pay her way just to be with me. She was already working for the government at the Green River Missile Base in Utah. She thought she might be able to transfer to my army post in Texas. She said she was willing to subsist on soda crackers and poverty stew to help pay rent on our own little place. I knew she was serious.

She also countered my arguments about war wounds. She told me that she wouldn't feel any different about loosing me to the war whether we were married or not. I might as well make her my wife because it would all be the same to her anyway. And, if I did come back wounded, she would follow me to hell before leaving my side, married or not. That's how she felt.

Unfortunately, in our culture, men have all the power. I wouldn't listen to her arguments. She offered her hand in love and all sincerity and I refused to reach out and take it. I reported to Fort Hood without her. She took it as a sign that I didn't want her anymore.

The rejection hurt her deeply. She began to wonder if maybe the farmer's daughter wasn't glamorous enough to be the wife of an Officer and a Gentleman. I would have been embarrassed and ashamed had I known she felt that way. But then, I should have been embarrassed and ashamed anyway for shunning her noble sacrifices after her many months of faithfully waiting for me.

We didn't officially break the ties that bind as I rode off into the dust of Texas without her. Over the next few months we wrote letters and spoke on the phone once in a while. We were still friends, but there was an empty space between us. She decided to move on with her life. She started making plans to transfer with her job to California and make a new start. She began to make the necessary arrangements.

At Fort Hood, after the Six-Day War scare, I buried myself in the manure pile of motor pool paperwork. There were endless forms, requisitions, and reports to file. My unit also spent weeks at a time out in the boondocks with the cannons, training the gun crews we didn't have for the Six-Day War. I was very busy and completely committed to being a good soldier. I didn't think about Jeannie, or getting married, often.

I had thought that the shadow of Vietnam hung heavy before I was drafted into the Army. But now, the shadow was suffocating. Everyone at Fort Hood was on the Vietnam Express, some going and some coming. Everyone had been there or was on his way. Those just back told endless stories about battles, booby-traps, and body counts. Some even had bullet wounds and shrapnel scars to use for show and tell. Those soon to board the outbound train walked around with deep and brooding eyes, quietly suffering. Those of us still in limbo and waiting for orders, hung around the bulletin boards anxiously, waiting for the ax to fall. There was a small chance of being sent to Germany or Korea, but deep in my heart, I knew where I was going.

Each day that I waited for orders to Vietnam was like a day in front of a firing squad. I was blindfolded, helpless, and tied to a post (an Army Post). Each morning I waited for the morning dispatches like I was waiting for a bullet. The mental torment was maddening. I started working hard at being a drunk. Alcohol numbed the pain of anxiety and disinfected the uncertainty. Good Mormons do not partake of alcohol, coffee, tea, or tobacco, but at that point in my life, I was not living the high standards of the faith of my fathers.

On Thanksgiving Day, after turkey and gravy at the Mess Hall, Jeannie called me on the phone to ask if I was coming home for Christmas. I told her no. I wanted to save what leave I had accrued so I could have a couple of weeks at home when the Vietnam order finally came ... whenever that was.

She surprised me by offering to fly to Texas to spend some time with me. I didn't know it at the time, but she wanted to sort things out before she closed the door on me forever and moved to California. She had been busy too. Like a fool, I told her that I didn't want her to come to Texas. I told her to wait and I would be home soon. I would surely be getting orders in a matter of weeks.

I was desperately trying to keep her at arm's length. I was afraid that if we spent any time together she would charm me into getting married, and I was determined that I didn't want to be married yet. We quarreled on the phone. She grew angry, and then came tears. In frustration and disgust, she told me that I had a deadline. If I wasn't home by Christmas it was all over: don't call, don't write, and don't bother. In the interim, she would be dating other guys. She was tired of waiting for nothing. I hung up on her, and spent the rest of the evening with my old friend Jack Daniels, brooding.

The next few weeks were complete hell for me. I knew her well enough to know that she was serious, and it tied my guts in knots. I tried to be a macho man about it. I told myself that it really didn't matter, and I resolved to find some waterfront wench at the Officer's Club to spend Christmas with. But, deep down inside myself, I knew I couldn't do it. I loved her dearly, in spite of myself.

As I brooded about it, I became angry. Jeannie was too pushy. Why couldn't she just sit on the sidelines like a China Doll and wait for me to win the damn war? Girls were supposed to wait at home while the guys did the man stuff. I was up to my baby's bum in alligators here in Texas, and surely even a woman could understand that? And, Vietnam was waiting just over the horizon. I needed to stay focused to stay alive. Wait a while, Sweetie Pie, and let me get the soldiering done. And, why get married now anyway? Kiss at the altar and then go overseas for a whole damn year? Now that sounded romantic. Women! I've never been able to understand how they think.

I let my anger turn to spite. In mid-December, I took a girl from Texas on a date, but it was a real wipeout. I've had more fun changing a flat tire in the rain. The girl from Texas wasn't Jeannie, and for the first time I realized that I was comparing every girl I met to the girl back home. No one measured up. It was a sobering revelation.

I brooded, fretted, and got orders for Vietnam. The First Sergeant handed me the order one morning with the practiced indifference of a traffic cop. Vietnam! It had finally happened. I had expected that sentence for many fretful months, but it was still a shock. I was to report to the Army Processing Center in Oakland, California for deployment overseas. I was to leave California for Saigon on the fifth day of February 1968.

The order came on December 21st, just four days before Christmas. I was crushed. I had two weeks leave saved up, and I wanted to use it just before I shipped overseas. I would have to wait until the middle of January to go home. I would spend Christmas all alone in Texas, sitting on my duffle bag again and thinking of loved ones as I waited to go to war.

But then, for the second time, I was given a reprieve. The First Sergeant told me that since I was going overseas for a year, I could borrow a month's leave against next year and sign out as soon as I could clear the post. I hadn't been aware of that. I could have kissed that multi-stripped and grizzled old Soldier. Young officers get saluted, but it's the old Sergeants who know where the treasures are buried in the military paperwork.

It took three days to clear the post. I had to turn in all government equipment, clear payroll, sign the motor pool over to some other guy, and get in line for lots of shots. I had to get a medical and a dental checkup too. Luckily, my status as an officer let me cut the long lines, and for the first time in my military career I took full advantage of the privileges of rank. I didn't even blush.

The airlines were jammed with holiday travelers. It was impossible to fly home on military standby status and expect to be home for Christmas. With just hours left before Santa Clause came, I didn't have time to even consider taking a bus or a train. To hell with it, I dug deep into my bank account and bought a ticket on a jet plane at full-price. I bought a round-trip ticket. My car was in a garage having the transmission fixed. I would need to fly back to Texas and pick it up later.

I didn't tell anyone at home that I was coming. Part of every soldier's daydream is to come home unannounced. The fantasy is to suddenly appear unexpectedly when you are supposed to be on a distant battlefield, and see the pretty woman drop a basket of wet laundry and run to meet you. It's a Norman Rockwell moment (wink).

The next day, as the big 707 taxied out on the runway, I realized that I couldn't wait to see Jeannie. I felt like a puppy who had just spent a long night all alone in a big box. I wanted to scoop her up in my arms and smother her with happy puppy dog kisses. But then, I remembered that we had sorta broken up. The last time I had spoken to her she was mad and in tears. She might not be glad to see me at all. The love of my life might even have another beau by now. The realization was sobering. I just couldn't imagine going home and Jeannie not being there to meet me.

As the plane angled up through the Texas cloudbanks, clawing for thirty thousand feet, I began to reflect about my life, my future, and my status as an ex-boyfriend. I sat quietly, looking out over an ocean of clouds, and went deep inside myself. I reviewed my life, my beliefs, my innermost fears, and my deepest emotions. For the first time in a long time, I took inventory. Now that Vietnam was a sure thing for me and I was facing the real possibility of my own death, I could be completely honest with myself.

What is life all about? I didn't know the answer at the time. I was young and it was still a mystery to me. But then, a second question: What is life worth without a pretty woman? I decided ... not much. I realized that the things I loved most in all the world were the red deserts of Utah and the farmer's daughter who wasn't waiting anymore. When I was completely honest with myself, I was shocked to discover that the Army really didn't matter all that much. When you got right down to it, the Army was just another job.

My conclusions were humbling. I had certainly made a mess of things. Was it too late to make amends? And, what would Jeannie think about my deathbed confession, now that I was on my way to a distant battlefield? What would she think when I told her that I loved her and couldn't live without her? I felt like a creep. My ex-sweetheart was a young woman of pride and character. I couldn't blame her if she told me to take a hike.

I looked down on a carpet of cotton ball clouds and realized that there was only one thing I could do to make it right. I had to ask her to marry me. It was a tough conclusion to come to. I could count a dozen reasons why it shouldn't happen. I was on my way to Vietnam, for Pete's sake. Who knew what my destiny might be? I might be badly wounded. I might not come back at all.

Oh well, she had told me once that it didn't matter. Maybe it should be a joint decision. I decided that we could at least get engaged. If I gave her a ring it would seal my commitment to her until Vietnam was done. If I did that, she would be waiting when I came home again. We could then tie the knot and live happily ever after ... damn the devil and damn the war.

As the airplane dragged it's afternoon shadow across Colorado, I took my wallet out and counted what money I had. I had closed my checking and savings account before leaving Texas, and my life's savings was in my wallet. It surely wasn't much, just a few hundred dollars. As a new Army Lieutenant, I made 300 dollars a month. It doesn't sound like much, but to put things in proper perspective, I had recently bought a slightly used Pontiac GTO for $2,600, and gas was .32 cents pr. gallon.

In spite of my limited resources, I resolved to buy a ring anyway. I would buy a ring and then ask Jeannie to sit down and talk with me - if she would still have me.

Buying a ring would pose a problem. I wanted to buy her something nice, but I had to live for a month on the money that was in my wallet. I had no other financial reserves. I also had to travel all the way back to Texas after Christmas and pick up the GTO. I could see that I was headed for financial disaster. Oh well ... be brave young soldier, you only live once. Damn the torpedoes and full speed ahead!

The plane landed in Salt Lake City, and I caught a taxi into the heart of town. It was early Christmas Eve and the ground was covered with snow. It was cold. I went to the Continental Bus Terminal and bought a ticket for home. The bus wouldn't leave for a couple of hours, and so I walked downtown and went shopping for rings.

There was a guy in a suit and tie working the counter in the Zales Jewelry Store. The store was all decorated for the holidays and the salesman was friendly and cheerful. When I told him I wanted to look at wedding rings, he asked if I knew my lady's ring size. Luckily, I did. Jeannie and I had talked about ring sizes when ordering high school class rings. (Women are so sneaky.)

The jewelry man sorted through his wares, and then he set a pair of pretty rings on the countertop. "These are the best deals in the store right now," he said. "And since it's Christmas Eve, I'll give you every discount I can scrape together."

There was no price tag on either ring, and so I asked how much. He scratched some figures on a notepad and then set a price on each ring. His prices were steep for my limited resources. It was a heavy blow. I winced and hesitated. What to do? In those days there were no credit cards, and making monthly payments to buy a ring was simply out of the question. Only houses and cars were bought on the installment plan.

It posed a serious financial dilemma for me. Buying a ring would take almost all of the money I had in the whole world. I could see that I would need to borrow money to get back to Texas and be able to eat for the next few weeks. It was distressing.

I looked the rings over carefully as I sorted through my financial problems and the deepest of my emotions. They were expensive, but pretty rings, sparkling diamonds to reflect the love-light in her eyes. She was worth it, and much more. What is money anyway?

"Tell you what," the eager salesman said. "It looks like you might be my last customer of the season. You meet my price and I'll pay the sales tax and give you the best box in the store to put the ring in. I'll even gift wrap it for free if you want."

"Okay," I said, trying to smile bravely.

I took a deep breath and made my selection. "I'll take this one," I said. "Good choice," the salesman smiled.

I bought the ring not knowing if Jeannie would accept it. It was very bold of me to assume that she would. Had she shopped around, she could have done much better than a soldier boy with an empty wallet and a ticket to Vietnam.

I didn't realize it at the time, but I had truly become one of those cocky and over-confident young Second Lieutenants, and maybe it was a good thing too. To win at love and war sometimes takes a fighter pilot's mentality. On that particular Christmas Eve, I knew that I couldn't be beaten – not by the Viet Cong, and certainly not by some civilian boyfriend who might compete for my lady's hand. I had made up my mind, and I was ready to claim my bride.

It was dark when the bus rolled into Price, Utah and snowing heavily. In the glow of streetlights, the huge snowflakes were like sparkling confetti raining down on my homecoming parade. The new snow was several inches deep and there were few tracks to mar the sidewalks. It was beautiful. There were very few cars or people in town when I got there. The stores were all closed and everyone was at home waiting for Santa Clause.

I called Jeannie's house from a pay phone in the bus terminal. Her sister answered the phone and almost had a coronary when I told her who and where I was. In a few moments Jeannie came on the line and I asked if she could come and pick me up at the bus station. She told me to hold tight and she would be right there.

I didn't know until more than a year later that she had left her date for the evening sitting on her mother's sofa when she put her coat on and left the house. The poor guy made small talk with her mother for most of an hour before he finally accepted the fact that he'd been stood up and she wasn't coming back. Jeannie has said that it is embarrassing to think about it now, but she was answering a higher call. She did call the poor fellow on the phone a few days later, unbeknownst to me, and apologized to him for standing him up like that. She is a good woman.

Jeannie came through the snowstorm in her dad's big Pontiac Bonneville, a pretty girl in a big white limousine, an appropriate homecoming I thought. I kicked the snow off my shoes and climbed into the passenger seat. We sat there looking at each other through the dim, yellow cast of the streetlights. The pale light flickered through the confetti of falling snowflakes. The windshield wipers chugged back and forth, and the car's heater fan was working hard.

"Hello," I said. "Remember me?"

"You creep," she said with a smile. "Why didn't you call?"

"I got orders for Vietnam," I said.

The words took me by surprise. They simply spilled out of my mouth all by themselves. I wasn't speaking - my heart and soul were reaching out to her. "I got orders for Vietnam, Jeannie ... I ship out in a month."

She reached out to me, and we embraced, there on the car seat, in the snowstorm, in front of the bus terminal. I held her to me, and smelled her hair, and we both started to cry. The sudden rush of emotion took me by surprise and there was nothing I could do about it. We held each other tight for a long time without speaking as our tears blended together between our pressed cheeks. All the pain and frustrations of breaking up, eighteen long months of separation, the war, and orders to Vietnam, were washed away.

Jeannie understood the depth of my anguish. She drank from the same bitter cup. My shameful display of emotion was safe in her keeping, but I felt like a geek just the same. Brave soldiers are not supposed to cry, especially officers, and never in the company of women.

Like kids, we drove out on Lover's Lane above town and

kissed and cuddled for a while. I regained some of my manly composure. I gave her the ring and she cried like a child. I told her that it wasn't as expensive a ring as I had hoped to buy for her, but it was the very best I could afford for now. If she wanted, I would get her a more expensive ring when we got to be rich and famous. She told me the ring would be with her always. Rings are only tokens, she said. I was the prize, not the ring. That pretty woman sure has a way with words.

We talked about our future. I walked her through my apprehensions again about being killed or badly wounded. She put a finger to my lips and told me to be still. She said the same thing could happen on the highway on our way home. For better or worse - damn the devil and damn the war. I told her that I would be shipping out in just a few weeks and, if she was willing, we could just stay engaged while I was gone and have a big wedding when I got back. She laughed like a schoolgirl.

"Oh no you don't," she said. "We've waited long enough. I want a husband and not a promise. We are going to be married tomorrow, or the next day, or just as soon as we can make it happen." My heart melted and I surrendered. We kissed tenderly to seal the contract.

When the Courthouse opened after the Christmas Holiday, we were there to get a marriage license. In those days you had to have a blood test too. We told our families what we were up to, and we caught a lot of flak. Our mother's were distressed. There was no time to plan a wedding. We were impatient and inflexible. No, we would not wait for a week or ten days to get invitations out. The minutes before Vietnam were ticking by like the broken white lines in the middle of the highway. We wanted to get on with it. I called the District Judge and asked if he would perform the ceremony. He knew my father, and he told me he would be honored.

We were married on December 30, 1967. Jeannie was

seven-weeks twenty. I was four-weeks twenty-one. Our marriage couldn't have been more bare bones had we eloped. We were married in the Judge's Chambers in the Carbon County Courthouse. Jeannie wore a pretty dress and I was in my uniform. There were no friends, flowers, photographs, or wedding cake at the ceremony. Our parents and a few siblings were the only witnesses. I have felt terrible in the years since that I didn't invite my grandparents whom I loved and deeply respected. Our marriage was a whirlwind wedding on the heels of a lightening strike engagement. We had taken everyone by surprise, ourselves included.

The man who tied our knot was Fred Keller, the famous "Cowboy Judge" from Southern Utah. Somehow, having him do the ceremony seemed appropriate. It was a pioneer wedding: no frills, no pomp and ceremony, and no putting on the dog. Jeannie didn't have a wedding dress or a bridal bouquet. Sometimes it hurts when I think about it. She deserved better.

But, in spite of the stark nature of the ceremony, we were both very serious about our pioneer wedding. We were totally committed to one another. I take you forever as my own. Hold my hand and we are one, come what may. We said our vows in the most humble of circumstances, but no married couple has ever honored those vows more than we have. Eagles mate forever.

Judge Keller refused the money I offered. He said soldiers were married for free in his courtroom. He had been a soldier during World War I. He shook my hand, looked deep into my eyes, and wished me the best of luck in Vietnam. He held my hand in a strong grip for a long time as if there was something else he wanted to say. Whatever it was, he didn't say it. Finally, he turned me loose, patted me on the back, and walked away.

We were finally married. I had taken a wife. What had I done? We were a couple of kids, holding hands and staring into the abyss that was the rest of our lives. Vietnam loomed just beyond the threshold like the Grand Canyon. How would we ever get across it? Where were we going, and where would we end up? Our future was scary. We clung to each other desperately.

To start our lives together, we borrowed five hundred dollars and flew back to Texas to get my car. Our leisurely trip home through Texas, New Mexico, and the red deserts of Southern Utah, was our honeymoon. The trip took three or four days. We stopped and saw some of the sights.

We stopped at a trading post in Shiprock, New Mexico, and I wanted so badly to buy Jeannie a Navajo necklace that she liked. The necklace was beautiful, a traditional design of silver squash blossoms with turquoise inlays, but it cost a hundred dollars. We just couldn't afford it. It broke my heart when she had to give it back to the saleslady ... maybe some other time. Sometimes it hurts your heart to be poor.

Almost thirty years were to pass before I was able to find a similar necklace and buy her that wedding present. My heart soared like an eagle when it finally happened.

> The bee shall honey taste no more,
> The dove become a ranger,
> The dashing waves shall cease to roar,
> Ere she's to me a stranger,
> The vows we've registered above,
> Shall ever cheer and bind me,
> In constancy to her I love,
> The girl I left behind me.

I love you Jeannie.

Wha Vyet namb?

As our hectic and war-troubled honeymoon came to an end, I packed my bags to go overseas. I tried to be cheerful and upbeat, but it was difficult. Jeannie too was sad and worried. We counted down those last few days by the minute. It was January, and cold in the Utah mountains. We were confined indoors most of the time. We spent much of our time in daydreams, making plans for a future we might not have.

It was hard for me to leave her. I held her pretty face in my hands and tried to memorize her features. The next time I sat at the train depot waiting to die, I wanted to have a clearer picture of her face in the clouds.

And then, as the day to depart crept closer, I began to worry that I might not be able to come home to her again. I felt guilty about having asked her to marry me, and I wondered if maybe we should have waited after all. She read my thoughts and told me not to worry. It would be all right. Damn the devil, and damn the war.

My parents went with us as we drove the three hours to the Salt Lake City Airport. I was in full uniform, polished brass and gold bars. It was a somber occasion. The sky was overcast and it snowed. At the airport, I kissed my mother and kissed my wife. I held Jeannie to me and felt hot tears on my cheek. She had been very brave, even stoic up to that point. I too, got all choked-up and couldn't talk. Officers don't cry in airports, and so I bit my lip, shook hands with my father, and marched to the airplane without looking back.

I took a window seat on the airplane where I could see back inside the air terminal. I could see my family, but they couldn't see me. Jeannie and my mother embraced for a while, and then they turned and walked away, arm in arm, going to the rooftop observation deck I suspected, to watch the plane take off. Dad stood there by himself and looked at the ground outside the window. He didn't know that I could still see him.

I felt sorry for my father that evening. It was a feeling I had never experienced before. Even from a distance, I could see the pain. Dad knew where I was going. He had faced the Japanese Navy and Air Force. He knew the horrors of combat. His little ship had been bombed and strafed. He had won citations for swimming out to rescue burnt and wounded men from oil fires on the water. He had been at the edge of the beaches as young Marines went ashore. He was so close to those beaches that men on his boat were hit by enemy rifle fire. He was no stranger to incoming mortars and artillery fire. He understood, in a way the women would never know, where I was going.

He looked old as he stood there. His head was bowed, shoulders slumped, his hands in his pockets. I felt bad for him, and I wanted to console him. I wanted to run to him and tell him it would be all right, but the big jet engines were beginning to whistle. The pilot came on the intercom and told us to put the cigarettes out. We would be airborne in just a few minutes.

As the big plane began to taxi to the runway, I watched dad for as long as I could. He never moved. He just stood there by himself, head down and looking at the ground outside the window. My heart reached out to him, and I whispered goodbye.

I flew out of Oakland the next day. It was a civilian 707, but a military charter flight. The plane was filled with soldiers bound for Vietnam. We were going into the Westerly wind, and the trip would take all of thirty hours. We would refuel in Hawaii and then on Guam. Our destination was Tan Son Nhut

Airbase on the outskirts of Saigon. There were half-a-dozen airline stewardesses in mini-skirts who tried to cheer us up, but with little success. We were on our way to meet the devil and there was fear in every heart.

I knew only a couple of guys on that chartered jet. They were people I recognized from the various training outfits I had served with. Everyone else was a stranger. Our only bond as soldiers was the common uniform we wore and the knowledge that we were being sent to the combat zone together.

During the past month of my whirlwind engagement and marriage, I had strictly avoided news reports about the war. I didn't want to be reminded, and it was nice to try to forget about it for a few weeks and give Jeannie my full attention. But now, on the airplane, I began to hear rumors of great battles raging all across Vietnam. Something big was happening, but the details were still sketchy. As fate would have it, we were in the sky over the blue Pacific, headed west, in the opening hours of the 1968 Tet offensive.

The world was beautiful from 30,000 feet, and it was good to be alive. The ocean was blue, the sky was blue, and the cotton ball clouds were as clean and white as freshly fallen snow. The silver wings of the great airliner glinted in the warm sunlight and the horizon faded into a misty haze. Out there somewhere, lovers walked hand-in-hand along sandy beaches, and young men ordered cool drinks in the shade of coconut palms. The world is divided into many different realities.

I had a lot of time to think during that thirty-hour flight. I didn't sleep a wink. There were no on-board movies, books, or piped-in music. It was a bare bones and no-nonsense charter flight - a boxcar with wings.

I sat the whole time and stared out the window at ocean and sky. I was trying to prepare myself to meet my fate, whatever it might be. As an officer, I knew I had to be brave and I had to set a good example. There would be no screw-ups and no excuses allowed. I was Teddy Roosevelt now: "Follow me to the top boys, we've got to take those guns." Could I really do it? And, did I have the right stuff?

I hoped I could be brave enough to live up to the old Marine Corps maxim: "Death Before Dishonor," but I wasn't sure I could measure up. What would I do when those bullets came for me and the shells came raining down? I didn't know, and I worried about it.

I wondered too, if this war was worth what I was putting into it. I was giving everything. I was putting my future, my body, my life, and my very soul on the altar of duty and patriotism. I could only hope that the cause I would fight for, and maybe die for, was worthy and just. I had to trust the decisions my government had already made for me. The war, it's causes and consequences, were beyond my control.

It was difficult. I was leaving behind a beautiful young wife to face an uncertain future by herself. She might even be pregnant, we didn't know yet. And, what if she was? Would the child she carried be my only legacy in this world of sorrow and tears? What would my child look like, and who would he be? If I were killed would he ever know who his father had been? Would my son grow up in another man's house with another man's name? Who would take him fishing? And, who would my pretty wife spend forever with if I didn't come home? How long would it take my family and my hometown to forget all about me?

I wondered too, what would my country and my family gain by my death, my noble sacrifice, on a far-off battlefield in a God-forsaken place like Vietnam? Would it really matter in the big scheme of things? What is an individual soldier's dying really worth? Does one man's death ever make a difference? Does giving that last full measure of devotion, as Abraham Lincoln coined it, ever change anything in the big scheme of things?

Vast armies engage each other en-masse, but soldiers always die as individuals. The thousands who fought and died at Gettysburg either won or lost the battle, but each man died alone, even if someone else was there to hold his hand.

Jeannie's cousin, Jimmy McBroon, had been killed in Vietnam just seven months before, in July 1967. His death was a heavy blow to the family. Jimmy was a draftee from the little town of Emery, Utah who completed basic training with my friend, Chester Housekeeper. He was then assigned to the First Cavalry Division in Vietnam. Jimmy died in an ambush, shot dead by a man who was hiding and who gave him no chance.

Incredibly, Jimmy had told Chester and others in his basic training company that somehow he knew he was destined to die in Vietnam. He went anyway, bravely shouldering that dark premonition, suffering in silence, and gave that most precious of gifts, his life, to the rest of us, knowingly. That gift is ours now, to do with what we will.

My thoughts turned to Jimmy as I looked down from that airplane over water and sky. I brooded over the tragedy and the loss of such a promising young life. Like those brave and noble soldiers Abraham Lincoln had talked about, he had been cut down in the flower of his youth. He had responded to his country's call with courage and dedication beyond anything most of us would ever know. And now, I was the young soldier sent to pick up the flag he had dropped and continue the advance across that same field of battle. I was honored to take his place in the ranks, but there was a lump in my throat and my heart was fearful. Would I follow him into eternity? Was it really worth it? And, what was it all about?

Back in OCS, we had been required to watch a film put out by the Department of Defense that featured President Lyndon Johnson as the principle narrator. The film was entitled "Why

Vietnam?" But, the way Johnson pronounced it in his deep Texas twang, it came out as "Wha Vyet Namb?"

In the film, Johnson knew he was talking to the soldiers he was sending to die, and so he tried, oh so hard, to convince us of the righteousness of the cause. He talked about communism, tyranny, oppression, dominoes, duty, honor, flag and country. He didn't quite get to motherhood and apple pie, but we all knew they were in the mix somewhere.

He gave it his best dramatic rendering, but sadly, he came across as phony. He was obviously performing. His sad and thoughtful countenance was scripted and counterfeit. In the middle of the film, my friend Martinez leaned over to me and said, "Would you buy a used car from that son-of-a-bitch?" We giggled, and were instantly reprimanded by the Tac Officers.

And yet, in spite of our premonitions about his dishonesty, as soldiers, we had no choice but to hope that he was telling us the truth. What were the options? And, in spite of his shifty eyes and patronizing manner, he did make it sound like a worthy cause. He told us we were fighting to preserve freedom, peace, and stability in the world. We were making a stand against the spread of world communism by rescuing a poor and needy nation from the clutches of evil. It was a war to liberate our Asian brothers.

Fighting for another man's freedom is noble, and that's what my friends and I were preparing to do, but I've always wished that Lyndon Johnson could have led us into battle. Wars were more carefully planned and more cautiously entered into in the days when the king was expected to lead the charge. We could have used the inspiration and the assurance that our president believed in what we were doing enough to put his life on the line with us. I could have had more confidence in his leadership had he been out front on a big white horse.

In-Country

The sun was going down and it was getting dark across the ocean. I was numb from lack of sleep and the long hours of mental anguish. My whole body hurt. It had been a long flight. I was ready to stretch my legs and get some sleep.

The pilot's voice came over the intercom and he asked for our attention. Then he said something like this:

"Gentlemen, we are approaching the Vietnamese coast. As you know, we are supposed to land at Tan San Nhut. However, I've just been advised that Tan San Nhut is under heavy attack and we are being rerouted to Bien Hoa. There will be MPs to meet us at the runway. They will direct you to the bunkers. Follow the MPs and do exactly as they say. All exits will be opened to accommodate a quick evacuation of the airplane. Be sure you take any personal luggage with you. You won't be able to get back on the plane. We will be making a very steep descent, so buckle your seat belts and hang on tight. I do wish all of you the very best. Welcome to Vietnam."

The stewardesses came back through the cabin checking seat belts and making sure everything was secured for an emergency landing. They smiled bravely, but looked terrified. It was obvious that this was not standard procedure.

We were not aware of what was happening yet, but the 1968 Tet Offensive was rapidly unfolding all across the country. The battle would rage for many weeks to come. It would prove to be the biggest single event of the Vietnam War.

The communist offensive didn't have a name yet, but we would soon learn that the battle for Hue was raging, Khe Sanh was under siege, and there was blood on the sidewalks of the American Embassy in Saigon. There were also hundreds of lesser battles in progress all across the country. The communists were going-for-broke and making their biggest play of the war.

The big plane slammed against the tarmac and the brakes were applied with full pressure. Tires squealed and then rumbled horribly as if the belly of the plane was being ripped apart. Engines roared as thrust was reversed and soldiers were thrown forward against the seatbelts. The big plane shuddered, moaned, and swerved drunkenly down the runway. There was a collective groan from the troops in the dark airliner cabin. All lights had been turned off during the decent and landing. The cabin was pitch black. Outside, everything was dark too, but we could see MPs in jeeps racing alongside, hurrying to keep up. The plane ground to a stop and the doors were immediately thrown open.

In spite of the anxiety and the helplessness that I felt at that moment, I will never forget the smell and the feel of the air that gushed in through those suddenly opened doors of that airliner. After spending thirty hours in air-conditioned comfort, it was like going underwater. The air was thick, heavy, and wet. The vapors that flooded into that airplane cabin were foreign to anything I had ever experienced before. It was like opening the visor of your space helmet in the alien swamps of the planet Mercury. The air was hot and humid, a virtual steam bath, and the smell of it was like a rotting compost pile.

The air had a strange after-taste too. There was a sweet, high-octane taste that lingered inside your nose and mouth like a film of grease. It took a while to realize that it was the smell of burning shit. There were hundreds of diesel-soaked honey-buckets smoldering near latrines all over the base. There was no indoor plumbing and no sewer treatment plants in Vietnam. Human waste was set afire in the open air. The stench was awful, but there was nothing else to breathe.

The MPs piled us all into jeeps and trucks and sped across the runway and toward a bunker complex. We passed fuel trucks racing to recharge the tanks on the airliner. The big plane made a juicy target sitting out there all alone on the runway. Everyone was scurrying to get the job done like the deck hands on an aircraft carrier. There was an urgency bordering on panic. The rockets and mortars could arrive at any second. The airliner crew had stayed with the plane. I worried about the stewardesses in their mini-skirts.

The jeeps and trucks skidded to a stop in front of the bunkers and the MPs jumped out and started to herd the new soldiers into the bowels of the earth. I was one of the first to reach the bunker door, but instead of going in, I stepped to the side and stood there as the others filed past and down the steps. An MP Sergeant came over, touched my arm, and told me to, "Please go inside the bunker, Sir." I told him I would when all the troops were safely inside. The Sergeant snorted like a dolphin, and then he said, "Yes Sir, as you wish Sir." He then walked away, shaking his head.

It was okay. I was Teddy Roosevelt. I was setting an example and taking care of "my" men. In spite of the possible danger, I would be the last man to enter the bunker. Several other officers filed past and down the steps.

In my thirty-plus hours of sleepless, anxious mental preparation to meet the devil, I had over-prepared. I had become General Washington. I was out in front of the troops setting a fine example - an Officer and a Gentleman. Hit me if you can, Ho Chi Minh. Fortunately, my sense of knighted chivalry would not last for long. After a few hours of sleep, I was better able to put things into proper perspective. And besides, my gallant show of raw courage and officer-like self-sacrifice was wasted. No rockets or mortars showed up as promised.

The MPs took us to a holding area in the middle of the base camp later that same night. We were given a bed and told to stand down until tomorrow. Then, we could start processing. Our orders and connections to units had been all messed-up by our arrival at the wrong base. It would take a few days for things to catch up and be sorted out. There were bunkers near the barracks, and we were told to go there in case of a rocket or mortar attack. The base camp soldiers told us they had been shelled several times in the past few days. The sirens did sound a couple of times that week, and we ran to the bunkers.

In spite of the exhaustion of a trans-Pacific crossing without sleep, I couldn't go to bed for a long time that first night. There was just too much going on and too much to see. So this is Vietnam? I stood outside the barracks in the dark and watched with fascination.

Bien Hoa was completely dark in the night, all blacked out and hunkered down. The lights had been turned off to deny the enemy gunners any reference points. In the dark, it was hard to judge how big the place was. I had no feel for what was around me and the uncertainty was maddening. I was anchored to one tiny spot of known territory in a vast and strange new world. All around me, everything was dark, threatening, and hostile.

The night had an odd feel about it too, something I had never experienced before. There was a strange, anxious tension in the air that permeated the darkness; a fretful knowing that death lurked in the shadows all around us. This was the heart of a war zone, and somehow, even the elements of nature seemed to be uneasy with the knowledge.

And, I could see and hear the war happening all around me. Far off on the dark horizon, yellow flares floated down on parachutes over a distant firefight. Strings of tiny sparks that were tracer bullets arched high into the night sky, fading as they went deeper into darkness, and then came the sounds of distant explosions. It was like watching a distant fireworks display on the Fourth of July.

And then, the rumble and roar of jet engines came from the nearby airfield as a pair of fighter/bombers streaked skyward. I couldn't tell the type of aircraft in the dark, Phantoms probably, but maybe Thunderchiefs. The bright glow of hot tailpipes shot across the dark sky and disappeared into the clouds. The sound of the jets was followed by the echoing, whop, whop, whop of distant rotor blades that told me that a helicopter was out there somewhere too, and maybe ferrying wounded from the distant battle.

Somewhere beyond the Mess Hall, and surprisingly close in the dark, an artillery battery began a fire mission. There was a loud CRACK and the flash of cannons in the night, and then the hiss of heavy shells slipping through the damp air on their way to the killing fields. A few moments later, far off and on the horizon again, came the silent flash of the shells exploding against a black sky. I could calculate the distance to the firefight by the time it took for the sound to come back to me, a measured count by the seconds, and then a distant rumble of thunder. The bright flashes and the distant rumblings reminded me of thunderstorms on the Utah desert that I loved, but this storm had a different feel. Somewhere out there, and very close to those bright flashes of light, a Forward Observer was applying his trade in earnest. My pulse quickened as I took it all in.

In the turmoil of the battle that was Tet, and with the compounding elements of arriving at the wrong place and my orders going somewhere else, I was stuck at the holding area for most of a week. I was lost in the chaos and confusion of the war. It was frustrating. I wanted to get on with it. I kept checking with the clerks for orders, but none were forthcoming for what seemed like a terribly long time. I was sitting on my duffle bag again with nothing to do but wait to die. The stress and anxiety was terrible. I paced the barracks floor like a caged cat.

The people who ran the place told me that it was customary for new guys like me to be put through a weeklong orientation course before joining a regular unit, but the course had been suspended because all the instructors had been sent to the battle areas as replacements. I hung around and watched and waited and ate and slept and fretted my time away. I wrote Jeannie a few letters, but it was frustrating because I didn't have a return address yet. I didn't know where I would serve, or with which unit.

At night, I sat out on the steps and watched the war on the horizon. There was always something to see. The nearby gun battery roared all night long and the jets and helicopters stirred the hot night air. Bright yellow flares trickled down through the clouds on distant horizons all around the base. The war was going on without me.

Finally, on the fifth or sixth day, I received orders. I was to join the First Infantry Division - The Big Red One. They were stationed north and west of Saigon, just a few miles up the road (Highway 13) from Bien Hoa. I was put on a supply convoy to the First Division Headquarters Camp at Lai Khe, and told to report to Division Artillery Headquarters.

The convoy was my first look at the country outside the wire. Rural Vietnam was a primitive, almost stone-aged culture set in a very pretty place. It was a completely different world to me. Everything was green and there were rice fields everywhere. The country was well watered and well forested. Little villages and humble farmsteads were scattered haphazardly and tucked back into the tree lines everywhere. There were footpaths leading to many of the villages instead of roads. People walked or rode bicycles and motor scooters. There were no cars on the roads, only army trucks, jeeps, and armored vehicles.

The houses were grass huts with walls made of plaited grass mats and strips of bamboo. Roofs were a thatching of palm leaves and grass. The floors were dirt. Chickens, pigs and dogs wandered through the houses. Groves of banana trees decorated village courtyards. Stale and damp wood smoke permeated the air around the villages. Thin waifs of whitish smoke could be seen rising from dozens of little cooking fires. With the smoke came the smell of sewer and animal dung. Small herds of monstrous black water buffalo, great beasts of burden with huge horns, grazed near the farmsteads. The buffalo watched us pass with evil eyes. Each buffalo had a metal ring in his flat, black nose.

The people were small, skinny, and scantily dressed. Some of the women, mothers with small children, walked around with their breasts exposed. Little kids ran around completely naked. No one wore socks. Grown-ups of both sexes wore black pajamas, sandals, and conical straw hats. Some of the men wore shorts or loincloths. Women carried burden-bearing poles over their shoulders with baskets attached at each end. Everyone smoked, even the kids, and the older women chewed betel nut, a mild narcotic that turned their teeth black.

This was the battlefield, and these poor people were both the enemy and the ally. It was everything I had been told that it was: primitive, foreign, and threatening. Older people watched us drive past with cold, indifferent, and unfeeling eyes. Children ran to meet us with big smiles and outreaching hands. The kids were calling excitedly, "chop-chop, chop-chop." A few of the soldiers smiled and threw candy, C-rations, and even cigarettes to the kids.

I felt like a fool riding along in that convoy with no weapons and only a clean shirt between me and the war. The soldiers around me all wore helmets and flak jackets and they carried guns. I noticed that they watched the people closely, even swinging a machine-gun barrel around to greet a cluster of people standing by the side of the road. I felt like a foreigner, an uninitiated trainee, naked, helpless, and terribly vulnerable.

At Lai Khe, I reported to Division Headquarters and was assigned to the Eighth Battalion, Sixth Artillery. There, I was finally allowed to draw weapons and jungle uniforms. I was given a steel helmet, a ten-pound flak jacket, a brand new M16 rifle, and an officer's .45-caliber pistol. The weapons gave me status as well as comfort and protection in the war zone. The new jungle fatigues, with a Big Red One patch on the shoulder, made me a member of a warrior tribe. I was proud to be assigned to that division. The Red One is a good division with a long and proud history of noble service to the country.

I then sat on my bags for another two or three days and waited for orders. Things move slowly through the bowels of the military paperwork monster, even in a war zone. The war went on without me for a few more days.

Cavalry Trooper

The Major looked hassled. He was drawn, tired, and in a foul mood. Another young Second Lieutenant and I were ushered into his presence together. I didn't know the other guy. We were both new in-country, and there to receive orders to specific units.

The Major spread some papers out on his desk, and then he said, "I have two critical assignments that must be filled this afternoon. One is commander of a 4.2-inch mortar battery; the other is a Forward Observer for the armored cavalry. McCourt, you have date-of-rank, you choose."

My heart stood still and my mind raced. The mortar battery was the safer job. Four-deuces were heavy mortars usually kept in rear areas for static defense. We all knew where an FO with the armored cavalry was headed. The choice was mine. I choked.

My mind, intuition, common sense and conscience, all screamed at me to choose the mortars, but my heart and soul were with the cavalry. The cavalry! I would never have dared to dream. The Major didn't want me for the lowly infantry, down in the mud, muck, and filthy trenches; he was offering me the cavalry. The cavalry was fluttering flags, gleaming sabers, and thundering warhorses - a young boy's dream come true. My heart was numbed with fear at where that assignment might take me, but deep down inside myself, it was the fulfillment of every adolescent hope. No soldier ever stood taller than a cavalry soldier.

But, I couldn't do it. I thought of Jeannie and the vows we had so recently made. She was waiting faithfully, and counting on me to come home again. She might even be pregnant, we didn't know yet. I had promised her that I wouldn't do anything foolish. I had promised faithfully that I wouldn't volunteer, I wouldn't take chances, and I wouldn't be a hero. I was a married man now with family responsibilities. As sad as it made me, I just couldn't volunteer for the cavalry with a clear conscience.

But then, I really didn't want to spend the war inside a barbed wire enclosure counting mortar rounds and getting trench foot in a muddy gun pit either. The days would be long and boring and the war would pass me by. I knew that if I stayed with the mortars, I would always watch those tanks roll past and wish that I had been brave enough to go with them.

I was caught in a dilemma. I didn't want to be stuck with a mortar battery, but I couldn't volunteer for the cavalry either. I did the next best thing.

"I will defer to Lieutenant Jones," I heard myself say. It was a brilliant move, but a weasel's way out - let the other guy choose. The Major looked annoyed, but Lieutenant Jones (not his real name) almost swallowed his tongue. "Mortars, sir!" he gasped. "I'll take the mortars!" And the thing was done.

I smiled on the inside. I could go to the cavalry now with a clear conscience. I hadn't volunteered. The Major handed me the papers and told me to go pack my stuff. The cavalry was sending a driver to pick me up.

I walked out of the Major's office terribly excited and terribly afraid. I knew that I would soon meet the devil and be a real FO. I also knew that I might have sealed my fate forever by letting the other man choose. But, I was optimistic. Somehow, in the bottom of my brave soldier's heart, I knew that it would be all right. This was something I was destined to do. I had known it for years.

The jeep pulled up in front of the office. I threw my gear in the back and climbed aboard. A PFC in a filthy uniform was driving and a Spec-4 (Specialist Fourth-Class) with a rifle was riding shotgun in the back. They were both wearing dirty yellow cavalry scarves.

The Cavalry soldiers were not very talkative. I had to pry information out of them. They said the unit was in camp to re-supply and they were headed back into the boondocks tomorrow. They said their headquarters camp was at Dian (pronounced Zee-on), but they were operating out of Phu Loi for now.

They said they were from the First Squadron, Fourth Armored Cavalry, known as the "Quarter Cav" because the numerical designation was written like a fraction, one over four (1/4). They said the unit was a ready reaction force for the whole First Division. Any unit in the Big Red One's area of operations might call for help and the cavalry would be sent to the rescue.

I could see that those two soldiers had been going to the rescue a lot lately. They were dirty and they looked very tired. They also had very old and very sad eyes for young men. They told me the unit had lost a lot of good men in the past couple of weeks. The Tet Offensive was still in high gear.

They took me to Phu Loi, a few miles back down the road toward Saigon, and there we found the Quarter Cavalry in a frenzy of activity. I was fascinated. There were tanks and armored personnel carriers parked all over the place, bristling with guns and radio antennas. The back ramps of several personnel carriers were down and troopers were literally using scoop shovels and push brooms to clean machine-gun brass from inside the vehicles. In some places, mounds of empty shell casings were piled more than a foot deep in the dust behind the tracks. Troopers were storing hundreds of ammo cans back inside the tracks, stowing boxes of C-rations, cleaning guns, and changing radio batteries and fuel filters. No one paid any attention as I walked through the yard in my brand-new jungle fatigues.

I was taken to the Headquarters Section and introduced to the Artillery Liaison Officer. He was a Captain with a fresh shave and a very short haircut. He was wearing clean and starched fatigues that looked completely out-of-place in his current surroundings. He looked too clean to be a member of that sweat-stained and dirt-impregnated combat unit. I never knew for sure, but he had an air of West Point about him. He introduced himself as Captain Rice.

The Captain gave me a quick overview of the cavalry operating procedures, area of operations, and support units. He then gave me a codebook of radio frequencies and shackle codes, and told me to keep it in the cargo pocket of my pants and to tie it to my belt loop with a nylon strap. He made me sign for the book, and he told me that I would be court-martialed if I lost it. He also gave me an artilleryman's lensatic compass and a canvas dispatch pouch filled with laminated maps. He then told me to report to Captain Daniels of "B" Troop.

It was getting dark when I walked into the building that served as Bravo troop headquarters. I was wearing my clean, new gear, and my duffle bag was over my shoulder. My rank and artillery specialty was on my collar for all the world to see.

The First Sergeant was frazzled. He was hoarse from giving orders and beat to a pulp by the frenzied activity of re-supply. He was an older guy, a brown boot soldier, and the stress, heat, and lack of sleep were taking their toll. He looked over at me as I came through the door, and then he said right out loud, "Good God, not another one!"

I must have given him an angry look, because he then apologized, stiffened to attention, saluted, and said it had been a terrible week. I found out later that I was the second or third new Lieutenant to report to the outfit within just a few days. The Quarter Cavalry was using up new Lieutenants pretty fast.

The First Sergeant told me the Captain was at a staff meeting with the Colonel, and I would have to wait to meet him. He said the unit would be moving out again first thing in the morning, and he was sorry, but there wouldn't be much time for the niceties of getting acquainted. He told me I would be riding with the Captain on the Command and Control (CC) Track, and he called a young trooper over to show me where to go.

I was introduced to the three enlisted men who served on the CC track with the Captain: Sergeant Jenies Mobley, PFC Robert Ivie, and SP4 Jerry Poirier. They all looked me over cautiously. New Lieutenants are always a little scary to enlisted men. It's a lot like getting a new dog. They don't quite know how to handle the new dog at first, until they find out about his temperament. Some dogs bark, some bite, and some just growl a lot. A few want to be petted. Young officers have a lot of power over enlisted men, but they must earn their respect and their confidence.

The guys on the CC track all had the same tired and sad eyes I had seen in the face of my driver and guard on the way over. They were veterans of many fights and many long, dusty miles on the vehicles. They gave me long, sideways glances as I stowed my gear and asked, what were to them, obvious and stupid questions.

It wasn't all my fault that I asked stupid questions. There was no one at the troop level to brief me about my new job. There would be no formal change of command. The man I was replacing was in a body bag or a hospital bed somewhere; the troopers weren't sure which. He had been loaded aboard a helicopter, bleeding and unconscious, and had disappeared forever into the Asian sky. That's how it was in Vietnam. The helicopters swallowed up the wounded and you never saw or heard from them again.

There was no one to pass the baton. As a battlefield replacement, we often didn't get to meet the guy we were replacing. We simply picked up where the other man had fallen, and did our best to figure it out and carry on.

The guys on the track showed me where to stow my gear, and they showed me which of the vehicular radios was mine. I fired up the radio and made several communications checks with the various artillery units in the area. My call sign was Dragoon Niner-two. The designated call sign for anyone in the Fourth Cavalry was Dragoon, followed by a letter prefix that identified the troop, and then a number that identified the man's job. The Captain was Dragoon Bravo Six. Just as a point of interest, in the olden days, a dragoon was a soldier who rode a horse to the battle and then fought on foot like the infantry.

The troop was made up of three platoons of armored cavalry and a headquarters section. A lieutenant commanded each platoon. Each platoon had three tanks and six APCs (armored personnel carriers). The personnel carriers were aluminum M113 models that were used as fighting vehicles. They were called ACAVs, a military acronym that stands for "Armored Cavalry Assault Vehicle." The ACAVs were deployed in battle like small tanks. Each ACAV had a fifty-caliber machine-gun mounted in a revolving, open turret called a cupola. Each also had a side-mounted M60 machine-gun and an M79 grenade launcher on board. The crew was three or four men, depending on how fat the unit was at any given time.

The tanks were Korean War vintage. They were old and obsolete, fifty-two ton, M48 models. The newer, M60 tanks were all facing the Russians in Europe or the North Koreans on the DMZ. The old M48s sported a 90mm main gun with a coaxially mounted machine-gun in the turret. Each tank also had a fifty-caliber machine-gun mounted on top of the turret. The tank commander fired the top-mounted fifty.

The Headquarters Section included the CC track for the troop commander, a couple of other ACAVs in support that included communications and medical personnel, and a huge VTR (tank retriever) with a team of mechanics. Also, the troop often had other elements temporarily attached, such as a pair of M132 flamethrower carriers or a brace of M125 APCs rigged with 81mm mortars. The First Sergeant and a headquarters staff stayed in the rear areas and took care of logistics, maintenance, and personnel matters. The full troop was authorized to have 197 people, but I don't think our field (fighting) strength ever exceeded 120 souls.

Since the unit was moving all the time, the crews lived in the tanks and ACAVs. Conditions were very crude and very cramped. Men slept in hammocks strung inside the tracks at night or dug fighting/sleeping holes alongside the vehicles. They took most of their meals from C-ration cans while on the go. There was almost no room for personal gear. The interiors of the tracks were filled with endless metal boxes of machine-gun ammunition. The boxes were stacked in neat rows, two or three high, along the inside walls of the track. The rows of ammo boxes formed a bench the troopers sat on when they were not manning the guns.

I spread my new maps out on the deck of the track and started trying to orient myself as to where we were and what was around us. Spotting artillery is scary business if you don't know where you are. The Captain showed up an hour or so later. We were introduced, but he didn't have time to talk. He met with his First Sergeant for a while, and then called for a meeting with his platoon leaders. I was told to attend the briefing and I would be introduced to the officers and the top Sergeants.

We had not begun the meeting yet, when sirens started screaming and rockets came whistling down on the base. We ran to the tracks for shelter. All the lights went out and we could hear the heavy Krump, Krump, Krump, of exploding shells off in the distance. The base artillery came alive, and dozens of big guns sent shells screaming back out into the night. I turned my radio on to see what was happening.

And then came an order over the cavalry command frequency. Scramble the unit, saddle up and deploy, the VC were making a push on the perimeter near the airfield. The word was that they were coming through the wire and we had to stop them before they got in. Bravo troop was ordered to charge right down the runway and hold the ground at the edge of the wire, just behind the perimeter bunkers.

There was a mad scramble to the guns. Big diesel engines coughed and then roared to life. We were off on a wild counter-attack in the middle of the night. I hadn't been with the unit for five hours yet.

The ACAV roared and bucked as we charged through the back streets of the military camp and toward the airfield. We were flying along all blacked-out, no headlights and nothing to guide by but starlight and the distant glow of parachute flares. The tanks and tracks rumbled and growled and kicked up great clouds of billowing red dust along the darkened back streets. The mechanical monsters followed each other through the night in a single file like a great herd of migrating dragons. I could feel the power of the ACAV beneath me, a great metal warhorse with a heart of steel. The big machine flexed her muscles, sending tremors through her thick, armored skin as the engine rumbled and track plates bit into the dirt, squealing in protest.

The yellow glow of the flares cast an eerie light through the boiling clouds of dust. The light penetrated the dust as if filtered through a canopy of silk. The pale, amber light flickered and shimmered as the flares drifted down on their parachutes, swaying from side to side. The soft, pulsating glow created weird, moving shadows and strange silhouettes on everything it touched. The moving tanks and helmeted gunners were bathed with a strange, otherworldly sheen, made all the more eerie by deep, dancing shadows that flickered and faded. The scene was surreal.

I was completely taken by the moment. With awe I drank in the sights, sounds, and realities of my new assignment. In the middle of the night, in a strange, foreign land, I was charging into battle with a troop of armored cavalry soldiers. My heart was fearful, but I have never been more proud.

As the new guy, I was shocked to discover that the troopers rode on top of the machines, out in the open, up-top as they called it. They sat by the gun mounts with the dust and dirt swirling over them, grim and resolute. They looked rugged and mean in the flickering yellow light of the flares, dusty warriors in full battle dress: tanker's helmets, flak jackets, and weapons at the ready.

The troopers were terribly exposed to hostile fire riding on top like that, but I was soon to learn that when facing RPGs (rocket-propelled grenades), it was the safest option. Better to take a bullet up-top than be shredded by steel splinters and globs of molten aluminum down inside the machine. An RPG could take out an M48 tank, and an aluminum-sided ACAV had virtually no chance. The redeeming features of the fighting vehicles were their massive firepower and mobility.

We charged onto the airfield and right into the rocket barrage. The bad guys were shooting at airplanes and probably didn't know that we were even there. The rockets came crashing down on the tarmac, splattering shrapnel and throwing chunks of asphalt everywhere. The bursting shells lit the night sky like huge flashbulbs followed by a mighty clap of thunder. For a millisecond, the flashes of light revealed maintenance sheds, hangars, and parked aircraft in revetments, and then came the concussion with a sound that stopped your heart. We dropped down inside the vehicles and buttoned-up (closed the hatches).

We moved on across the airfield and took up our blocking position behind the perimeter bunkers.

There was no frontal attack to repel. Some clown in the bunkers had panicked and summoned the cavalry for nothing. We were now sitting ducks, out in the open and fully exposed to the rocket barrage. The North Vietnamese gunners were aiming at aircraft parapets a few hundred yards behind us, but the rockets were falling short and landing all around us.

The concussions of the 122mm warheads rattled our teeth and buffeted the armored vehicles violently. The whole thing reminded me of those old war movies about submarines enduring depth-charge attacks. We were buttoned-up inside the tracks with only the glow of instrument panels and red-filtered flashlights to see by. The concussions would shake the whole vehicle, everyone would duck, and dirt would trickle down from the closed hatches.

It was impossibly hot and hard to breathe inside the closed-up tracks. The dim lights of the instrument panels showed that every face was streaked with ribbons of sweat. My clothes were wet. My heart was hammering in my chest as I fought to breathe, and to overcome an irrational impulse toward claustrophobia. I struggled to show a brave heart. The nearby flashes of light and the WHAM of explosions went on for what seemed like a long, long time. Holy Cow! Welcome to Vietnam!

The several radios in our command vehicle created a background jumble of different sounds in the darkness. Each radio was on a different frequency. Our internal vehicle intercom, squadron, troop, and artillery radio channels were each filled with different voices and different call signs, each competing to be heard and understood. It all blended into a roaring babble that was hard for a new guy like me to follow and decipher. It took a while to learn what to listen to, and what to disregard.

Like all battles, there was a great deal of confusion as to

what was happening. Were the bad guys really coming through the wire? Did we have infiltrators in among us? Should we move back out of the shellfire? There were calls to bunch up and calls to scatter out. There were calls to stand to the guns and calls to remain buttoned-up.

And then, came a call for medical assistance. "Bravo Six, Three-five has been hit!" an out-of-breath voice thundered in the headset. "We've got a possible KIA (killed in action) and another WIA (wounded in action) over here Captain. We need some help."

Our CC track backed out of line and started toward the disabled track, but we became entangled in concertina wire at the edge of the runway. One of the few things that will stop an armored vehicle is barbed wire. If it gets wrapped up in the track pads and sprockets it will completely disable the machine. Our vehicle ground to a halt amid the screech of twisting wire. The Captain cussed, and then jerked the door open and ran through the night to where his wounded soldiers waited. The worst of the barrage was over, but intermittent shells were still crashing down around us.

The driver worked the track back and forth but it wasn't coming free. "We've got to cut the wire out," the track commander said soberly. "We don't want to be caught here and unable to move if the bastards do come through the wire." He opened a toolbox, fished out a pair of wire cutters, and then hesitated, looking upward at the ceiling of the track, listening for the scream of incoming rockets. Even in the dim light of the instrument panels I could see the fear etched into his face.

"You got another pair?" I heard myself ask. He looked over at me with a question in his eyes. "Got these," he said, holding up a pair of pliers. "Let's go," I said, as I reached out to take the pliers. The Sergeant smiled and nodded. He hadn't expected that.

"Don't touch nothin' Jerry," the man called to the driver.

"We're going to have our hands in the sprockets." Then he said, "Ivie, you stay with the radio and be ready to man the fifty. This shouldn't take long." With that, I followed Sergeant Mobley out into the night.

The last couple of 122s slammed into the aircraft parapets several hundred yards behind us as we were leaving the track. The enemy gunners had finally gotten the range, now that they were out of rockets. Luckily, that was the end of the rocket barrage, but we didn't know it yet.

By the dim light of the flickering, yellow flares, we dug frantically at the wire, cutting, twisting and pulling for all we were worth. We were motivated, and our efforts were adrenaline charged. It was terrifying to be out in the open like that. My ears were tuned like radar beacons for the scream of another rocket and my heart was thundering in my chest. In no time at all, it seemed, the track was free. Captain Daniels came running back through the dark about the time we were clear. He had blood on his hands and blood on his uniform.

Nothing I could have done that night would have won me more respect than going out into the shellfire to help free that ACAV. I made a great first impression with the troops. I hadn't been there long enough to know everyone's name, but by the time the sun came up that next morning I was a member of the team. The guys accepted me and looked after me. I had a lot to learn in a hurry, and they all knew it, but they all tried to help.

For a while, we waited in the dark for the attack that never came. Then, we went back to the headquarters area, finished loading up, and tried to get a few hours of sleep. Tomorrow would be Judgment Day - my first full day in the field as a combat soldier and a Forward Observer. At first-light we were going after those VC who had failed to come through the wire. My heart was filled with anxious excitement and my stomach was full of butterflies. I didn't sleep at all that night.

Into the Valley of the Shadow

The next morning, before it was fully light, we were outside the perimeter and sweeping through the area where the enemy had been spotted the night before. There were shell craters and broken trees everywhere from our own artillery, but no bad guys to be found. We continued our sweep out into the brambles and rice paddies of the former French Indochina that was a strange new world to me.

It was my first morning in the field, and everything was new. I was in a new country, on a new continent, in a new hemisphere, on the dark side of the world. Everything was different: the trees, foliage, farm fields, sky, people, houses, animals, and even the air itself, was different from anything I had ever known.

The new world was lush and green, but somehow dry too. Our vehicles kicked up great clouds of chalky red dust that settled down on everything. The troopers told me that the wet (monsoon) season would begin in another couple of months. When it did, the red dust would turn into gooey red mud. Vietnam had only two seasons of the year: dry and hot, and wet and hot. I got there in February, during dry and hot.

The cavalry was strange and new to me too. I had been trained as an infantryman and as an artilleryman. Armor was the combat arm I didn't know yet. Armored vehicles, armored tactics, and the armored cavalry mindset were new to me. The mobility, weaponry, and the excellent inter-unit communications were exciting, but I felt terribly exposed sitting on top of the ACAV with only a flak jacket and a green shirt to stop the bullets. It took a little getting used to. All that beautiful armor plate seemed to be going to waste, protecting only the engines, ammunition, and fuel tanks.

It was hard for me to believe that sitting on top was the safest option, but when I saw all the troopers doing it, I accepted that it must be true. I took my place on an improvised seat cushion on top of the ACAV, wrapped myself tightly in my flak jacket, and hoped for the best. The flak jacket weighed just over ten pounds, but it wouldn't stop a rifle bullet. It was good for stopping shell fragments, and a lot better than nothing, but it offered only limited protection.

I soon learned that the troopers didn't stay up-top all the time. When we started to draw heavy small arms fire, or when shells were bursting close, like on the airfield the night before, we dropped down inside the tracks. When standing inside the track, we could shoot over the side of the ACAV with only our heads and shoulders exposed. There were many times, however; when RPGs were coming thick and fast, when we chose to stay up-top and brave the rockets, shell fragments, and bullets.

In the months to come, I would see several tanks and ACAVs hit with RPGs while men were riding on top. In most cases, the crewmembers survived, even though some were blown completely off the machine by the concussion of the explosion. Those men caught inside the vehicle were usually not so lucky.

My place on the ACAV was next to the Captain. I was to stay close so we could communicate face-to-face and share a map when necessary to coordinate our efforts. My job was to work for the Captain and do only what he told me to do. He was the unit commander, and if he wanted artillery, he would tell me where and when.

The Captain and I were still strangers to one another. Because of the rocket attack the previous evening, we had yet to have a staff meeting or even a formal introduction. I was trying hard to stay out of his way and yet anticipate what he might want me to do. I still had a lot to learn.

My primary responsibility was to know where we were at all times so I could start a fire mission in a heartbeat if we were ambushed. I rode with a map spread across my lap and with my compass tied with a nylon strap to the buttonhole on my shirt pocket. I made frequent radio checks with the local artillery batteries and had them keep a few gun tubes pointed in our direction, just in case.

We had been out beating the bushes for an hour or two when we got a call that a truck convoy had been ambushed near a small village just a few miles away. Someone else had found the bad guys we were looking for. We put the spurs to the tanks and ACAVs and charged to the rescue.

As the ACAV bucked and roared across unfamiliar ground, I followed our progress on a map, checking off terrain features with a grease pencil and alerting a gun battery to stand by for a possible fire mission. The grim faces on the soldiers around me were disconcerting. I could read fear as well as anxious resolve in their countenances. They were veterans, and they knew what was coming.

As we came thundering down the road, we could see trucks and jeeps up ahead scattered along the roadway. A couple were on fire. Two or three helicopters were over the scene, shooting wildly at targets on the ground. The radios were boiling over with hyper-excited radio traffic. The helicopters reported there were enemy troops in the bushes everywhere, dozens and dozens of them, not VC militia, but North Vietnamese Regulars in full uniform. My pulse rate shifted into overdrive. This was it - the real thing.

The Captain had the tanks and ACAVs leave the road and spread out in a battle formation as we approached the area. We swept parallel to the convoy, clearing the ambush site and driving toward the village, pushing the enemy soldiers before us. The tanks were firing canister shells into the bushes and machine-guns were ripping off long bursts of fire into the shadows. I had the artillery swing more gun tubes in our direction, and told them to stand by, but the helicopters were in the way and the Captain hadn't ordered a fire mission yet.

We received intermittent sniper fire as we approached the village, but no strong, organized resistance. The enemy troops were apparently running. I wasn't surprised. How could infantry stand and fight a column of tanks? We swept into a tree line in front of the village ... and there the devil was waiting.

There was a tremendous flash and a BANG on the turret of a leading tank – an RPG hit. The fifty-caliber gun mount was blown completely away. The tank commander was thrown back, and his body hung down over the back of the turret. His legs were tangled inside the tank, and he hung there, suspended over the back of the turret. His head was gone and a hand was missing above the wrist. A river of blood and lumpy clots of gore slid down the dark steel turret and then bubbled and cooked on the hot engine cowling. The driver of the tank seemed unaware of what had happened, sealed up in his driving compartment as he was, and the big machine kept its place in formation and continued the attack with the mangled body of its commander spilling out from the open hatch. It was like a scene from a horror movie.

The whole world exploded. Thousands of bullets, shell splinters, rockets, grenades, and tree limbs sailed through the air. Dust and smoke boiled everywhere. "Hit 'em! Hit 'em! Hit 'em! Move it up! Move it up! Support that tank!" the Captain screamed through the headphones in my tanker's helmet. Every man was bent over a weapon of some kind, and the sound of it shattered the blue glass dome of the sky.

It was my baptism by fire, and the horror of it shook me to my very soul. I had thought I was ready to face the cannons, but this new reality hit me like ice water. I had been through the very best of American training, but there are some things they just can't prepare you for.

For one thing, the noise of combat is beyond description, especially with an armored unit firing tank cannons and dozens of heavy machine-guns. Sound itself becomes a physical punishment. Shockwaves of sound smash into your face and you actually squint and duck your head into the storm of sound. You can feel the concussions, the ultra-sound impulses, pounding at the vital organs deep inside of your body. To be buffeted by such intensity of sound makes you draw deep inside yourself for shelter. You try to make yourself very small. Your first impulse is to want to curl up in a tight little ball. You must fight to overcome that impulse.

And then, there are the smells of mortal combat. From my training, I had expected the smells of gun smoke, hot gun barrels, diesel smoke, dust, and napalm. I had even anticipated the smells of human slaughter: warm blood and open intestines. What I had failed to factor in was the effects of heat, fire, and tropical sunshine.

The enemy troops we faced that day were some of Ho Chi Minh's best. They were professional soldiers, and ready to meet our armored column. They had dug in, prepared the battlefield, and they had a plan. Several of them hid in spider holes and let our lead elements pass over them. Then, they popped up behind us and cut down the men in the rear. They were going for the soft targets: medics, mechanics, and the headquarters people. Our CC track was up front and just behind the lead tanks when we got a call that the rear elements were being shot to hell. The Captain divided his force and sent several ACAVs back to help. They got a few of the bad guys, but most of them slipped away into the bushes.

The NVA (North Vietnamese Army) battle plan had worked well. We had several men down, both wounded and killed, and a lot of the enemy soldiers got away. Whoever the commander of that enemy outfit was, he was a good strategist. It was a perfect way for dismounted infantry to fight tanks. As a student of tactics, I was impressed.

The Captain sent one of the men on our ACAV back to drive one of the headquarters tracks whose crew had been hard-hit. That left our M60 machine-gun unmanned. He asked if I could take over. He didn't know that I had been a star pupil at machine-gun school, and I didn't have a chance to tell him.

I was thrilled to man that gun. In the middle of a big fight like that one, there could be no greater comfort than to wrap your arms around a warm and friendly machine-gun. I embraced her like a lover.

Manning that gun was a godsend for me. It gave me something to do. I was the new guy and still searching for my place within the unit. I hadn't been ordered to shoot artillery, and until that moment I had been only a spectator, horrified and helpless as I took in all that was happening around me. Now, as a machine-gunner, I had a job that gave me focus. I had a mission to fulfill.

Our formation was moving slowly forward and I slapped a few rounds into the shadows as we approached the village. It was great to be able to shoot back, but I was completely frustrated by a lack of targets. There were bullets, rockets, and shrapnel flying everywhere, but no bad guys to shoot at. The bushes, trees, and shadows were thick, and I just couldn't see the enemy. It was maddening.

And then, a frantic call came through my radio headset from the driver of our track. "There's one in that pagoda on your left, Lieutenant! He's shooting from that little window!" I looked left, and sure enough, at about the distance of a football field away was a beautiful little pagoda at the edge of a cemetery, just in front of the village. Pagodas are small, sacred buildings in the Far East, and in Vietnam, they are usually made of stone and contain only one room. An enemy sniper was using the little Buddhist shrine for cover and concealment as he hammered away at us with a rifle. He might have thought we wouldn't shoot at the sacred building - he was wrong. A church is a church when it is used for worship. A shrine used as a fighting position becomes a legal target.

I aimed the gun at the little window and squeezed off a short burst. The bullets went where I pointed, but the soft stone absorbed the impact. The stone crumbled under the force of the slugs and blew away as chalky dust. A few bullets went through the little window, but to no apparent effect. The stonewalls were thick and the building was like a bunker. A couple of machine-gunners on other ACAVS opened up on the pagoda too. We peppered the building good, but with no discernible damage to the NVA soldier inside.

It was frustrating. We had to keep moving to support the tanks. If we left the sniper hiding in there, he might pop up and get some of our people from the rear elements as they moved through behind us. They had pulled it off once already. We had to take this guy out somehow.

As our ACAV moved abreast of the building, I saw that there was only one door in the little shrine and it was on my side. The doorway was a small, narrow opening, and there was no door that could be closed. I could see into parts of the interior of the building. Portions of the back wall and floor were visible, but I could not see into the corners where the enemy soldier was hiding.

In desperation, not knowing what else to do, I aimed low at the floor of the shrine through the open doorway and squeezed off a short burst. The effect was more profound than I could ever have dreamed. The bullets zipped through the open doorway, skipped off the stone floor, and bounced around crazily inside the small building. It was like batting tennis balls into a closet. Yes! I held the trigger down and gave him half-a-belt, at least 100 rounds. We could see the flash of tracers ricocheting around inside the pagoda, and a few bounced back outside through the doorway and the hole that was the little window. A gunner on another ACAV several yards away gave me a big grin and a thumbs-up salute. And then, mission accomplished, we moved on to support the tanks.

As the ACAV surged ahead to rejoin the tanks in formation, I looked back at the chalky dust that hung in the air outside the open doorway of that little shrine. Did I get him? I didn't know. The unit was moving and we couldn't dismount to check it out. We had to maintain the battle formation. Maybe the sniper was still hiding in there behind another barrier? It was even possible that there was an underground room or underground passageway that we couldn't see. And then, the man might have escaped before I ever started shooting. I never did see him. We would have to check it out later when the battle was over.

What I did know was that I had tried very hard to kill a man ... and it was just a mechanical process after all. Getting him killed was a problem to solve. The emotions at play had been fear for my own safety and frustration at not being able to get him in my sights. He wasn't a person - he was a target. I had been trained, drilled, and coached about using that machine-gun as a tool, and there, across that open and deadly space, I had been able to narrow my focus to the mechanics of the task at hand. How best to hit the target? How best to take him out? There was no hate and no pity in the equation. I was doing a job.

I was enraged a few moments later when I saw men shooting pigs as we moved through the village. Even in the terror of the moment, I was outraged. As a farm boy, I went over-the-top when I saw dumb animals being mowed down for no apparent reason. The pigs were screaming and thrashing around on the ground. I grabbed one of our men by the shirt-sleeve, and over the roar of a hundred guns I asked what the hell was going on. He looked at me with wild eyes, and then he yelled that they were enemy pigs. They belonged to the VC. The pigs were enemy rations and our guys were shooting up the enemy supply depot.

The concept of "enemy pigs" was new to me, and I balked at the very suggestion. On my own, I made my first command decision in Vietnam. I keyed the radio switch in my tanker's helmet and ordered the troopers to leave the damn pigs alone. The guys on my track all looked at me like I was crazy, and maybe I was.

I was suffering from shock, and I may have gone a little over the edge. It was my first major battle and my mind was rebelling against the horrors. I had seen the headless horseman. I had felt the terror of bullets coming for me, and RPG rockets zipping past. I had endured concussions that threatened to burst my eyeballs. I had suffered endless screams in the radio headset from wounded, desperate, and panicked men. My beating heart had almost exploded in my chest from an overload of fear, panic, and shock. I might have just killed a man, against every moral principle I had ever been taught - but the pigs were inno-cent. For God's sake, at least let the pigs live.

I was the new guy and completely out-of-line for interfering with anything going on during that battle. I had no command responsibility over any of those troopers. I still had a lot to learn. But then again, I was with that unit for most of a year, and I don't remember seeing a man shoot another pig.

We found 87 enemy bodies after that fight, and several blood trails leading out into the boondocks. I don't know how many of our people were wounded or killed. There were several.

The NVA soldiers who hid in the spider holes had gunned down most of the men in our maintenance section. The guys on my track said we also lost a good medic, a man I hadn't even met yet.

Incredibly, I had served in my first big fight in Vietnam as a machine-gunner and not as an FO. Who could have guessed? My Captain never ordered a fire mission. Dark Horse, the Cavalry Air Wing, had provided close support with helicopter gunships.

It was also amazing to me that I had participated in a battle where a hundred men had been killed and I never saw an enemy soldier to shoot at during the whole fight. I saw dozens of them dead in the bushes, and tracer bullets coming at me from out of the shadows, but not one bad guy on the hoof. I had burned up a few hundred rounds of machine-gun ammunition, but my targets had been only shadows, muzzle flashes in the bushes, and the little Buddhist shrine.

After that fight, our people policed up the battle area, made the body count, and collected weapons and documents. I stayed at the temporary command center near where the headquarters track was parked. I had seen enough for my first day in the field. I was trying to catch my breath, gather my wits, and be a professional soldier, in spite of my shaky knees. And besides, I wasn't anxious to put my hands into any bloody pockets to search for documents and maps - maybe next time.

When one of our men came back to the track with an armload of captured rifles, I asked if they had checked inside the pagoda. He said they had. He told me there were three dead enemy soldiers in there, and it was a mess.

I didn't go to see. What I had learned on the gunnery ranges at Fort McClellan was true after all. Machine-gunning is a gruesome business, and not a good line of work for a man with a conscience.

God, Gooks, and Patriots

We've all heard it said that there are no atheists in foxholes. It may be true, I don't know. I do know that some men become angry with God during wartime. They seek to blame God for the misery and the carnage that we mortals wreak upon ourselves. I don't believe that God ever starts wars, but I do believe He is always there when they happen. Sometimes, I think He influences the outcomes.

War is the ultimate clash of opposites, the struggle between good and evil. War brings out the very worst and the very best in men. Perhaps that's why God tolerates our constant warring. War reveals the true character of a man and a nation. Life is a test. We are here to show God who we really are. We validate the eternal judgments of God by our actions. The battlefield is one of those places where all of the elements, and the potential, for good and evil come together ... and we can choose.

I have always believed in God, but while in Vietnam, I didn't pray often. I surrendered to the will of God early in my combat tour. It's interesting how that happened too.

When I first arrived in-country, I prayed constantly. I was desperate to live. I pleaded with God for my life, my limbs, and my future. I found myself willing to bargain with God. I was frantic to appease Him and keep Him on my side. I begged God for His personal attention to my safety and survival. There was nothing more important in the whole world than my life.

And then, I got to the killing fields. I began to do what I had been trained to do, and what I had been sent to do. My job was to kill other men. I saw those other men, dead in the tall grass, and it bothered me. In those quiet moments when I could go deep inside myself, I could see the war and my place in it differently now.

I had been taught that all men are the children of God. Behind our different cultures and our different uniforms we are brothers. Why should I be so presumptuous as to assume that God would favor me over my brother? Was I arrogant enough to believe that American sons are more important to God than Asian sons? And, as an individual, what made me more worthy of life than those NVA soldiers who died in that little pagoda? Didn't they have wives, families, and futures too? Didn't they want to live as much as I wanted to live? Did they beg God for their lives too? Were we unknowingly asking God to choose between us? I brooded over it for several days.

I finally resolved the conflict with a prayer. I got down on my knees and told God that I was leaving it all in his hands. I would not beg for my life ever again. It was all up to him.

I reminded God that I had a soldier's job to do, and there was nothing I could do about that. The war, its outcomes and its consequences, were beyond my control. I was trapped like a bulldog in a wire cage, facing the opponent of my master's choosing. I was a slave, fighting as a Gladiator in Lyndon Johnson's Asian coliseum.

I didn't hate my opponent. Hell, I didn't know him. But, I had to fight him and I had to kill him or I would die. I was in a position where I had to defend my life and the lives of my cavalry troopers. Those fine young men were counting on me to do my job and do it well. None of us would ever see our homes and families again if we didn't all do our jobs. We were locked in a brotherhood of mutual dependence. We had been thrown into the bullring and we were duty-bound to fight the bull. Anything less would bring shame and dishonor upon us, our families, and our nation, forever.

I did promise God that I would be a soldier of honor. I would be principled, disciplined, and as merciful as I could be in my current circumstances. But, the outcome was entirely up to Him. He could choose between us, my Asian brothers and me. I would accept His will. I told God that I wouldn't bother Him about the matter again, and I didn't.

Back home, my extended family joined in regular Sunday afternoon prayers on my behalf. The family would kneel in a circle and hold hands as they prayed. The prayers were organized by my maternal grandmother, Bertha Winn, a Mormon Saint who knew the pain of having a son wounded and almost killed in World War II. Grandma saw the world through the eyes of faith.

As I prepared to go to the killing fields, my grandmother gave me a small, pocket-sized bible with a steel cover plate. It was the second time she had given that same gift. Her oldest son had carried it to the Pacific Islands in World War II and it had brought him home in spite of his wounds. The little bulletproof bible was worn and stained. The steel cover plate was scuffed and scratched and the leather binder was rotted and cracked. Uncle Glen had surely carried it through the tropics.

I was honored to receive such a gift from her, and I carried grandma's little bulletproof bible with me everywhere in Vietnam, but not always in my pocket. It was fragile and worn when I received it, and wearing it next to my sweaty body was sure to ruin it completely. And then too, it was too bulky to wear in my shirt pocket under my flak jacket, next to my heart where grandma wanted it to be. As a compromise, I kept it wrapped in plastic with my shaving kit in my rucksack. It was always close, and a reminder of grandma's love and faith.

I gave that little bulletproof bible to my oldest son, Army Sergeant Rex McCourt, as he prepared to leave for Somalia with the Tenth Mountain Division in 1993. Rex shot it out with Al Qaeda thugs in the back streets of Mogadishu several times and came home unhurt. He still has the family talisman ... and a nine-year-old son named Dillon who says he wants to be a soldier.

I have no faith in amulets, lucky charms, rabbit's feet, four-leaf clovers, or Saint Christopher's medals. I believe in God; I believe in destiny; and I believe in the power of self. On the other hand, grandma's little gift of a bulletproof bible was a wonderful, physical manifestation of her love and concern for me. With it and her prayers, she was doing everything she could to bring me home. I loved her for it. I felt the comfort of her presence every time I held that hopeful little gift in my hand. It was like a lock of my fair lady's hair, a scented hand-kerchief to be tucked into the corset of a knight's armor. Only a son going to war could ever make me part with it.

The man I worked for in Vietnam was Captain Daniels. I spent a great deal of time with him those first months I was in-country. We sat next to each other on the ACAV and we covered a lot of miles and a lot of battlefields together.

Captain Daniels didn't have a first name, at least not to me. He was Captain Daniels, Dragoon Bravo Six, and that's all I ever knew him by. In the four months we were together, I never did learn his first name. I didn't need to know it. I was his subordinate. I called him "Captain," or "Sir." He referred to me as "Mac," "Lieutenant Mac," or most often by my radio call sign, "Niner-two."

Captain Daniels was a good soldier and a capable and competent commander. He would one-day be an Army Colonel. I trusted his judgment and his leadership. He was an American Centurion when I knew him, leading 100 men into battle with iron chariots and weapons of war. I was told that he and I were both replacements sent in during the early days of the Tet offensive. He had joined the troop only a week or two before I got there.

The previous Captain and Forward Observer had gone down together after offering a North Vietnamese soldier a chance to surrender and live. I was told that during a battle in the opening days of Tet, they had spotted the bad guy in a spider hole and got the drop on him with the machine-guns. The Captain ordered that no one shoot the guy, and he had the driver take the ACAV right up to the enemy's fighting hole where he ordered the NVA soldier to Chieu Hoi (surrender). The bad guy stood up with an AK-47 on full automatic and took out most of the track crew. He got the Captain, the FO, and the Sergeant who was the track commander.

Of course, the enemy soldier's bad manners bought him a ticket to hell, and his calloused indiscretion caused serious repercussions for others of his tribe in the weeks and months to follow. In the months I was with the cavalry we took very few prisoners. During Tet, the war became a grudge match. No quarter asked, and no quarter given.

We were actually fighting two enemies in Vietnam, the Viet Cong and the North Vietnamese Army. The Viet Cong were guerilla troops. They were local South Vietnamese communist militia who farmed during the day and set booby-traps and land mines at night. Their weapons were a blend of modern Chinese equipment and a packrat's assortment of relics gleaned from battlefields going all the way back to 1940.

They often sniped at us with rifles and RPGs, but we seldom fought them in pitched battles. They usually fired a round or two and then ran like hell. They always got the first shot from ambush, but lucky for us, they were lousy shots. However, the law of averages was on their side. Once in a while they got lucky.

The Viet Cong were sneaky-peeky hit and run guys who always kept us on our toes. They didn't wear uniforms and they tried to blend in with the local civilians when we came after them. Some of them were women. Some even worked for Americans during the day as laborers, laundry girls, and janitors, and then set tripwires for us at night.

The North Vietnamese troops were professional soldiers and Ho Chi Minh's finest. Those we encountered in the III Corps area sometimes wore navy blue or pale-green uniforms instead of the usual black pajamas. They were well armed, well fed, and with good leadership and combat discipline. They were good soldiers, brave and confident enough to attack our armored columns with a purpose. Captured weapons after battles showed that in some of their units, one man in every three or four carried an RPG anti-tank rocket launcher instead of a rifle. Sometimes they used heavy, anti-aircraft machineguns and recoilless rifles (big, tripod mounted bazookas) to give our tanks and helicopters something extra to worry about. They were tough soldiers. An American was a fool if he didn't respect and fear them.

All Vietnamese, be they military or civilians, good guys or bad guys, were relegated to the status of "Gooks." Some have said that this is a sure indication of the racial-biases of the white, ethnocentric Americans, but it was more than that. It was a self-defense mechanism. When you've been sent to kill people, you must alienate yourself from them as far as possible to protect your conscience and your inner sense of well-being. You've got to get the job done and still be able to think of yourself as a good person. It's a moral dilemma common to soldiers.

You can't, in good conscience, kill people who are like you and your loved ones, and so you make them into something different, something less than human and worthy of being killed. You find yourself playing mind and word games. It happens in every war. My father's generation fought "Nips" and "Krouts." Americans fought "Chinks" in Korea and "Towel

Heads" in Afghanistan. Even during the more genteel days of the American Civil War, when white, Anglo-Saxon, protestant Americans fought each other, the two sides were relegated to "Johnny Rebs" and "Damn Yankees." When the other guy is "different" from you, it is easier to shoot him.

The Vietnamese were easy to de-humanize. Theirs was a third-world culture and economy. They were bare-footed rice farmers who lived in leaky little grass huts in primitive, Dogpatch-style villages. They ate fermented fish stew and made do without toilet paper. Pigs and chickens lived in the house. They were "Gooks," and the term had more to do with culture than race.

It didn't take me but a few days in the field to discover that the Vietnamese hated us. Even our friends in South Vietnam hated us, at least those rural farmers I had contact with. In his classic, Academy Award-worthy film debut, "Wha Vyet Namb," President Johnson had assured me that the South Vietnamese were grateful to my fellow soldiers and me for our noble sacrifices. He said they looked to us as their saviors and protectors from Communist oppression. But now, on the ground in Binh Duong Province, I discovered that it was all a myth. The Vietnamese people hated us.

I could never speak Vietnamese, but I can read body language, and people talk to you with their eyes. The unwashed masses of the countryside didn't seem to give a damn about anything but wanting the war to stop.

I could understand it. We were foreigners, and we were ruining their country. We were killing their people, both on purpose and by mistake. We were depopulating large areas of their country and moving the people into concentrated "resettlement areas" where we could "better protect them." Ancestral homes, farms, and cemeteries were being turned into deadly Free Fire Zones. Before the war was over, an estimated ten million South Vietnamese, almost half of the native population, would be refugees. Native customs, social patterns, and centuries-old village traditions were being erased by the demands of the war.

We were defoliating their beautiful forests with an acid rain of Agent Orange. We were polluting their rivers and ruining their fields and livelihoods with the chemical toxins. We were destroying nature, wildlife, and all forms of plant life indiscriminately. The chemical compounds got into irrigating water and drinking water sources.

The countryside was scarred by the devastation of war. Farm fields were dotted with huge bomb craters, a vexing frustration to farmers without tractors. The innocent children of peasant villagers, for the next two or three generations, would loose lives and limbs to forgotten mine fields, booby-traps, and unexploded bombs and shells.

The country suffered economically. In some areas sawmills were forced to shut down because shell fragments in the trees tore saw blades to pieces and injured workers. The rubber industry was decimated. Farmers were relocated far from their lands and the fields of their ancestors. The Americans and South Vietnamese set up "relocation" camps to feed and clothe the refugees, but many desperate and destitute civilians turned to drug dealing, prostitution, and a lucrative black market to survive.

Foreign soldiers were always pointing guns at the people, and bombs and artillery shells came from out of the night, indiscriminate and at random, like meteorites falling from unknown regions of the sky without conscience or accountability. Families slept in foxholes dug in the dirt floors of their humble homes. The Americans called it Harassment and Interdiction Fire (H&I). It was meant to terrorize the enemy and disrupt his redeployment and re-supply efforts.

The shells were aimed at places where the bad guys might be passing in the night, trail junctions, river crossings, known staging areas, or anywhere else the intelligence wizards told us to point a gun. There was seldom any scouting done to see what was really in the area, or any follow-up after shooting to check for results.

The people were prisoners of their villages. They could not travel without the risk of being imprisoned or killed as an enemy combatant. At any given time, vast chunks of the country were designated as "Free Fire Zones" where any Vietnamese national could legally be shot on sight like a predatory animal. Sometimes the rural farmers failed to get the message that their backcountry farms had been made bull's-eyes by an executive order in Saigon.

South Vietnamese government agents came with guns and taxed the people and conscripted them into military service during the hours of daylight, and then left them to the mercies of the Viet Cong at night. The Viet Cong came with guns and taxed the people and conscripted them into military service during the hours of darkness. The South Vietnamese would imprison them as traitors if they failed to fight with the Americans. The Viet Cong would shoot them as traitors if they did. The humble farmers were trapped in a living hell. The Vietnamese people were living a horror beyond anything the fat and happy Americans could even imagine.

And, Americans were only the latest in a long line of foreign soldiers to occupy the country. First had come the French, then the Japanese, and then the French again, and now us. It had been happening for five generations, for over 100 years. We were people from the other side of the world who were bigger, richer, better educated, and better armed than they could ever hope to be, and we looked down on them with haughty contempt as we tore their world apart.

The gods of war must have hated the Vietnamese to bestow upon them such long-term misery and bloodshed. I looked into the eyes of the fourth and fifth generations of Vietnamese who knew nothing but oppression and war, and I saw hatred, anger, and deep sadness there. They were tired of the fighting. They didn't seem to care who we were, where we came from, or what the hell we were doing there. Most just wanted us to go home and leave them alone.

I was soon to learn too, which side believed in what they were doing. The North Vietnamese, and most of the Viet Cong, fought like tigers. They came at us valiantly, recklessly, even hopelessly. They fought with courage, tenacity, and conviction. I had to admire them.

Ho Chi Minh had told the Frenchmen in 1946 that they could kill ten of his men for every one the French lost, and he would still win the war – and he did. They were fighting for different principles, the Frenchmen and the Vietnamese. And now, we had picked up the fallen French standard and we were losing our one man to ten, and Uncle Ho was winning a second time.

Our "allies," the South Vietnamese, were slothful soldiers. I'm sorry, but it's true. The ones we worked with were reasonably well trained and well equipped, but with hearts of lemon Jell-O. They lacked courage, conviction, and competence. Most were unwilling conscripts who fought timidly for their freedom. When we worked with them, they got in our way. They bunched up behind our tanks like herds of sheep and we ran over them trying to maneuver. We couldn't trust their leadership, artillery, air force, or intelligence. Whenever they were shot at they dropped on their bellies in the mud and squealed like pigs on the radio for the Americans to come and rescue them. We often moved through their cowering ranks to take the fight to the enemy. I became contemptuous of the very pretense that they represented a fighting force.

It played good to the American people, but I knew from the start that Nixon's plan for the "Vietnamization" of the war, his plan to let the South Vietnamese take over, would never work. The South Vietnamese military, in spite of endless shiploads of American equipment, and in spite of world-class military coaching, was a mob and not a real army. They didn't believe in what they were doing or what they were fighting for. Unlike their communist cousins from the North, with whom they shared a common history and DNA, there was no fire in their belly. It was rather sad. It is hard to fight for another man's freedom while he cowers in a ditch several hundred yards behind you.

It was no surprise to me in 1975 when the South Vietnamese Army threw down their guns and ran like rabbits when the North Vietnamese came at them with a purpose. They abandoned the world's third largest air force on the tarmac (all American supplied), and left American tanks sitting in the middle of the road with the engines running. They ran to the coast and waited for the Marines to come back and save them. I watched it all on TV with tears in my eyes. It's too bad that Lyndon Johnson and Richard Nixon didn't ask for my opinion in 1968. I could have predicted the whole thing seven years before it happened.

And, it didn't take but a few weeks in the field for me to know that our efforts were less than noble. We were there to kill people, pure and simple. The body count was the only measure of success in Vietnam. Promotions and careers depended on the numbers. Instead of taking the high ground and marching on the enemy capitol, we fed bodies to Robert McNamara's statistical analysis machinery. The college boys in the air-conditioned offices in Washington had it all figured out. If we expended "x" number of bullets and used up "y" gallons of fuel for the tanks, we had damn well better kill "z" number of enemy soldiers or we were not doing our job.

And, as it all turned out, we just couldn't win. The deck was stacked against us. The North Vietnamese hated us, the South Vietnamese hated us, and our friends and neighbors back home hated us. The newspapers from home showed people protesting the war, burning the flag we were fighting for, spitting on soldiers like us, and calling us all baby killers. It made my heart hurt.

The war was a long way from being over when I was there, but I could already see the futility of our situation. Our position was untenable. We had no clear course to victory. We were treating the symptoms of a disease called communism without going to the source of the infection. Without a radical change in policy, we were doomed to failure.

In retrospect, I suppose I must have felt much like a Confederate soldier of a hundred years before. I was caught up in something that I could see was hopeless, but I couldn't quit. I had to fight for my friends, my honor, and to defend my own life. I had sworn an oath to serve. I couldn't turn my back on that commitment.

Noble ideals are always the first casualties of war, and yet I remained ever the idealist. It was the one bright hope I could cling to. I was proud to be an American, and I was proud to fight for another man's freedom, even if he didn't fully understand or appreciate what I was trying to do for him. My intentions were noble and my sacrifice real. I had placed my sacred honor, my body and soul, on the altar of that sacrifice. I was fighting for my country and defending democracy on foreign soil because it was the right thing to do. In spite of the many obstacles and the taunts of the protesters, I served with a sense of pride. My king was unworthy, but my countrymen were inherently good. I was proud to serve them.

The draft notice I received from my government told me that my friends and neighbors had selected me, to represent them, in the armed forces of the United States. And, like that brave Japanese pilot of World War II, I was giving it my all, delivered with honor and all earnestness to a lost cause.

It was the charge of the Light Brigade after all.

"Forward the Light Brigade!
Was there a man dismayed?
Not tho' every soldier knew
    Someone had blundered.
Their's not to make reply,
Their's not to reason why,
Their's but to do and die,
Into the valley of death
    Rode the six hundred."

In the Belly Of the Beast

The Fourth Armored Cavalry was a ready reaction force for the whole First Division. We were the guys on the big iron horses sent to the rescue. Our rapid mobility and heavy firepower was always in demand. We charged up and down the length and breadth of division operations, from the Newport Bridge just north of Saigon to the Cambodian border near Loc Ninh. We would join a big fight or a big operation for a day or two, and then pull away and charge up Highway 13 for forty, fifty, or a hundred miles to join another big fight or another operation already in progress. We covered a lot of ground and we expended a lot of ammunition – more than our share. There was very little down time. We lived in the armored vehicles.

During those early months of 1968, in the wake and the aftermath of the Tet Offensive, we were involved in some kind of combat incident, an ambush, a sniping, a land mine, a booby-trap, a fire fight, or a pitched battle, every two or three days. We were always on the move and always at the battle's front.

It was constant combat and our casualty rate was very high. We were loosing men, both wounded and killed, at a steady rate of two or three each week, and sometimes as many as six, eight, or ten all at once. Our troop had a field strength of about 120 souls. At our rate of attrition between February and May, we would have ceased to exist as a fighting force had it not been for a steady stream of new blood from the States.

As Forward Artillery Observer for the unit, I enjoyed a unique status. My job was much different than being a platoon leader or a tank commander. I was a specialist, an artillery technician "attached" to the cavalry unit with no command responsibility. Technically, I worked for Division Artillery and not for the Captain I served.

And, I was the only artilleryman in the troop. Cavalry FOs were not assigned a radioman or a rifleman/scout to cover their back as was common in the infantry units. I worked alone, and I was in charge of things and not people. I carried a tremendous amount of responsibility, to be sure, but I had only my maps, radio, codebooks, compass, and personal weapons to look after. Captain Rice, the Squadron Artillery Liaison Officer, was the first link in my chain of command back to Division Artillery. But, I didn't see him often. Day-to-day, I sat at the right hand of Captain Daniels of "B" Troop.

My unique status gave me a good deal of flexibility within the unit, and sometimes, when my artillery skills were not needed, I could choose who I wanted to be. Depending on what was needed at the moment, I might fill in as a substitute machine-gunner, rifleman, grenadier, medic, or infantry squad leader. I enjoyed the relative freedom and the flexibility.

Those months I spent on an ACAV are a blur to me now. Most of it is jumbled and lumped together after all these years. I can untangle some of it through the letters my pretty Jeannie saved, but perhaps it's just as well not to do that. The Vietnam War was not a sequential series of events anyway. Progress was not measured by territorial gains, cities captured, or rivers crossed. The whole thing was a sinkhole. One day was very much like the next day. It really didn't matter where we were or what we were doing or what day it was. It was all the same.

What follows is but a handful of memories, examples of our cavalry forays into the valley of the shadow, unique only because of some special terror or event that keeps them fresh in my mind after all these years.

Baptism by Fire:

As a Forward Artillery Observer, I had been trained well, but trained on the prairies of Oklahoma to direct shellfire on the steppes of Russia. Vietnam was a whole different world. In Vietnam, everything was close. It was a world of trees, vines and heavy foliage. Visibility was often restricted to a few yards at best. My first fire mission in the jungle was an exercise in terror.

Captain Daniels was reluctant to use me in the first few fights we fought together. He was afraid of me. I was offended at the time, but I realize now that he was a wise man for feeling that way. With my radio, map and compass, I controlled more firepower than all of the tanks and armored vehicles in his whole unit. I was a young and inexperienced Second Lieutenant, barely twenty-one years old, and I had all the muscle of Division Artillery at my beck and call. I certainly had the potential to be dangerous.

We had our backs to the wall when Daniels first told me to bring fire from the sky. The bad guys had ambushed us on a narrow road in thick trees and we could not maneuver. Our column was stopped cold and unable to attack or disengage. The NVA had planned it well, and our troop was being shot up pretty good. The only thing that kept them from overrunning us was the overwhelming firepower of the armored vehicles.

The NVA used that tactic often when they picked the ground and initiated the fight. They would catch us where we couldn't maneuver, and then attack from well-prepared fighting holes that were very close to our vehicles. They always tried to get close enough that we couldn't use artillery or air support without getting our own people killed. The safest place on the battlefield was always where we were, and the NVA tried to get right in among us and fight at close quarters.

It seems incredible that dismounted infantry would actually pick fights with our column of tanks, but they did, and they did it often. They had great faith in their RPG rockets. Our ACAVs had aluminum armor that was easily penetrated, and our tanks were Korean War relics.

In this particular fight, the NVA were in well-prepared fighting positions that were so close we were throwing hand grenades at each other. The trees made it impossible for us to overrun them like we usually tried to do. They had bottled us up on the road by knocking out a couple of armored vehicles at the front of the column. We couldn't disengage without leaving dead and wounded men and functioning weapons behind. We wouldn't do that, and it was becoming a desperate fight.

The Captain turned to me with wild eyes and told me he wanted artillery in behind them, and bring it in as close as I could. I could see in his eyes that the poor man was almost as afraid of me as he was the NVA, but he didn't have a choice. I was the only artilleryman he had and all his cards were on the table. Artillery was the ace that hadn't been played yet.

I was terrified because of the trees. Tall trees complicate a close-support fire mission considerably. To get artillery where we needed it would be difficult. The mission would be very dangerous.

It was also hard for me, that first time, to give my full attention to what I had to do. Amid violence, carnage and chaos, I had to close my mind to the horrors going on all around me and focus my thoughts on gun/target angles, compass bearings, and radio call signs. I had to get it right and I had to do it in a hurry. And, as I worked out the logistics of the thing, I couldn't watch for danger or cover my own back. I had to trust the men around me to protect me while I plotted coordinates, checked compass azimuths, and worked up the fire mission. I had to narrow my focus to the engineering and mechanical principles of killing people from long range, even though I was in great danger and right up against the target.

Somewhat surprising to me, I was able to pull it off. As the battle raged around me, I became an isolated pocket of introverted, studious reasoning, with a map spread across my knee, a grease pencil in my hand, and radio speakers in my ears. I did everything by the book. I was scared to death, and the sound of my heart beating in my ears almost drowned out the incoming radio traffic. The cavalry troopers covered my back.

A lot depended on the mechanics of the thing. I used a 105mm howitzer battery (six guns) because I could see that to be effective I had to go danger-close. A 105 has a tighter killing radius (about 35 yards) and is safer to use in close support. I also knew that a point-detonating fuse might give me an airburst in the trees and I didn't want that to happen. A close airburst would get my guys too. I ordered delayed fuses, the kind usually reserved for busting bunkers. I reasoned that if a delayed fuse hit a tree limb, the shell would most likely be at or near the ground before the shell detonated.

As per standard procedure, I sent the first few shells into an area several hundred yards away so I could locate the point of impact and then walk the shells back to us in measured increments. The first rule in artillery spotting is to always put that first round someplace you know you're not, and then direct the shellfire from there.

I soon discovered that I couldn't see the incoming shells because of the trees, but I could hear the far-off detonations over the roar of the battle. The shells were exploding out in the boondocks someplace behind the bad guys. Good Lord, I had never considered that in combat I might have to direct shellfire by sound. I hadn't been trained to do that. The gunnery ranges of Oklahoma are flat and you can see for miles. We never practiced in the forest or the jungle. But, there was hope. I could hear the shells bursting off in the distance, and that told me that my coordinates were good and the artillery battery and I were at least on the same page. Judging from the sound alone, I walked the artillery back in increments until it was much closer.

I was afraid to bring it all the way home, but I had no choice. My Captain and the cavalry troopers needed me. The battle was growing desperate. My firepower was wasted if it wasn't on the target. I had to walk the shells into the enemy positions, or as close as I possibly could.

"One gun for adjustment, drop one hundred, we're bringing it home," I screamed into the headset over the roar of the battle. A few moments later, there was a heavy CRUMP back in the trees somewhere. The sound told me that the shells were closer than I had thought, but still too far away to be effective against the NVA spiderholes. I had to get them closer. My hands were trembling.

I punched the toggle switch on my tanker's helmet to talk to the cavalry troopers. I said something like· "This is Niner-two guys. I've got incoming artillery on the way. Now listen close ... when I yell "Splash" you better duck. You'll only have a second or two."

I toggled the switch to the artillery channel again. "One gun for adjustment, drop fifty, danger-close, and give me a splash." "Roger that" came the almost too-cheerful voice on the artillery command frequency, "One gun, drop fifty, danger-close, request splash." Splash is an old artillery term that is used to give the FO a three to four-second heads-up before the shell hits the ground. The Fire Direction Center can calculate the time-of-flight that close ... or you hope they can.

I was filled with terror. Where would the damn thing land? I was guessing, directing only by the sound of the exploding shells above the roar of the battle. Had I cut it too close? Would it land where I wanted it to land? Would it go off in the trees above us? There was no way to be sure. I was sick with apprehension. My military career, my reputation with these good men, and maybe my very life, depended on where that next shell landed. Luckily, the Captain and none of the troopers knew of my anguish or the questions I was asking myself.

I stood in the ACAV, crouched down and looking out past the M60 gun shield. My only weapon was a radio. Bullets and grenade fragments were flying everywhere and I ducked my head and squinted my eyes tight. I didn't want to be shot in the face by some NVA guy in a spiderhole, but I really needed to see where that next shell landed.

"Splash" came the call in my headset. I already had my thumb on the toggle switch of the cavalry channel. I punched it and screamed "SPLASH!"

Everyone in "B" Troop of the Fourth Cavalry ducked and covered – but me. I watched the fireball go off just above the ground. A big piece of shrapnel hit me between my right eye and ear. I had cut it just a little too close. Luckily, the shell fragment glanced off the gun shield and then hit the very edge of my tank commander's helmet. The ricochet slowed it down and the helmet stopped it. The impact stunned me a little, but I was not hurt – just a red mark where the edge of the helmet slammed into my head. I thanked God later that none of my cavalry soldiers were injured. I had sprinkled them with hot metal fragments and wet wood chips, an errant FO's baptism by friendly fire. I was embarrassed. It's not supposed to happen.

"Add fifty, fire for effect," I screamed into the headset. I was moving it back but keeping it as close as I dared. It was the best I could do under the circumstances. The shells came thundering in by the dozens and the jungle exploded behind the bad guys. There was a constant roar of impacting shells and bright flashes of light from deep in the shadows. Tree limbs and dirt clods sailed through the air and a great cloud of dust and smoke filtered through the trees. I couldn't quite get close enough to get the NVA spiderholes, but the North Vietnamese were now the people who were trapped. They were unable to maneuver, retreat, or reinforce. We shot them all to hell with the tank cannons, grenade launchers, and heavy machine-guns while the artillery sealed the escape route.

I learned a lot that day. I walked the shells back and forth in front of our line and tore that patch of jungle apart. I was able to lend real support to the unit and it was a great confidence builder for me. We were able to get our people out of the ambush kill zone and onto better ground. We were able to bring our disabled vehicles and our dead and wounded soldiers out with us. We also got several of the bad guys.

My Captain actually complemented me for doing a good job when the battle was done. He was impressed by the "Splash" call and how close I was able to get the shells without taking out his unit. He used me in almost every fight after that. Many times over the next weeks and months I would direct artillery fire to within 50 yards of our armored columns. It was risky business. We lived in a world that was danger-close.

I don't know if anyone ever told the Captain that I hit myself with shrapnel that day. I never did. It wasn't something to be proud of. After the fight, I found that ragged chunk of metal. It was lying at my feet amid the thousands of spent bullet casings on the floor of the ACAV. I carried that piece of shrapnel in my pocket for the rest of my Vietnam tour. I still have it.

Meeting the enemy:
In the terror of the dark of night, and amid the glow of parachute flares, bursting shells, and the crack of incoming bullets, I imagined my enemy to be six feet tall and with the muscles of a

professional wrestler. I could see him with my mind's eye. He had cold and steely eyes, a cruel smirk on his evil face, and he was coming for me with a screwdriver-tipped bayonet. I imagined him as a brutal and merciless killer, older than me, bigger than me, tougher than me, and more willing to die than me. I was terribly afraid of him, and I fought savagely to keep him and his flat-tipped bayonet from overrunning our defensive position.

As the morning sun chased the shadows from the battlefield, our enemy melted into the jungle and the shooting stopped. We soon made a reconnaissance sweep out in front of our positions to determine where the enemy had gone and to assess the results of our late-night fight. We had lost a few good men, and we were already under pressure from headquarters to get a body count so the Generals could determine if we had won the fight, and by what margin.

I was humbled and embarrassed when I finally met that enemy soldier face to face. He wasn't at all what I had expected. I found him lying on his side in the thick bushes out in front of our fighting position. He had died sometime during the night, and he had died in agony. His knees were drawn up against his stomach and both hands were curled like claws over his lower chest. His lips were pulled back over his teeth in a grimace of pain that now looked almost like a defiant sneer. There was a large, dark bloodstain on his clothing, and dried blood was smeared over his mouth and nose. His eyes were open to the morning light, but they were glassy and without life. The blowflies had already found him. The flies were happily exploring his sightless eyes and open mouth.

The man was wearing civilian clothes, and he didn't look much like a soldier. He was probably VC instead of NVA. There were no papers in his pockets to tell his name or his unit. There was no weapon near the body either. I guessed that he had crawled away from his weapon, or one of his buddies had rescued it from the battlefield before the sun came up. Our people found the bodies of half-a-dozen of his friends scattered in the bushes around our perimeter.

It surprised me that I felt pity for that young man lying there in the bushes. He was so small. He was short, skinny, and not at all the Sumo Wrestler I had imagined in the dark. I was ashamed that I had been so afraid of him. He couldn't have weighed more than a hundred pounds and he didn't look to be more than fifteen or sixteen years old.

We left him there, where he had fallen, to the mercy of the flies and his friends and family if they dared to come and find him. We never buried the people we killed. We just counted them.

The life that young man lost that night was registered as a check mark on a chart at Division Headquarters. He was only a statistic now, a number in the all-important body count. But, he had served a useful purpose in our effort to win the war. By being killed and being counted, he had helped to tip the balance sheet in our favor.

A Landmark

Soon after I joined the cavalry, in mid-February, we had a firefight near a small hamlet not far from the Dian (Zee-on) Base Camp. We killed a few bad guys. One of the enemy soldiers went down along the dike of a rice paddy near the road. He was lying out in the open. We dutifully counted him, took his weapon, cleaned out his pockets and left him there. We were busy, and we went on to other adventures and other firefights.

A week or so later, we passed by the same area and discovered the body still lying where we had left it. No one had buried the man or dragged his carcass away, even though he was quite close to the road and close to the tiny village. He was slowly succumbing to the ravages of nature and the tropical climate. The stench was awful.

I'm speculating, but evidently the local folks didn't want to bury the man because to do so would make them appear to be his friend. They couldn't afford to be friends with our enemy, and so they did what we did. They just left him lying there where he had fallen. They walked around the dead man and went about their business.

We traveled past several times in the months to follow, and the dead man was always there. He became a landmark, a milepost on our journey. We watched him slowly rot away as little animals and the elements of nature scattered his remains. The last time I saw him, he was only a grinning skeleton with tattered shreds of uniform still clinging to his ant-covered bones.

The Vietnamese villagers pretended that he wasn't there. Like a lot of the ugliness of the war, life went on in spite of the horrors. That rotting, stinking, human body was just one more reminder of the unpleasantness. The farmers plowed around him like he was a stump or a big rock in the field.

Borders:

We had chased a retreating NVA unit as far north as we could legally go, and then we circled the wagons. The night became as dark as the inside of a coalmine. When the mortar shells came whistling in, we could see the flash of the tubes on a distant ridgeline. It was a rare event, an opportunity to zero in on the enemy position and clobber them with artillery. I quickly calculated the coordinates and called for a fire mission.

I was waiting anxiously for the big shells to arrive, ducking as the mortars burst around us, when the gun battery called back.

"Dragoon Niner-two, this is Dynamite Battery. Be advised that your coordinates plot over the border into Cambodia. We cannot fire this mission, over."

"Dynamite, this is Dragoon Niner-two, be advised that we are under attack from an enemy emplacement at those coordinates. We have visual contact. We can see the flash of the mortar tubes, over."

"Your mission is denied, Dragoon, we will not shoot across the border without higher authorization, over."

I responded with urgency and with anger. "Dynamite, this is Dragoon Niner-two. Rules of engagement dictate that we can shoot across that border when fired upon. We are under fire at this very moment. I can actually see the gun emplacement and I have the position plotted. I can get those bastards if you will shoot the damned artillery! Over."

"Stand by Dragoon, we will check with battalion for clearance, out."

Over an hour later came a call from Dynamite Battery. "Dragoon Niner-two, we have clearance for your fire mission. What is your pleasure, over?"

"Forget it Dynamite. We have no enemy contact at this time. They ran out of ammunition and went home a long time ago, out."

Incredibly, my request to shoot back was passed from the gun battery to Battalion, to Brigade, and then all the way to Division before anyone would make a decision to let me shoot over that magic line into the enemy sanctuary. It was probably a General who finally Okayed my self-defense fire mission. By then, it was too late. Vietnam was a strange, political war.

Shooting the Back Azimuth:

I don't remember where I learned it. It was never taught in my stateside artillery training. It must have come from that body of personal experience and shared knowledge passed on in Vietnam from FO to FO in the base camp Officer's Clubs, or while sitting in the shade along some jungle trail. However it happened, after only a few weeks in Vietnam, I learned to shoot the back azimuth.

If you knew how to read the signs, the shell crater from a Chicom (Chinese Communist) 82mm mortar round would tell you where the enemy mortar crew was. A Chicom 82 left a distinct footprint in the soft dirt. For one thing, the tailfin of the mortar round was always found lying in the shell hole. It happened every time. It was a calling card from our enemy that identified the shell crater as one of theirs. And, when the mortar shell exploded, the metal fuse in the nose of the shell would be driven deep into the dirt leaving a little round hole that burrowed several inches deep. The softer the ground, the deeper and more distinct the fuse hole.

If you put a nice straight stick down the fuse hole, it would give you the "angle of fall" (trajectory arc) of the mortar shell and the back azimuth to the mortar tube. This was critical information. The angle of fall would tell you how far away the mortar was. The back azimuth would tell which direction the shell came from. In the base camp areas, this information was gleaned using radar. We didn't have the luxury of radar in the outback. We improvised.

The back azimuth was determined with a compass. We held a compass over the stick in the fuse hole and took a compass bearing along the axis. This gave a direct line to the mortar tube.

The angle was also critical, but the science was not as exact. You had to guess. A mortar throws a shell in a high-angle arc. If the shell came down steep at almost a ninety-degree angle, you assumed they were very close. If the angle was flatter, closer to forty-five degrees, you guessed they were near maximum range. If you knew the effective range of the mortar, which we did, you could then make an "informed" decision about how far away you wanted to drop your own artillery shells along that back azimuth line. And, if you plotted the line on a map, sometimes terrain features near the estimated range would help make the decision for you.

With my radio, map, and compass, I was the only guy in the troop who could challenge the enemy mortar crews. The Army calls it counter-battery fire. Counter-battery is when you shoot your guns at their guns when fired upon. You had to have indirect-fire weapons to do it, high-angle and long-range howitzers. Tank cannons and machine-guns are direct-fire weapons. They can't reach enemy mortar tubes behind the cover of trees or on the backside of a hill.

The only disadvantage in shooting the back azimuth was in gathering timely information. To get the data in time to do any good was one of the most dangerous jobs in Vietnam. Generally, it was a good idea to wait until the bad guys stopped shooting before you ran to a shell crater to gather the necessary information, but by then, they had usually expended their ammunition allotment and were packing up to head for the tall timber. We had to be fast to catch them before they got away. Sometimes, if you were angry, highly motivated, or just a little crazy, it was tempting to race with the devil and move too quickly.

I kept an eighteen-inch-long wooden dowel rod near my radio on the ACAV. It was my back azimuth stick. Whenever we were mortared, as soon as I judged they had stopped shooting (an inexact science), I would run from cover to the nearest shell crater and work the wizardry with my compass and back azimuth stick. It took only a few seconds. I would then run like hell back to my radio where I already had an artillery battery standing by. In minutes, we would commence to pound the back azimuth.

Unfortunately, in spite of my best efforts, I almost never knew how effective my counter-battery fire was. We were seldom able to follow-up. But, it did make me feel like a stud horse to be the one guy in the unit who could always shoot back.

Signals:

It was the Captain who first noticed it. Whenever we approached the town of Chaun Thaun on Highway 13, a white kite would rise like a ghost above the trees. And then, as we got closer to the village, the kite would disappear.

We charged in quickly a couple of times to apprehend and question the kite flyer, but we were always too slow. With innocent, poker-playing faces, the local civilians swore that they had never seen the kite or the kite flyer. They assured us that they were all good, communist hating, loyal subjects of the South Vietnamese government.

The fabled, white kite of Chaun Thaun became something we looked forward to seeing on our journeys. That ghostly apparition, that only Americans could see, always peeked over the trees and hung suspended in the air for just a few minutes, and then disappeared as we got closer.

Tripwires:

Vietnam was a war of booby-traps, mines, and shots fired from ambush. It was a lot like the French and Indian Wars on the American frontier in the early 1700s. The wild men of the forest hid in the shadows, picked off stragglers, and sent flaming arrows into the stockade at night.

Vietnam was also a war of tunnels. Our enemy lived underground. When we approached, they melted into Mother Earth like hunted animals seeking refuge in their burrows.
We always destroyed their tunnels when we found them. And, in most cases, our people explored them first, searching for weapons, documents, or bad guys to add to the body count.

It took a special breed of soldier to volunteer to go into the enemy tunnels. I never did it. The tunnels were dark, stinking, and dangerous places. They were full of rats, spiders, snakes, and evil men with guns and long, ugly knives.

My friend Smokey Clark was a tunnel rat. Smokey was a rodeo cowboy from my hometown, a bull rider unafraid of man or beast. I never ran into Smokey while in Vietnam, he served with an infantry unit, in another area, at another time. Smokey, and others like him, went into the tunnels with a pistol, a flashlight, and a heart of tempered steel. I salute any man who ever did that.

Like most tunnel rats, our guy was a volunteer, a young man who loved the excitement and the adrenaline rush of crawling into the unknown regions of the enemy burrows. He had done it several times. His willingness to face the devil in the dark gave him an exalted status within the unit.

The tunnel rat stripped off his flak jacket and chambered a round in his pistol. He then peered into the hole for a long time with a flashlight, searching for snakes, tripwires, punji stakes, or mines. He found none. He then got down on his belly and started into the hole, headfirst. His boots were still in the sunlight when there was a muffled CRUMP from inside the hole and a thick cloud of white smoke came pouring out of the tunnel.

We grabbed his feet and pulled him from the hole, and as we did, we began to gag and choke from the gas. It was a CS grenade, tear gas, the kind used by riot police. CS is not supposed to be lethal, and the VC sapper who prepared the trap might have thought it was a white phosphorus grenade when he set the wire.

The gas canister had exploded right in the man's face, and it took six or eight of us to hold him down while the medic worked him over. His eyes were burned and blistered horribly, and the skin of his face, neck, and hands was scorched a deep red. I don't know what had happened to his lungs. His eyes, nose, and mouth were bleeding freely and swelling terribly. He made sounds that haunted my dreams for years. We used all the water we had before the medivac got there, five-gallon cans of it, trying to wash the burning crystals out of his eyes and from the flesh of his face and mouth. When we finally got him on a helicopter, our medic threw up.

I don't remember that young man's name, and I never knew how it all turned out, but many times in the years since, I have thanked God for my eyesight.

Willie Peter:

During my tour with the cavalry, I went into an area known as the "Iron Triangle" three times. The Iron Triangle was Northwest of Saigon between Highway 13 and the Cambodian border. The town of Ben Cat was at the point of the triangle, and Tay Ninh marked the southern boundary to the West. It was a vast area of uninhabited and foreboding jungle that was a stronghold and a staging area for NVA infiltrators who sneaked across the border from Cambodia on the Ho Chi Minh trail. There were always large numbers of NVA soldiers in the triangle.

The job of the American Army in Vietnam was not to storm the enemy castle or to capture the enemy king. Our job was to kill enemy soldiers wherever we could find them. When they wouldn't come to us to be killed, we had to go to them. Whenever our busy schedule would allow it, the General would send us into the Iron Triangle to stir up the hornet's nest and "get some."

To search and destroy in the Iron Triangle was like hunting tigers. We were the bait. The cavalry was the sacrificial goat tied to a stake to entice the tiger. Our job was to find the bad guys and get them out in the open where the artillery, helicopter gunships, and Phantom jets could send them to hell in large numbers.

Being tiger bait was always dangerous. The hunt was unpredictable. Our enemies knew the game too, and it was difficult to draw them into a pitched battle. They would seldom bite, but they often nibbled at the bait. They sniped at us often with rifles and RPGs. They planted mines, set booby-traps, and lobbed mortars and rockets into our perimeter at night. Then, like wary and often hunted tigers, they slipped away into the vastness of the jungle.

We always knew they were out there and watching as we passed by. We could feel their evil presence around us. Sometimes, we could even smell them too. The wild men of the jungle had a distinct smell. It was an odd mix of campfire smoke and fish oil tainted perspiration. We would find their sandal tracks in the dust, still-warm campfire ashes, tunnel entrances and staging areas, but we could only find the bad guys when they wanted to be found. They fought only when they were ready, and they always got the first shot. We lost a lot of good men in the Triangle using them as tiger bait.

In the early morning hours of darkness, the rockets and mortars would come screaming down on us and the enemy would test our defenses. We couldn't just duck and hide from the mortars. We had to stand to the guns to protect ourselves from a ground assault. The communists were always searching for a weak spot and trying to find a hole in our lines where they could get in among us. Large NVA units were always in the neighborhood, and we never knew how many we might be facing in the night. The possibility of being overrun was very real. Being tiger bait in the Triangle was scary as hell.

Our enemy always preferred to fight in the dark. Those were the days before night vision devices, and darkness gave the enemy an advantage. Our Phantom jets, helicopters, and artillery spotters were less effective in the night. We couldn't see them, and they could maneuver and concentrate large numbers of troops in a way they couldn't do in the daylight without being shot to hell. They would run from us in the light of day, and then attack with a vengeance from out of the darkness.

It is terrifying to fight for your life in the dark. You always feel so very much alone. You can't see your friends and you can't see your enemy. You don't know what is happening around you. Every small sound is frightening. You always worry that your neighbor has been overrun and the devil is behind you with a big knife or a hand grenade.

They often came from out of the night with bayonets fixed. You never knew how many, or how determined they might be. And, when they got in real close like that, the effects of our artillery and air power were minimized. We couldn't get them without getting some of us. It was a real challenge for an artillery observer.

We always had defensive artillery targets pre-plotted around our perimeter to cover our enemy's likely avenues of approach and retreat. When they made a rush at our lines, my job was to get artillery coming fast and close to try to break up the attack before they got through the wire. We shot thousands of rounds of artillery in the Iron Triangle.

One night, quite by accident, I learned how best to break-up a night attack against our defensive lines. I found that it didn't matter how many of them there were or how determined they might be, I could make them run. The trick was to shoot white phosphorous in the dark.

A white phosphorous artillery shell (the artillery designation is Willie Peter) is an insidious device. The shell scatters a waxy powder that ignites when exposed to oxygen at room temperature. The exploding shell sends long streamers of the burning substance over a wide area. The powder will burn for as long as it has oxygen or until it is entirely consumed. Fortunately, it burns itself out in just a few seconds. After a Willie Peter shell has detonated, a lingering cloud of dusty white smoke is left hanging in the air. The shells are most often used by artillerymen to start fires or to mark targets for highflying aircraft. When used against troops, white phosphorous is every bit as sinister as napalm. It causes severe burns.

In the daylight, a Willie Peter shell throws out long streamers of boiling white smoke that glow at the ends like sparklers. It is scary all right, but not something that will buckle your knees. It is the enhanced visual effects of Willie Peter in the dark that gives it that extra boost of terror that makes men's hearts fail them. No soldiers, no matter how disciplined, no matter how brave, will stand and face that glowing chemical monster with the reaching fingers when it comes for them from out of the dark.

Willie Peter doesn't kill as effectively or as efficiently as high explosive shrapnel rounds, and we didn't use it often against troops, but it became an ace up my sleeve. It was a card to be played in the most desperate of circumstances - a weapon of terror and intimidation. A few times, when our perimeters were under night attacks and we were fearful of being overrun, I brought Willie Peter as close as I could to our defensive lines. Each time the bad guys broke ranks and ran.

We were coming back to an NDP (night defensive position) in the Iron Triangle late one afternoon. We had been out all day beating the bushes. It was Injun territory and there were lots of hostiles out there, but we couldn't goad them into a fight. It was frustrating.

All day long, our enemy had tormented us without mercy. We had triggered a few booby-traps and ran over a few mines. We had been sniped at with rifles and RPGs, and then the wild men of the jungle ran away. Some of our friends had been badly injured: torn, bleeding, and writhing in pain. We had called in medivac helicopters and then gunships, but to no avail. The bad guys were still out there, and stalking our every move. Now, we were heading back to camp to circle the wagons. We were angry, tired, dirty, and dispirited.

We knew what was coming as the light began to fade. Every night we had been there, for over a week, the bad guys had mortared our positions and tested our perimeter in the wee morning hours. We were completely exhausted from the tension and lack of sleep. We had been on the razor's edge and without rest for a long, long time.

As we approached the NDP, I spotted half a dozen freshly dug foxholes on a low ridge just a few hundred yards outside of our wire. Our vehicles were passing right by them, but no one else seemed to notice they were there. I could see that the foxholes were in a perfect place to be used as a staging area to coordinate attacks against our perimeter. It was also a great place for an enemy Forward Observer to take shelter while directing fire on our camp. I was amazed when I realized what I was looking at.

I told our driver to stop for a moment, and I stepped off the ACAV and told them to go ahead and I would catch up later. We were near the front of the armored column and there were many vehicles coming down the trail that would provide cover and protection while I checked it out.

With rifle in hand, I trotted over to the newly dug foxholes and looked it over. The dirt was still damp and the holes were not yet as deep as they should be. I knew the bad guys would be back later in the night to finish the holes and probably use them against us. I took my compass out and took two or three readings on prominent terrain features, and then plotted the intersection of the lines on my map. I pinpointed the location and set the coordinates. I then caught a ride back to our defensive positions on one of the last vehicles in the column. I had a plan.

I talked it over with my Captain and then the Colonel. They were both enthusiastic and gave me their blessing. I called a heavy, 155mm gun battery that was several miles away and told them I wanted them to register (sight-in) their guns for a special fire mission later in the night. I told them there would be no adjusting of the shells to hit the target. They were to fire on one point, all six guns simultaneously. I told them we would be using Willie Peter shells with point detonating fuses.

My intent was to surprise old Victor Charley (the VC) and light up his life. We owed it to him. From ambush and without warning, he had taken down a few good men today. Their blood was crying for revenge. I was angry, and with the information I had gleaned from studying the enemy foxholes, I was a guy who could even the odds.

The NVA always seemed to hold the initiative, and with it, the high ground of troop morale. I wanted to change all of that. I wanted to seize the initiative and take charge of the battlefield. I wanted to gain the advantage that comes with shooting first. And, I wanted to scare the hell out of my opponent as much as I wanted to kill him. I wanted to do psychological damage even more than physical damage. I wanted to change his attitude and humble him. I wanted to erase his haughty smirk and put his self-confidence in the toilet. I wanted him to wonder how we figured him out and how we knew where he was in the dark. I wanted to give him something to worry about. It had to be something very dramatic and with extreme shock value, something he would remember for a long, long time. Willie Peter in the dark would be perfect.

The fire direction officer at the gun battery caught the vision, and he laughed when I told him what I was up to. He told me they would be happy to help. He said they would fine-tune the gun sights and stand by for my orders.

The NVA were good soldiers, but they were fairly predictable. They usually fired their mortars and rockets around two in the morning. I figured they would be setting up and getting ready to strike around one-thirty, and so that's when I called for the shot. I alerted our perimeter that some-thing big was about to happen, and I told the cavalry troopers to hunker down and hold on tight.

I told the gun battery to fire "battery four" (six guns to shoot four shells each, for a total of 24) on the pre-determined coordinates. It was certainly overkill, but I was going for maximum shock value. I told them to fire when ready and to give me a "shot" and "splash" before the shells touched down.

I waited fretfully. It was exciting to finally have the tiger in my sights, but I was anxious too. Had I guessed right, and had I timed it correctly?

There came one word in my earphones, "Shot!" That meant that the shells were in the air and on the way. I repeated the word into the radio for my cavalry troopers, "Shot!" There was an anxious silence for several seconds, and then we could hear the shells rippling through the air high overhead as a voice screamed in my headset "SPLASH!" I too yelled "SPLASH!" into the cavalry radio channel, and this time I ducked with them. The shells came screaming down through the darkness.

It was one of the most incredible things I have ever seen. The Fourth of July fireworks display at our nation's capitol couldn't hold a candle to it. Earth and sky came alive with fire and light and we had a front row seat. The horror and the magnificence of it were breathtaking.

It was a completely dark and stormy night when those big shells came thundering from out of nowhere and impacted into that one small area. The white-hot flash of it lit the jungle as bright as day for a mile around. And then, the big shells just kept coming: Crump, Crump, Crump, in rapid succession. The glowing, boiling, thumping, luminous cloud pulsated like a beating heart that grew larger and larger and brighter and brighter as each new shell impacted into the target area. Huge burning streamers of phosphorous arched hundreds of feet into the air, boosted ever higher by the new explosions. The tentacles of the monster spread out over the tops of the trees and enfolded a great patch of enemy jungle. The spreading streamers radiated a glowing white luminescence that smoldered with bright red and yellow sparklers in the tips of the chemical fingers. A great shower of glowing sparks rained down over the jungle, lighting up the shadows and chasing the night away. Some of the streamers reached out toward our positions and landed just a couple of hundred yards short of our concertina wire. An audible gasp went up from soldiers all around our perimeter. The shot was Perfect!

The big shells finally stopped coming. Weak streamers of burning sparks trickled down through the trees as the white-hot glow faded and collapsed in upon itself. The night came crowding back to reclaim the jungle. And then everything became quiet, the lights went out, and the stormy night reclaimed the Asian sky. The night air was completely filled with a chalky-white chemical smoke. Here and there in the inky darkness, a glowing ember persisted.

The world was hushed by the overpowering spectacle. There was not a sound to be heard as the brightness faded into black. We sat in stunned silence as the darkness settled back around us.

There were no mortars, rockets, or self-confident enemy warriors on our perimeter that night. It was one of the few nights in the Triangle when they failed to try us.

The next morning we found pieces of web gear, shovels, ammunition bandoliers, rucksacks, AK-47 clips, and a dozen unfired RPG rockets scattered in the bushes near the enemy foxholes. There were even a few bloody bandages. But, there were no bodies to count and no weapons to claim. Ho Chi Minh's warriors had cleaned up the battlefield in the dark before we got there. You had to admire the bastards.

The Prisoner:

We drew rifle fire from a thick grove of rubber trees. Our guns spun to meet the threat. People in black pajamas were seen running through the trees. The machine-guns took them down. We charged into the trees to gather them up, collect weapons, and make the body count.

Unfortunately, we got the wrong people. When we got to the site there were three of them lying in the grass: an old man, a teenaged boy, and a middle-aged woman. Around them were scattered the tools of rubber plantation workers. There were no weapons. It was a mess. Heavy fifty-caliber machine-gun bullets had almost severed the old man's head. The boy had taken multiple hits through the torso. The woman was still alive.

The woman had taken a rifle bullet through her upper arm. Miraculously, it was her only wound and the bone was not broken. We found her laying on her back in the tall grass, bleeding, her face a stoic mask. She was calm and resigned, waiting to die. Around her lay the bodies of what might have been her father and her son.

Our medic went to her and dressed and bound her wound. We loaded her into our track. She was weak and hardly able to walk. We were going to take her to a South Vietnamese aid station and leave her there. We left the bodies of her family where they had fallen. We would notify Vietnamese authorities at the aid station.

We sat the woman on a seat cushion on top of a long row of boxed machine-gun ammunition inside the ACAV. I was sitting above her on the splashboard where I could look down at her. Her bandaged arm was in a sling and she held it tightly against her side. She winced in pain as the track bucked and jostled down the rough backcountry road, but she never made a sound. I was impressed by her strength and quiet dignity in the face of such pain and misery.

The Colonel called and told us that he wanted her interrogated before we turned her over to the aid station. She might know who it was that shot at us. He told us to treat her as a prisoner. We had found no other people near the rubber grove, and it was entirely possible that she was VC or a VC sympathizer. It might even be that her little group did shoot at us and then managed to ditch their weapons somehow. There were a lot of women in the ranks of the local VC units.

I watched that woman for a long time as we traveled down that long and dusty road. Her pain, misery, and quiet, resigned suffering overcame me. It was unbearably hot and she had lost a lot of blood. I knew she was dying for a drink of water.

We were not supposed to give prisoners food, water, or cigarettes before the intelligence wizards had a chance to work them over, but I couldn't take it. I dropped down inside the track and drew a dipper of water from the water can. I sat down next to the woman and offered her the ladle. She gritted her teeth, closed her eyes tight and ignored me.

I moved in front of her where she had to look at me, and I offered the water again. She just sat there. I took a tiny sip from the ladle to show her it was all right, and then I offered it to her again.

Tears welled up in her eyes and she clenched her teeth tightly. Her dark gaze bored a hole right through me. With shock, I finally recognized in her face the eyes of my enemy. The woman hated me, and she would not take water from my hand.

Chieu Hoi (Surrender):

The fight happened in an open area where the trees had been cut down by bulldozers (Rome-plows we called them). A poorly led VC militia unit had tried to hide out in the open, apparently believing that we would be looking for them in the deep jungle. Evidently, they forgot about the helicopters flying overhead.

Our people got a good twist on them, and shot them up pretty good, mostly from the air. As the afternoon shadows grew long, our tanks and ACAVS were sweeping the battle area and policing up weapons, documents, and making the obligatory body count. There was sporadic shooting and the occasional concussion of a grenade being tossed into a hole or a suspicious brush pile. I was riding up-top with my rifle and artillery map spread across my lap, watching for danger. We were finding a few of bodies.

From out of nowhere, a VC soldier in civilian clothes stepped out from behind a tree with his hands held high above his head in a signal of surrender. There was another ACAV between where we were and where he was. The VC was surrendering to the other ACAV. A young soldier on the other ACAV had a rifle in his hands and was pointing it at the surrendering enemy. The American soldier was a new guy, a recent replacement from the States. No one was behind the M60, and there was no track commander behind the fifty. For some reason, everyone else had dismounted the vehicle. The young Private was alone in the back of the ACAV.

I watched it happen from a few yards away. I saw the grenade as the man stepped out from behind the tree. The enemy soldier held both hands high above his head, but there was a grenade in one of those hands. He was walking directly toward the ACAV where the bewildered young soldier covered him with the rifle.

"Kill him!" I screamed. "Kill him ... kill him!"

I jerked my rifle to my shoulder to do it for him, but the Private was in my line of fire and I couldn't shoot.

"Kill him! I screamed again, becoming frantic at what I knew was about to happen. "Kill the Bastard! Kill him!"

I jumped to my feet on top of the track, scattering maps and grease pencils, trying to get a better angle of fire. My man was still in the way.

"Kill him!" I screamed in desperation, as loud as I possibly could, my voice breaking from the strain.

The enemy walked right up to the young soldier and handed him the grenade over the side of the track. The PFC reached out and took it. Still holding the grenade in his hand, the Private motioned with his rifle for the VC to get down on the ground. The enemy meekly complied.

I vaulted over the side of the track and ran to the young soldier's assistance. By the time I got there, everything was under control. The young man had set the grenade down on top of the track. It was an American grenade, and the pin was still crimped and in it's place. The enemy soldier was lying facedown in the dirt, his arms stretched out above his head. The Private had him covered with the rifle.

"You idiot!" I cursed, angrily. "Don't ever let one of them approach you like that! He could have killed you with that grenade!"

The young soldier gave me a wild and angry look. He was shot full of adrenaline and shaking like a leaf. He did not appreciate having his butt chewed, especially by someone not in his immediate chain of command.

A moment later the young soldier's Sergeant came running up and congratulated him for doing such a fine job. I was incredulous, but I held my tongue. What the hell? I shook my head, bit my lip, and walked away. I was just the stupid FO and not the unit commander. Better learn to keep my mouth shut and just take care of my job.

Innocence met innocence on the battlefield that day. Miraculously, they both survived.

Self-Inflicted:

A supply convoy was ambushed from a small hamlet near the road. We were operating nearby, and we got there in minutes.

We were working with an American infantry unit, and together we swept through the village looking for the bad guys, tanks supported by dismounted infantry. We moved slowly, checking each house for VC, weapons, and tunnel entrances. The village was deserted, but we did receive a few rounds of sniper fire. There was sporadic gunfire and the sounds of explosions as our people probed the shadows and dropped grenades down suspicious holes, trying to dislodge the people who had shot at us.

As we moved through the hamlet, a young infantry Private was walking alongside of our track. He must have been a new guy. He walked up to the open doorway of a little Vietnamese hut, flattened himself against the wall and yelled "Chieu Hoi" (surrender) over his shoulder. When he got no response, he chucked a hand grenade into the confines of the small, single room. It was like something you might see in a John Wayne movie.

I'm sure it would have worked well in Europe where the houses are made of stone. The trouble was, the wall of that jungle homestead was only a grass mat.

I saw it happen in slow motion. In complete disbelief, I screamed at the soldier to duck. He froze. He just stood there, looking at me stupidly, his eyes filled with fear, panic, and confusion. I ducked. The grenade exploded.

The grass walls and roof of the hut were blown apart by the blast. Tufts of grass came fluttering down through the boiling smoke and dust. The soldier was flat on his face in the dirt, half covered by the shredded grass mat, stunned, bleeding, and trying to crawl away from ground zero. Thank God, he was wearing a flak jacket.

I vaulted over the side of the track to help him, but a couple of his buddies had grabbed him by the arms and were dragging him away by the time I got there. One of them came back a few minutes later and gathered up his rifle, helmet, and canteens. I don't know how badly he was hurt.

Friends:

The injured man was lying on the ground waiting for a helicopter to take him out of the jungle. He was seriously wounded. We had bound his wounds and treated him as well as we possibly could, but he was slipping into shock. His face was fish-belly white and his eyes were getting dreamy. We had covered him with a blanket and propped his legs up, but he was slowly sliding toward unresponsiveness. It looked bad. We were growing anxious.

A friend of the wounded man came running to him. He had just gotten the word that his buddy was down. He ran over to the wounded man and got down on his knees at the man's side. He reached out and took the wounded man's hand. The two of them just looked at each other for a while. No one spoke. It was obvious that the wounded man was in bad shape. He might not make it.

Finally, the wounded man's friend smiled wickedly, leaned close over his injured buddy, and said, "Bob, if you're going to die, can I have your watch?"

There was stunned silence from those of us gathered around.

Incredibly, the wounded man began to smile and the color started to come back to his face. He painfully turned his head a little toward his friend and said, "Screw you!"

The two of them started to laugh. Evidently, it was an old joke between them. The two of them talked, joked, and laughed some more before the helicopter finally found us. The signs of deep shock started to leave the wounded man. When we put him on the medivac there was color in his cheeks, and he had the strength to feebly wave goodbye to his buddy as the helicopter went airborne.

He was still wearing his watch.

Celebrities:

We were coming out of the jungle after a long operation. We were dirty and exhausted. Our armored column was in a long, single file that snaked down the road and toward the gates of the base camp. It was late afternoon and a great cloud of dust heralded our arrival.

As we approached the base camp, we could see that something strange was happening just outside the main gate. There was a large group of people there, and some of them were running around with movie and TV cameras on their shoulders. There were even sound guys with microphones attached to long poles. Some guy in civilian clothes was standing at the edge of the roadway, directing some of the tanks and ACAVs to pull over by the side of the road. Most ignored him, but a few did pull over. The Captain was angry when he saw it, but he didn't raise any hell over the radio. He wasn't sure what was going on either, and he didn't want to step on any high-ranking toes.

As we got closer, we could see that it was comedian Joey Bishop and his stateside entourage. The Captain cussed like a pirate. Joey Bishop was a big time TV personality back then.

I was filled with righteous contempt when I saw what was going on. The shameless pretender (Joey Bishop) was all dressed up in filthy jungle fatigues with his hair all disheveled and his jungle boots all scuffed up. He hadn't shaved for two or three days. His makeup guy had done his best to make him look like one of us. Everyone around him was dressed in clean civilian clothes or an odd mix of civilian and military attire. Joey was the only guy in the bunch with messy hair, dirt-streaked face, and dusty eyelashes.

His clean and well-groomed photographers were standing with their backs against the wire of the base camp, posing the man in front of our column of tanks with nothing but pristine jungle as a backdrop. Just a few feet above them and out of the range of their cameras, a couple of grinning perimeter guards were leaning over the sand bags of a watchtower while taking pictures with their own hand-held 8mm movie camera. Everyone was laughing and shaking their heads at the blatant masquerade. The man knew no shame.

To the people back home, good old Joey Bishop was a brave and noble patriot who went deep into the jungle to entertain the troops. Who could dispute it? He had pictures to prove it.

A volunteer:

Staff Sergeant Williams was a member of the Fourth Cavalry Artillery Liaison Team. He worked for Captain Rice. He, Captain Rice, and a couple of other guys traveled with the Squadron as a part of the Headquarters Section. The Sergeant's job was to keep track of the three or four FOs like me who served with the fighting units in the field. He monitored our radio traffic and listened in as we fought battles and tempted the tiger. I spoke with Sergeant Williams often, and we became good friends.

Sergeant Williams was not happy. In his relatively safe job, he began to feel that somehow he was less a soldier than those of us who faced the devil in the course of a day's work. He told me that he wanted to go out into the field "just once," to see what it was like to bust jungle and be tiger bait in the shadows. He volunteered to go on a couple of night ambush patrols but was never allowed to do so. He was not a trained artillery observer or a light-weapons infantry guy, and his skills were better utilized with the Headquarters Section.

And then, in mid-April, the Forward Observer for Alpha Troop was scheduled to go to Hawaii for R&R. The cavalry was critically short in the Forward Observer department, and we had no one to replace the man while he was away. The Tet Offensive had gobbled up all of the available FOs at Division Artillery too, and they couldn't help.

Somehow, some way, Sergeant Williams sweet-talked his way into the temporary assignment. It was the fulfillment of his dreams and he was happy. For a week he would be a full-blown Forward Observer with a front line cavalry unit.

For some reason, I don't remember why, I was given the responsibility to train him for his temporary assignment with the other troop. I had only a couple of evenings to bring him up to speed. Luckily, his regular job was to monitor our radio traffic, and so he knew all about procedures, call signs, maps, and technical terms. My job was to teach the man to shoot using only his radio, map and compass. We practiced at the edge of our jungle perimeter. He called in 105s and beat-up the jungle while I stood at his elbow and coached. It was a crash course, but he was a willing and able student. Within just a couple of days he was competent enough to be trusted in the field.

On the appointed day, Sergeant Williams proudly took his place on an ACAV next to the Alpha Troop Commander, Captain Serio. Captain Serio was new in-country, and new to his combat command. I never knew him well, but I admired the man tremendously. He was everything an Army officer was supposed to be: intelligent, charismatic, well-educated, well-groomed, proper mannered, and self-assured. I would have followed him anywhere.

Captain Serio also had a great sense of humor. At the conclusion of a staff briefing before going north on that fateful operation, he had brought the house down with a rare and wondrous display of comic relief. When the Colonel had finished his presentation and dismissed everyone, young Captain Serio stepped up to the large panels of briefing maps, and with a perfect Peter Seller's German accent, he began to swing his arms in wide arcs across the maps and give a second, and fictitious batch of orders.

"Zee First Panzer Division vill attack along zis axis. Zay vill show no mercy to ze enemy! Zee Second Panzer Division vill zwing down zis vay an cut off ze enemy retreat. All prisoners vill be fed wieners an sauerkraut until zey talk!" He went on and on. It was hilarious, and the whole command staff laughed until we cried. It was wonderful to see such humor in the face of true adversity.

Only a few days later, on a bright and sunny Asian morning, Sergeant Williams and Captain Serio took their places atop an ACAV and ventured into the jungle and into eternity together. Before noon, a single RPG rocket, fired from ambush, killed them both, instantly.

Ambushed:

It was late afternoon in the Iron Triangle. We were tiger bait again and searching for a North Vietnamese base camp. We had been busting jungle all-day and we were exhausted. We had been on the razor's edge for hours and our search had been unsuccessful. We were on our way back to a night defensive position where we could hunker down and wait for the enemy mortars and rockets to keep us awake again all night.

Armored vehicles are not well suited for jungle fighting. Our movements were restricted in the heavy jungle. We were channeled. There were places where we couldn't go. If the ground was swampy, or if the trees were too thick, we couldn't go there. We had to plan our routes of travel carefully. That made us predictable. Our enemy too could figure out which route we might take and where we might pass by. That always put us in the bulls-eye.

On that particular afternoon, we were traveling slowly in a long armored column, single file, down a narrow jungle trail. The vehicles were spaced several yards apart and the jungle crowded right up close. Tree branches and vines swept down over the gun turrets and we often had to duck. Snakes and the nesting pods of huge red ants were a real concern. We could only see a few yards into the wet, greasy shadows of the damp and stinking jungle.

The men stood behind the guns with fingers on the triggers and peered anxiously into the depths of this strange and menacing world. We were at the mercy of the tigers. We couldn't see them, but our growling diesel engines and the metallic rattle and squeak of our track plates kept them informed of our whereabouts.

It might have been a premonition that compelled us to ride inside that day, or maybe it was just that the jungle was too close. We were standing inside the track and looking out over the sides, weapons at the ready, as we sought refuge from the limbs, snakes, and ants. The Captain was with the Colonel. There were four of us on the track: Mobley, Ivie, Poirier, and myself.

Poirier was sick. He had been gassed by diesel fumes while helping the mechanics recover a disabled vehicle that had run over a mine. Sergeant Mobley had temporarily taken his place as our driver. Poirier stood behind the M60, groggy and seasick. Ivie was in the cupola manning the fifty. I stood looking out over the side of the track with a rifle at the ready and my artillery map under my elbow where I could read it.

We came around a long, looping bend in the trail and for a millisecond I thought that a mortar shell had landed in the trees alongside us. There was a blast and a shower of sparks in the shadows – and then I saw the RPG rockets coming for us.

Everything stopped. The motion of the track, the noise of the diesel engines, my beating heart, all froze in a single frame. The rockets hung suspended in the air. There were three of them. I was dead.

I don't know how it happens, but at moments like that you enter a different level of consciousness. Time stops. Everything happens in ultra-slow motion. Your mind is processing information faster that the physical world can keep up. Your mind outruns your body. It can outrun bullets too.

The rockets were coming at me in a lazy slow motion. The stabilizing fins were spread wide and the rockets were spiraling slowly as they came. A faint trail of smoke followed each one.

And then, they had passed us by. One went close over our heads and exploded in the trees behind us. One passed inches over the side of the track and zipped across the empty spot where the Captain and I usually sat, again exploding in the trees behind us. The third went into the dirt just behind our vehicle. The explosions showered us with dirt clods, wood chips, leaves and twigs, but none of us caught any shrapnel.

And then came the machine-gun bullets. It all happened so fast there was no time to duck. I was now looking right into the muzzle flash of a machine-gun that was only a stone's throw away. A glowing, dotted line of tracer bullets came sailing out of the shadows and right for me.

Again, it was all in ultra-slow motion. The bullets floated lazily through the air and then zipped overhead with a terrible CRACK. Everything was frozen in time. My body seemed not to be responding but my mind was going faster than the bullets. Incredibly, as I watched those bullets coming to me, I remember thinking very clearly that the stupid bastard was shooting too high.

I hadn't been singled out. That machine-gunner was shooting at all of us. He was shooting at our armored vehicle. He had pinned the trigger in a long and ragged burst of fire, and lucky for us, he wasn't much of a gunner. He was shooting wildly. It was obvious that he wasn't using his sights. He was missing everything. But then of course, from our perspective, any tracer bullet coming to you looks like it's coming up your nose. Both of our gunners ducked and covered, leaving our machine-guns unmanned. Our driver never faltered, and our track continued to roll down the trail as the rockets, and then the machine-gun bullets, came after us.

Like Captain Serio of Alpha Troop, I'm sure our track was singled out because of all the radio antennas. Several other ACAVs had passed the spot unmolested before we got there. The too-many antennas told the enemy that we were the command and control vehicle. The commander of the unit was on our track. They had waited for us specifically before springing the ambush.

At the Fort McClellan Infantry School, I had been taught to attack an ambush. The old brown boot sergeants taught us to never duck and try to hide in the middle of an ambush. "You are in the killing zone. You are where the enemy wants you to be. If you duck and try to hide he will kill you. If you run he will kill you too. You can be sure he has your escape route covered. The way to survive is to fight back. Go right at him. Don't hesitate and don't hold back, go right at him. It's your only chance."

We had practiced it in the swamps of Alabama. When surprised, when ambushed, we learned to fight like hell. The old Sergeants would kick us in the butt if we ducked and covered our heads.

Without thinking, in that critical, deadly moment, I did as I had been taught. I attacked the ambush. I was in a perfect position to do it. By chance, the bad guys had caught me hiding behind the sights of my rifle. The ambush was happening right in front of me and I was looking at the action down the barrel of an M16. All I had to do was hit the trigger. The rockets had started my response, and I was already reacting when the machine-gun bullets started. My bullets passed his bullets in the air. In real world time, my thoughts and reactions were instantaneous.

My mind was running faster than the bullets, and several thoughts came to me during that critical moment when time had stopped. A whole list of survival responses came on my radar screen in a single millisecond. I knew we had to make the bad guys duck and keep them from aiming. We had to keep them from reloading the rocket launchers, and we had to pin them down until the tank behind us could bring a gun to bear. I knew that I had to make my shots last for a few seconds to help make it happen and to give the tank time to aim. All of those thoughts raced through my mind as the tracer bullets floated lazily overhead in super-slow motion and my finger hit the rifle trigger again and again.

I was shooting into the deep shadows of the ambush site. And, unlike my opponent, I was aiming as best I could from the moving vehicle. The flash of the machine-gun muzzle was my only reference point in the darkness of the jungle. Reflexively, I framed it in the sight ring. There was no man for a target, only that flickering point of light in the shadows.

As always, my rifle was set on semi-automatic, but in the excitement of the moment my trigger finger was super-charged and it took only seconds to empty the magazine. Incredibly, in the suspended animation of the moment, I actually counted each round as I hit the trigger: one, two, three, four, ... all the way to eighteen, and then my rifle bolt locked open on an empty chamber and I was done. Almost immediately after that, there was a terrific blast as the tank behind us sent a canister round into the ambush site. A steady roar of machine-gun fire from our side followed the canister into the trees.

The whole thing lasted an eternity, but in earth time it was only a few seconds from start to finish. From the time the rockets came, until the tank took out the ambush site, couldn't have lasted more than ten or twelve seconds. It takes much longer to tell the story than it did to live it. During the ambush, everything I describe here happened all at once. Our ACAV continued to roll down the jungle trail through the whole encounter, and the enemy gunner fired probably fewer than fifty rounds. In fact, it is possible that the enemy soldier was firing an AK-47 on full automatic and not a machine-gun at all. An Ak-47 rifle magazine will hold thirty rounds.

Somewhere in the middle of my eighteen rounds of rifle fire, the enemy tracers stopped coming (our defective M16 rifle magazines would hold only eighteen rounds and not the designed capacity of twenty). The enemy gunner might have run out of bullets, he might have seen the tank bearing down, or, I might have hit him. I don't know. I will never know. We kept moving and didn't stop to sweep the ambush site. The wild men of the jungle had picked the ground well and it was a terrible place for us to initiate a big fight. We couldn't maneuver. Our people were strung out on the trail for most a mile and it was getting late fast. We would wait and meet them another time when the odds were more in our favor.

God was good to us that afternoon. I will never understand how four of them missed from such close range. That machine-gunner and his three rocket-firing friends were no more than fifty yards away when they opened up on us. An ACAV is a big target. The odds of four of them missing under those circum-stances are incalculable. They must have been very excited, very fearful, or very unskilled. Incompetence and fear and are two of the things you always pray your enemy has plenty of. Grandma's prayers were being answered on my behalf.

Over the years, I have often thought about my response on that fateful afternoon, and marveled about it. I am not a brave man. I have proved it many times. There were other times in Vietnam when I was the first man to duck, cower, or run for cover. I think what happened that day was that I was taken completely by surprise with no time to think about it. I reacted instinctively, like slapping at a bee. I also reacted exactly as I had been trained to react. The whole thing lasted only seconds, and before the enormity of what was happening soaked in to my consciousness, it was all over.

None of our people were hurt in that ambush, but I was an emotional train wreck. It was embarrassing. Within a few minutes of that attack we were back at our NDP and I was so weak from the adrenaline overload I couldn't walk. I got out of the ACAV and collapsed against the side of the track. My hands were shaking so badly I couldn't drink a cup of coffee one of the men brought to me. I spilled it all over me. Someone else had to light a cigarette for me. I couldn't hold a match still enough to light the smoke. One of the guys laughed and slapped me on the back and called me John Wayne. My teeth were rattling together so hard I couldn't smile. Someone called the medic. He came over and filled me full of "give-a-shit" pills. In just a short time, I was mellowed-out and ready to wander off into the jungle and pick flowers with the hippies.

The next day, for the first and only time, I wrote Jeannie a letter and asked her to pray for me. I didn't tell her what had happened, but the ten months of Vietnam that still lay before me weighed heavy on my mind and soul. The future was dark with thunderclouds, lightening and rain. I knew I was taxing the odds. In just seven weeks of field duty I had used up half-a-dozen of my nine lives. It was becoming very clear that I would be damn lucky to get through this thing alive.

Let There Be Light:

An American fire support base was surrounded and under siege near Loc Ninh on the Cambodian border. The cavalry was given the order to charge to the rescue and take a unit of infantry with us on the armored vehicles. The problem was, there was only one road that could take us there, Highway 13, and the intelligence wizards told us that the enemy was anticipating our intervention and they were digging in somewhere along the route on ground of their choosing. They were preparing the battlefield for our arrival and planning to stop our tanks. It was sure to be a costly fight. And, if they could delay our relief column long enough, the firebase might be overrun. The fighting there had been bitter for a day or two already and the base was critically short of ammunition and supplies. The firebase was very small, and re-supply from the air almost impossible. There was no airfield, and it was a pitifully small target for parachute drops. Heavy anti-aircraft fire was keeping the helicopters away.

The Colonel held a staff meeting to discuss the situation and make a battle plan. It was early afternoon already. It would be dark before we got that far north and the enemy would have another advantage. It would be a journey into the valley of death for sure.

Someone reminded the assembled officers that there was a vast area of Rome-plowed (bulldozed) and defoliated forest to the east of Highway 13 for miles and miles toward An Loc and Loc Ninh. There were also a few back roads and jungle trails less frequently traveled. Could we surprise the bad guys and make an end run around their left flank? They wouldn't expect us to come at them from anywhere but down the highway. We could confuse and upset their battle plan if we could pull it off. It was a great idea, but risky.

The staff plotted a possible route through the forest and farms on their many maps, and sent helicopter scouts to check for barriers and obstacles before it got too dark. The whole squadron would participate in the operation and it was decided that "B" Troop would be the spearhead for the night advance.

The Colonel spoke with me personally, and told me he wanted artillery illumination along the entire route. It would be too risky for the unit to use headlights. Headlights would identify the exact location of individual vehicles and give our enemy specific targets to shoot at. Artillery illumination would make it much more difficult for them to pick out individual targets in the dust and the moving shadows of the flares, especially at long range.

The Colonel said he wanted me to plan it, coordinate it, and shoot the mission. I was thrilled, and proud to be chosen for such an assignment. Normally, it would be the Artillery Liaison Captain on the Colonel's staff who would plan and implement such an ambitious undertaking, not a Second Lieutenant serving as an FO on the ground.

I plotted the route on my stack of maps, circling the firing radius of each artillery unit in our area of travel. We would be busting through trackless wilderness for many miles, strung out in a line well over a mile long. I would have to keep dozens of parachute flares in the air at all times so all the drivers could see and follow the trail. It was sure to be the Mother or all Illumination Missions. I had never heard of anything like it before.

There are some safety considerations, even with an illumination mission. When an artillery illumination round pops open, the "butt plate" of the projectile falls to the ground. The butt plate is a steel lid from the back of the shell that weighs a few pounds - the weight varies with the size and caliber of the shell. The flares must be planned so they don't pop open directly over friendly troops or the butt plate might kill someone as it comes crashing to the ground. And then, once the flare is ignited, the hollow shell casing of the artillery round continues on its merry way for several hundred yards downrange. The mission must be planned to allow for the trajectory of the empty casing so as not to cause any friendly casualties.

I don't remember how many gun batteries I used that night. I know there were well over a dozen. Some were 105s, and others were 155s. I used every artillery unit that could reach us. I had them firing from different fire support bases, from different directions, and at different angles over our column. As we outdistanced the shooting range of one battery, I would call for another from a different fire support base to fill the gap.

It was an incredible thing to witness. For a distance of more than two miles, the night sky was lit with a continuous string of dancing yellow lights high in the heavens. There were as many as three-dozen in the air at any given time. As each flare drifted slowly toward the ground, swaying on a silk parachute, another would pop open above it. Often, there were three continuous layers of lights over our column all at once: one nearly spent and near the ground, one higher in the sky, and a new one just popping open, high against the stars.

As our column moved forward, the string of lights moved with us. New flares popped open in front of our leading tanks as the lights at the end of the procession winked out. The string of lights crawled slowly through the night sky, marking our progress and inching ever closer to our objective. I'm sure it was one of the most spectacular light shows of the Vietnam War. The glow of it lit the night sky for miles and miles and it lasted for many hours.

I was too busy to fully enjoy the spectacle. I marked our progress on a map, continually talking to the various artillery units and coordinating with the guns. I had to call for each new shell at the head of the column, and check-fire the ones at the end of our column as they were no longer needed. By the time we approached Loc Ninh, the dawn was breaking in the east and I was hoarse from talking on the radio all night. I was also completely exhausted.

We got past the North Vietnamese ambush along the highway without firing a shot. We took them completely by surprise. They must have watched our marching column of lights circle around their flank in bewilderment and disbelief. It was not ground suited for tanks, but we moved a whole armored squadron through the uncharted forbidden forest. Like Hannibal and his elephants, we crossed the forbidding Alps and entered the field of battle behind our enemy's lines. They broke ranks and ran.

We pushed through to the beleaguered fire support base later in the morning. The 105mm gun battery at the base had expended all of their "hard" ammunition by the time we got there. All they had left to shoot was illumination rounds. They were firing the illumination shells direct-fire without fuses, aiming the guns directly at the bad guys and sending the illumination rounds at them like thirty-five-pound rifle bullets that wouldn't explode. Those artillery guys were happy to see us.

Phantoms in the night:

It was a very dark night and our enemy was persistent. We were on the Cambodian border, working as part of a task force. We had a self-propelled 155mm gun battery with us in our night defensive position, and by sheer luck, the VC had put a mortar shell right inside one of the big ammunition carrier vehicles. There was a huge fire. Hundreds of pounds of gunpowder and diesel fuel from the vehicle's fuel tanks were burning, and tons of artillery shells were cooking-off. The steady Thump, Thump, Thump, of exploding shells rocked our perimeter. Sparks and red-hot chunks of metal rained down over the tops of our vehicles. To escape the fire and the whistling "friendly" shrapnel, we were all hunkered down inside the tracks like sweaty gophers in steel cages. The hatches were sealed tight and we were suffocating in the heat and smoke of the big ammo fire.

The big fire lit our perimeter as bright as day, and that gave the bad guys a real advantage in the dark. They could see us clearly while we were forced to stay buttoned-up. We could bring fewer than half of our guns to bear without exposing ourselves to great risk from our own exploding ammo. The enemy troops were taking full advantage of our misfortune, and they were getting bolder. They were lobbing RPG rockets and American M79 grenade rounds into our positions. We were shooting back as best we could.

I had tried to direct artillery fire from inside the buttoned-up ACAV, but gave it up as too dangerous. I couldn't see or hear where my shells were falling. What I had done so far hadn't done us any good. I had called for an AO in an airplane, but he hadn't arrived yet. We were a long ways out in the boondocks and far from the nearest airfields.

I was on the radio, desperately trying to make contact with the promised AO, when someone cut in on the artillery channel. It was a serious breach of protocol. Combat command frequencies were not to be interrupted for any reason.

"Unknown station, identify yourself!" I commanded.

It was quickly evident that the unknown station had been monitoring my radio traffic for some time. He knew who we were, where we were, and what our situation was.

"Dragoon, this is Eagles Six," he said. (I don't remember his true call sign. Eagles Six is close enough.)

"We are a flight of two Phantom jets orbiting your position. We understand that you are under attack and we can see the fire in your perimeter. We are returning from another mission up north and we still have ordinance onboard ... could we assist?"

"Wait," I said into the headset, wondering how this guy got on my radio frequency and how he had actually found us out there in the boondocks.

I was sitting inside the buttoned-up ACAV right next to the

Captain, but with the roar of the guns and exploding ammunition, it was easier to talk to him through the radio. We were both wearing tanker helmets with radio speakers in our ears. I punched the intercom button. "Captain, I'm in contact with a couple of jet aircraft overhead. They are offering to help. What do want me to do?"

"Anything they got!" the Captain replied, hopefully. He was up to his belt loops in alligators trying to coordinate the perimeter defense. He was busy on the other radio channel and he didn't have time to talk. "Anything they got!" he said again.

"Yes sir," I said excitedly. The Captain was leaving it all up to me. I was thrilled.

"Eagles Six, this is Dragoon Niner-two, happy to have your help. What's onboard?"

My heart sank when the answer came back "CBU." In military lingo, CBU stands for "cluster bomb units." Cluster bombs scatter like dumping a barrel of hand grenades from a fast moving aircraft. It was the worst possible thing we could use for close air support in the dark. It would be terribly dangerous to get them close enough to do us any good.

"Damn," I cussed into the radio speaker. "We got bad guys in RPG range just outside the wire, Eagles. I don't think we can get CBU close enough to help us out."

"Oh ye of little faith," the calm, self-assured voice came back through my radio speakers. "Give us a chance, Dragoon. We can take them out."

I liked the guy's attitude.

"Can you mark the outer edges of your perimeter?" Eagles Six asked.

"We can," I responded. "We have a few strobe lights."

"Purrrrfect," the jet jockey purred.

"Now," he said, "Mark your outer perimeter and give me a compass point to where the gooks are."

183

"Roger that," I said. I was becoming enthusiastic.

I got on the troop frequency, apologizing for interrupting the captain, and coordinated getting the strobe lights out. We carried strobe lights for just this type of contingency. They were shielded, and could only be seen from aircraft overhead. We usually used them for night helicopter medi-vacs and re-supply.

While I was on the cavalry channel, I warned everyone that we had close air support inbound, and I would give notice before touchdown. The troopers were used to close air support, but we usually had a FAC (Forward Air Controller) in a small plane to coordinate with the jets. This was my first time to dance with the Eagles when I could lead and control what was happening.

When the strobes were out, I got back on the artillery frequency and talked to the Eagles again.

"Strobes are out, Eagles, do you see them?"

"Roger that," the pilot said. "We see them, Dragoon." Then, with some astonishment in his voice, he said, "Damn, you guys are right in that fire aren't you?"

"That's affirmative," I said. "It's hot down here in more ways than one."

"Where are the bad guys?" the pilot asked. He was getting down to business.

"The gooks are south of us," I said. "I say again, Victor Charlie is south of us, compass bearing three-two-hundred from the center of our perimeter. You've got to get it close to do us any good, Eagles. Let me know as you start your pass so I can warn my troops. We are all in armored vehicles so a little over-spray might not be as critical as if we were dismounted infantry."

"Got it," the pilot said, deadly serious now. "VC south at thirty-two hundred, bring it close and heads up." And then he said, "We will make one pass and I will drop two pods. My wingman is flying empty, but he will follow me down and strafe with 20 Mike-Mike (20mm cannon) a little further back into the bushes."

"Roger that," I said. "We are standing by."

The next few moments dragged by, punctuated by friendly machine-gun fire and the steady, CRUNCH, CRUNCH, CRUNCH of exploding artillery rounds from the middle of our perimeter.

"We're rolling in, Dragoon." came the calm voice in my headset. "Roger that," I replied. I punched the switch to the cavalry channel. "SPLASH, SPLASH, SPLASH," I screamed into the radio mike. I had the cavalry troopers trained by then. Anytime anyone yelled "Splash" over the radio, the whole unit would duck and cover.

Above the noise and the light show in our perimeter, we didn't see or hear the jets coming down. Our first awakening was when everything to the south of us exploded. There was a long, rolling, roaring thunder as hundreds of bomblets exploded in the night. A shock wave of flashing lights, explosive concussions, dirt, smoke, and steel splinters roared past our defensive line like a freight train in the night. The flash and BANG of it made us duck even deeper toward the steel flooring of the armored vehicles. The ground shook and the ACAV shuddered. A huge cloud of dust drifted in over our positions. Holy Cow! Right on target!

I looked over at my Captain. His eyes were wide and his mouth was opened in shock. He had been busy with perimeter defense and hadn't been paying close attention to what I had been cooking up with the Eagles. "My God!" he said.

"Purrrfect, Eagles," I crooned into the radio speaker, trying to mimic the jet jockey's previous frivolity and his calm, casualness on the radio. "Got some!"

"Glad to help," the Phantom pilot smiled through the radio.

"We're outta bullets, low on fuel, and we gotta get outta here," he said. "Is everything okay down there?"

He was asking without asking, if any of us had been hurt by his close support.

"Things couldn't be better down here," I assured him. "You put it right where we needed it. I'll buy the beer and beefsteak if I can ever run you down."

"Don't worry about it," the pilot said. "Glad to help."

And then, the mighty War Eagle signed off. "This is Eagles Six, we are leaving this frequency. Good luck Dragoon. Make it home."

With that he was gone. The ammo fire in our perimeter burned all night, but there were no more RPG rockets, enemy mortars, or small arms fire from outside our perimeter.

The Magic of Confidence:

Someone screwed up. We had set up two NDPs (night defensive positions) within a short distance of each other and failed to link them. There was a thin strip of jungle between our two "friendly" positions little more than 100 yards wide. An enterprising enemy sniper figured it out and crept in there with a rifle.

From his position between our two units, the enemy soldier could pin down both perimeters and we couldn't fire on him without killing each other. It was almost funny that we had been so stupid and the bad guy had been so bold as to take advantage of our carelessness. We were in a real mess.

The infantry was gathering a fire team to sweep into the gap and chase the sniper out, but it would be a risky venture. The bad guy held the advantage of cover and concealment. He would surely get the first shot if he wanted it. It was likely we would have some people hurt. I felt bad for the infantry guys as I watched them prepare to face that dragon. They were brave and resolute, but their eyes had that far-away, weary sadness that betrays the inner turmoil.

I looked the situation over carefully, and then went to my Colonel. "I can take him out with artillery if you will let me do it," I volunteered. The Colonel seemed impressed by my audaciousness. He smiled. By radio, he talked it over with the commander of the other perimeter. They decided to let me go for it. The mission would be danger-close and scary, but better than risking American lives if I could pull it off.

I called a 105mm gun battery that had the proper gun/target angle for the mission, and asked them to alert their best gun crew and register (sight-in) the gun. I told them it would be one gun for adjustment, danger-close, and everything had to be absolutely precise.

I was standing by and waiting for the gun battery to get ready when the Colonel of the artillery unit came on the radio. He said, "Dragoon Niner-two, this is Danger Six. My battery commander (a Captain) has informed me that you intend to walk shells danger-close between two friendly units. Are you up to this Lieutenant, and what is the purpose of this mission?"

"I'm up to it, Sir." I shot back. "We have a sniper between our two units, Sir, and I've been given a green light by my squadron commander to take him out."

There was silence for a few moments, and then the big artillery boss said, "I'm going to countermand this fire mission, Dragoon. It's too close and too dangerous."

"With all due respect, Sir," I pleaded. "If your people are afraid of this mission, have them keep the nose plugs in the shells and I will hit this smart ass Victor Charlie in the mouth with the dud round." (The shells would not detonate with only a nose plug and not a fuse.)

There was silence again for a few moments, and then the Colonel keyed his radio mike. I could hear people laughing in the background. The Colonel was laughing too.

"You win, Dragoon," the Colonel said. "Your gun is preparing for the mission." But then he said, "Damn it, Lieutenant, you be careful. This is against my better judgment."

"Yes, Sir. Thank you, Sir," I said with a big smile.

I ordered both perimeters to button-up for close support, and I carefully walked the 105s between our two strands of concertina wire. With point-detonating fuses, I stitched holes in the ground every fifty yards through the gap between our lines, one shell at a time, overlapping the bursting radius of one shell and blending it into the bursting radius of the next, covering the entire stretch of ground with deadly shrapnel.

We never went to look for that enemy sniper. It was getting dark and time to prepare for the incoming mortars. I never knew the outcome of my little adventure, but the sniper didn't bother us again. A Sergeant from the infantry unit came by a short time later to thank me, and to shake my hand. I was happy, and proud too.

The Language Barrier:

We had to move from point "A" to point "B" in a hurry and the road had not been swept for mines. So, we moved the column twenty or thirty yards off the road and ran parallel to it. It was slower and rougher traveling out there, we had to go over paddy dikes and through ditches, but we could avoid any land mines and still reach our destination in a reasonable time. Unfortunately, by running off the road like that, our tanks and ACAVS did a lot of damage to the local farm fields.

We were passing a small farm hamlet, driving right through a small vegetable garden, when an old woman came running up to our track. There was fire in her eyes and she was screaming something in French at the top of her lungs. Most of the older

Vietnamese people could speak French. After all, they had grown up in "French Indochina."

The woman was obviously upset that we were tearing up her garden. Being a farm boy myself, I was probably the one guy on the track who truly felt her pain. But, the old gal had singled me out as the target for her attack. Perhaps she could read the officer's insignia on my collar. The woman ran up to our track, pointed her finger at me in righteous rage, shrieked something in French, and then with hands on her hips, she sneered defiantly with black, betel nut stained teeth.

Our ACAV slammed to a stop. Our driver, French-Canadian Jerry Poirier, vaulted from the driver's seat. He ran back to the old woman, pointed his finger in her face, and in perfect French he began to tell her where the moon went over the mountain.

The old woman's face couldn't have registered more shock had he hit her with his rifle butt. She threw both hands over her mouth in horror and her eyes grew wide and fearful. She turned and ran toward the houses. Jerry followed her for a few steps, still wagging his finger and reading her the Riot Act in French. People near the houses scattered as if expecting us to shoot.

Jerry ran back, jumped into the driver's seat and put his tanker's helmet on again. He then turned to me with a big grin, toggled the switch to intercom, and said, "You'd a shot that old woman had you known what she called you, Lieutenant."

"What did she call me, Jerry?" I asked.

"You don't even want to know," he said with a smile. "Besides, it was a pretty good line and I might want to use it myself sometime, in French, of course." With that, he grinned impishly, punched the accelerator, and we were off on the rest of our adventure for the day.

Several times in the following weeks I asked him what the old woman had called me. It always made him laugh, but he never would tell me. I can only imagine.

Jerry Poirier was a Canadian citizen. He told us he had developed contempt for all of the American draft dodgers flooding into his hometown, competing for jobs and the local girlfriends. And so, he decided to cross the border, join the American Army, volunteer for Vietnam, and see what those delicate peace-lovers were all so damned afraid of. He said he couldn't wait to go back to Canada to tell them what it was all about. I'm happy to report that Jerry Poirier completed a full combat tour in Vietnam, and went home to Canada as one of my heroes.

A Conscientious Objector:

The man didn't carry a gun. He was a combat medic with a front-line infantry unit, and he refused to carry a weapon. He was a conscientious objector, a man who didn't believe in killing. And yet, in spite of his moral objections, he was there to do what he could to help other young men of his generation who had been called to fight. I don't know how he had come to be in the army, or how he had come to be with that unit, but he was a legend in the First Division. Everyone had heard about the combat medic who never hesitated to go into the dragon's mouth to rescue his friends, but who refused to carry a gun.

We worked with that infantry unit one day, and I saw that man who was a legend. His unit was under fire, moving forward to support our tanks. The medic was in full battle dress but carrying only his medical kit. Bullets were popping through the trees and the soldiers were bent low as they advanced, moving cautiously, deliberately, and with deadly resolve toward the enemy bunkers. The unarmed medic moved with them, unfaltering, firm and resolute. A couple of riflemen seemed to stay close, as if hoping to protect him.

In the lives of such men, weak and sinful humanity is surely redeemed in the eyes of God. Such a display of raw courage, Godly virtue, honor, and duty in the face of moral conflict is seldom seen in the human creature. That good man won the respect of every soldier in Vietnam. May his tribe increase forever.

Chop-Chop:

Whenever we passed through a town, dozens of little kids would run to the edge of the road and beg for "chop-chop." I don't know what chop-chop meant in Vietnamese, but to us, chop-chop was candy, gum, cigarettes, or "government surplus" cans of c-rations. We got the candy and gum with our government rations. The government made a special "Tropical Chocolate" that wouldn't melt, tasted awful, and was the only thing I ever saw a kid throw back at us. American soldiers have always had big hearts, and throwing chop-chop was the highlight of our day. The kids loved it, and we always felt like Santa Clause.

Our squadron was passing through the town of Ben Cat one day, and when one of the troopers threw chop-chop to the kids, a few items skidded across the ground and inadvertently went under the concertina wire of an ARVN (Army of the Republic of Vietnam – our friends) compound. A little kid went under the wire after it and set off a tripwire. A booby-trapped grenade exploded, killing the little boy and badly wounding a couple of his friends. We stopped the column to investigate.

The local civilians were upset and wanted us to pay cash money for the kids. Our "friends," the ARVN Army people, thought it was our fault too. We shouldn't be throwing goodies and making friends with the kids. We should stick to business and kill VC. It was irresponsible of us to cause injuries to children by throwing candy.

We, on the other hand, were mad at the ARVN. The incident caused hard feelings. Things were said through interpreters that were best left unsaid. What the hell were they doing setting tripwires in the middle of town? So what if it was inside of their wire. Maybe they should get off their lazy butts once in a while and stand guard the way we did. They should never rely on booby-traps to cover their sorry asses in the middle of town where kids, dogs, pigs, and chickens wandered about.

I don't know how it all played out. We had to continue our journey to the battle's front. While we rode on to face their enemy, the local civilians negotiated the worth of a dead or damaged child with representatives of the U.S. government ... and the ARVN soldiers reset the tripwire.

Missing in Action:

"You've got to list him as: Missing in Action - Presumed Dead," the staff officer said. "You don't have a body to send home."

"We've got his foot!" The other officer said angrily. "We can't tell his family he's missing in action when we know damn well he was killed."

"If you don't have a body he is missing in action."

"No! That's not right. Several men saw the explosion and we know he was killed. We can send the foot home in a closed casket and let that do for a body."

"A man can live without a foot. To save problems later, you had better list him as: Missing - Presumed Dead, and let it go at that."

"Never! I won't do it!"

After listening to that argument for a few moments, I walked out of the headquarters' building and into the bright Asian sunshine. I didn't know the dead man they were arguing over, but I felt very sad just the same.

Friendly Fire:

Night in the Iron Triangle. A full moon cast pale shadows

over the distant edge of the jungle. We were set up in the middle of a large open area, a huge, abandoned rice paddy that gave us good fields of fire. The tension was unbearable. We knew that Ho Chi Minh's troops were out there somewhere, and there might be thousands of them. We were tiger bait, all sucked-up and hunkered down behind the guns, waiting for the attack that was sure to come.

As expected, the mortars came whistling in. Shells burst all across our perimeter with a thunderous CRACK and a shower of deadly sparks. Machine-guns opened up on the perimeter. Someone screamed into the radio, "We've got movement to our front Captain, they're coming at us from the north." The whole perimeter opened up with a flash and bang of wild night firing.

I punched the toggle switch on my tanker's helmet and yelled at the big guns several miles away. "Fire mission Dreadnaught! Defcon 3 (pre-planned defensive concentration number 3), shell Hotel Echo (high explosive), fuse Papa Delta (point detonating), battery one (six guns - one shell each), observed fire, will adjust."

In just a few minutes the shells came thundering in and lit the night sky with bright flashes at the edge of the distant tree line. They were big shells, 155s. "Drop two hundred, battery one, we're bringing it home," I screamed into the headset over the roar of tank cannons and machine-gun fire. Again, the exploding shells ripped open the darkness and made the machine-gun and cannon fire of the tanks seem weak and insignificant. It was impressive, but the shells were still too far out to protect our perimeter.

"Drop one hundred, battery one, danger-close," I commanded. The six shells came screaming in all together. There was a tremendous, ragged flash of light, a roar of earth-shaking thunder, and a monster cloud of dust and smoke along the edge of our concertina wire. Holy Hell! Way too close!

"Add two hundred Dreadnaught! Get it out of here! Check your plots and level your bubbles. That one damn near got us!"

I was shocked. Damn ... did I do that? Did I misjudge the distance?

The next series of shells landed far out in the middle of the field again, much too far away to be effective. Something was terribly wrong. I was not getting the measured distances I expected. "Drop fifty, Dreadnaught," I hissed into the mike through clenched teeth. I was moving it back to us again, but very cautiously this time. I was suddenly very much afraid. Something wasn't right.

And then came a call on the cavalry troop frequency: "Bravo Six, this is Two-Six (second platoon commander)! We got a man down by friendly fire, Captain! We need a medic! I don't think he's going to make it!"

My heart stopped cold.

"Check-fire the artillery!" came a call on the Squadron command frequency. It was the Colonel. "Check-fire the (expletive deleted) artillery! We've got to look into this Bravo Six. Keep your damned FO off the radio."

"Check-fire!" I screamed at the distant guns. "End of mission Dreadnaught!" And then, with a sick heart and shaking hands, I said, "Save your plots, Dreadnaught ... we have an incident here."

I threw my headset aside and ran to the track that had reported the friendly fire. Tracer bullets were still streaking out into the night and mortar shells were still exploding around us periodically, but it didn't matter. I got to the wounded man just as the Captain did. The track was sitting right in front of where the artillery shells had landed. My mind and my heart were numb.

There was blood everywhere. The upper deck of the ACAV was covered with blood, and the smooth, liquid surface glistened in the soft glow of the parachute flares. The man was dead. A piece of shrapnel had ripped through his chest.

The crewmembers of the track were incensed that I was there. It was my fault. I was the incompetent artillery spotter who had killed their friend. They glared at me through the dim glow of red filtered flashlights as the medics gave up on the dead man. I could feel the hate and contempt in their eyes more than I could see it in the dim, red light. I was devastated.

"Where is his flak jacket?" the Captain asked quietly. There was a long pause. "He wasn't wearing it," a man finally offered. "Damn!" the Captain cursed, angrily.

The mortars stopped coming and the firing on our perimeter slowly faded away. The NVA had failed to rush the wire. The parachute flares slowly winked out and the moon came back with silver shadows. Darkness and stillness soaked back into the night.

It was a pretty night. The big, full moon illuminated ribbons of silver clouds that floated slowly overhead on an ocean of dark sky. Stars twinkled like polished jewels high in the heavens. But, down in the moon shadows where I was, the beauty of nature was wasted. Nothing mattered anymore. I was crushed. I was physically sick. Was it my fault? Did I make a bad call? Did I misjudge the distance in the dark?

In spite of weeks of accumulated exhaustion, I couldn't sleep the rest of that night. It seems incredible to me now, but I actually sat out in the middle of that perimeter on a folding chair and smoked a couple of dozen cigarettes. I cupped them in my hand, but it was almost like I was daring the NVA to take me out. Nothing mattered anymore. Where was that sniper with a telescopic sight who picked up the soft glow of cigarettes in the dark?

My life was over. Somehow, I had killed one of my own men. It was an accident, but that didn't matter. I was an officer, a trained professional, and I was supposed to protect my cavalry troopers. Those good men looked to me for help and support. I wasn't supposed to kill them.

I might be court-martialed. I might be sent back to the States in disgrace. I might be drummed out of the army for incompetence. And, if not, how could I ever look these men in the eye again and feel that I held their confidence? I would have to be reassigned. I would be forced to leave the cavalry in disgrace. I would be sent to some place and some job where I couldn't hurt anybody. I would be a combat latrine orderly or a body-count clerk, buried somewhere in the bowels of Division Headquarters where a Colonel could keep an eye on me. I would be a failure as an officer, a soldier, and a man.

I couldn't bear it. It scares me now, but I wanted to die. I had been living in the mouth of hell, under tremendous stress and without rest for weeks, and now, to have the blood of one of my own men on my hands pushed me over the edge. I collapsed under the weight of it. I was numb. I was drained of all emotion. I had nothing left to give. I couldn't cry. I couldn't cuss. I couldn't run. I couldn't hide. I couldn't sleep. I sat on that folding canvas chair in the moonlight, out in the open and fully exposed to hostile fire. I smoked my cigarettes and waited for that sniper's bullet. I thank God that it never came.

The next morning, a helicopter landed just after daylight and an Army Major came looking for me. He carried a leather briefcase and he was wearing clean and starched fatigues. He was obviously a staff officer from an air-conditioned office in Saigon. He was there to investigate the friendly fire incident.

The Major introduced himself to my Captain. The Captain introduced me to the Major. It was all very formal for an open-air inquisition. We were standing in a barbed wire enclosure, in the middle of a jungle clearing, with no roof, walls, desks or chairs. We held our meeting standing in the dust alongside our fighting vehicle. We were all wearing flak jackets, helmets, and side arms. The bad guys were still out there somewhere, and probably watching.

The staff officer looked me over carefully as we stood there. He was sizing me up, and it made me feel uncomfortable. I was not the Hollywood ideal of a noble, competent warrior. We had been in the jungle for weeks and we hadn't seen clean clothes or a shower forever. I was as skinny as a snake and my uniform didn't fit very well. I needed a shave and a haircut. I had been awake for a couple of days and nights and I was bleary-eyed and groggy. But, I took consolation in the fact that I looked like all of the other men in the unit, including my Captain.

To begin, my Captain offered a glowing testimonial of my fire directing skills. A couple of the men on my track stepped forward and offered good words on my behalf too. I was grateful.

The Major then asked those assembled, including men from the dead man's track, for their assessment of what had happened. They all said they didn't know how it happened, but they all agreed that American artillery shells had landed very close to the edge of the perimeter.

The Major then excused everyone but the Captain and me while he took my formal statement. I told him that I didn't know how it had happened either, but I felt there had been plenty of safety margin for what I had called for. The shells were impacting in the open field where I could see them clearly. It was an easy call, and only one series of shells had landed too close.

I had anguished about it all night, and in my own mind, I thought I might have it figured out. I told the Major that I didn't know for sure, but I suspected that the Fire Direction Center at the gun battery had mistakenly doubled my request. Instead of dropping one hundred meters as I had ordered, they had given me twice that. By mistake, they might have repeated my first order instead of following my second one. It was a plausible theory. Such things did happen on occasion. The Major told me that he would check it out. The gun battery, and especially the Fire Direction Center, would be his next stop.

We went outside the wire, the Major, the Captain, and I, to find where the shells had landed. The grass was almost knee high. We went only a couple of steps beyond the wire, and there, right in front of the blood-covered track, was a smoking-fresh shell crater with the tailfin of a Chinese 82mm mortar imbedded in the dirt. The Major stopped and picked it up.

"Were you people under mortar fire during the fire mission last night?" the Major asked.

"Yes sir, we were," the Captain offered, "heavy mortar fire too."

The Major held the mortar tailfin in his hands and looked out over the grassy field. He said, "Captain, do you see any shell craters in closer proximity than this one?"
"No sir," the Captain replied.

"From this point, Captain, can you see any other shell craters at all?"

"No sir," the Captain said again.

The Major pondered it for moment, still holding the mortar tailfin in his hands, and then he turned to me. Very matter-of-factly, like he was talking about the weather, the Major said, "That soldier was killed by enemy mortar fire, Lieutenant."

He then turned to my Captain. "My investigation here is closed, Captain. Carry on." With that he went back to his helicopter and sailed out of my life forever. He took the tailfin of the mortar with him.

My Captain and the men on my track, Mobley, Ivie, and Poirier, walked through the perimeter, stopping at the various fighting vehicles and spreading the word about the outcome of the investigation. It wasn't my fault. I didn't do it. It was not friendly fire. I am forever grateful to those men for their consideration. I was with that unit for several more months, and I don't remember anyone ever mentioning the incident again.

In just an hour or so we saddled up and went back to the jungle to be tiger bait again. It was good to be alive. I was thankful that the enemy sniper hadn't found me in the moonlight. And, I was relieved that I could still be a cavalry trooper and take my place next to the Captain. Now, if I could just get some sleep.

The Major did the right thing that day. He did the right thing for me, for the artillery soldiers at the gun battery, for the family of the man who was killed, and for the Army. And just maybe, his conclusion that it was not friendly fire is the absolute truth. But, for years I've wished that I could know for sure. My shells did land too close that night, and the question of how it happened was never resolved.

Sometimes, even after all these years, when I close my eyes at night, I can still see, and hear, and feel, those big shells thundering into the tall grass at the edge of our perimeter. I can still see that huge cloud of dust and smoke in the moonlight, and feel the shock of having them land there unexpectedly.

Free Fire Zone:

A free fire zone was a political designation, and the idea behind it was simple. Large areas of the backcountry were declared hostile territory in order to isolate NVA infiltrators and make it easier for us to find and to kill them. In theory, all the "friendlies" had been evacuated and only the bad guys remained in the area. Any person (read that any "Asian" person) found in a free fire zone was a legal target. Gender, age, occupation, place of residence, political affiliation, or good reason for being there were of little consequence. If they were in a free fire zone, their government had declared them to be enemy combatants.

In most of Vietnam, at least in III Corps, American soldiers were not allowed to shoot unless fired upon. This gave the VC an advantage. Free Fire Zones were different. In a Free Fire Zone we could shoot first, and we did. Of course, most of us used some discretion, but we were always more aggressive in free fire zones. There were not supposed to be any "friendlies" in the area, and we often shot first and asked questions later.

The South Vietnamese Government often declared large tracts of land to be free fire zones to accommodate our search and destroy operations. Unfortunately, the backcountry peasant farmers sometimes didn't get the word. There was no TV, radio, or newspapers out in the boondocks, and the poorest of the poor scratched out a humble living in small jungle clearings that were a long way from civilization.

We were in such an area one day, searching for a unit of NVA infiltrators rumored to be in the area. I remember that it was a beautiful day of bright sunshine and fluffy white clouds. For once, it was not too hot and not too humid. To make things even better, we were finding no bad guys, no booby-traps, and no tripwires. We hadn't been sniped at all day. It was like being on vacation.

We did find an unexploded 500-pound bomb. It was lying on top of the ground in the tall grass where it had failed to explode when dropped from an airplane a few days or a few weeks before. We always destroyed that kind of unexploded ordinance. The Viet Cong cut dud bombs open and used the explosive to make mines and booby-traps to kill us. We had an engineer with us, an explosives expert, and the Captain called for him to rig a detonating charge. It would take a little while.

The Captain wanted to continue his search and destroy sweep of the area so we didn't have to come back to the same area tomorrow, and so he decided to continue on and leave the engineer at his work. We needed to be out of the area anyway before the bomb went off.

The Captain surprised me when he turned to me and said he wanted me to take charge of the detail. He would leave one ACAV for transportation and security while the engineer set the charge. When the charge was timed and ready to detonate, we could mount up and catch up.

"Yes sir," I said as I gathered up my rifle and steel helmet. The troop rode off over the hill. I was left out in the middle of nowhere with one fighting vehicle, one engineer, and three cavalry troopers with tired, dirty faces. I was the boss. They waited for orders.

"Okay guys, let's form a perimeter," I told them. "Johnson, you stay here with the track and stay behind the fifty. Fredrickson, you go south. Jones, you go north. I'll take the east side by the ravine. Go out about a hundred yards from the bomb and lay low. Mr. Engineer, you let us know when you are ready to get the hell out of here ... and please, do be careful." The Engineer Staff Sergeant grinned as he slid his rucksack over his shoulder and checked the .45 on his hip.

We all went to our assigned tasks. We were in an open, grassy area with relatively few trees. I took my rifle and went my hundred yards or so away from the bomb to the edge of a ravine where I could look down into a thickly wooded little streambed. I stretched out on my belly in the grass. The sun was warm on my back. Things got very quiet.

I was lying there in the warm sunshine, half-asleep, waiting for word from the explosive expert, when I caught movement in the trees below me. The adrenaline rush almost knocked my boots off. Holy hell! There were people moving through the trees below me! I was suddenly wide-awake.

I couldn't notify my troopers. We had no radio contact with each other. I couldn't notify the Captain and the rest of the cavalry squadron to come back to us either. The only radio we had was on the ACAV. The ACAV was 200 yards away and below the crest of the hill. I was on my own. My heart thundered in my ears like soldiers marching across a wooden bridge. Damn! What do I do now?

I focused severely on what it was I had in the trees. I could see only two of them so far. They were both wearing black pajamas and I could see that they were following a little path through the trees that would bring them within fifty or sixty yards of where I was hiding. I couldn't make out any details of the people yet, but I was convinced that it was the point element of a moving detachment of enemy soldiers. Always, when a unit moved, someone had to walk point. The job of the point man was to find the enemy forces and take the bullets or booby-traps before the whole unit fell into an ambush. I was sure I had a couple of point men coming to me. Who was behind them, and how many? My hands were beginning to tremble.

I was the only man aware of the danger. The job was mine to do. I looked it over carefully and decided that my best option was to shoot first. From their position, I was skylined on the crest of the ridge and they might spot me if I tried to sneak away. And then too, by sheer accident, I was in a good ambush position. I held the high ground with a good field of fire. I had no cover, but good concealment in the tall grass.

I reasoned that if I could stack-up the point men, the enemy unit would most likely take cover and then reconnoiter cautiously when the shooting stopped. That should give me time to gather up my people and get out of there. I would then lead the cavalry back to the spot, and with air cover and artillery we would send the devil some company. I had it all figured out.

I decided to wait until they were at the closest point and then kill both of them with one long burst of fire. Strangely, they were walking very close together and that would make it easy. I set the selector switch on my rifle to full automatic.

I selected a gap between two trees where I knew the men would pass, and I lined up the sights. My finger rested on the trigger. I waited. I kept my eye focused through the sight ring, but through my peripheral vision I watched them approaching the kill zone. In just a second or two they would walk through my gun sight and I would drop them. My heart was hammering and little ribbons of sweat ran down my face. My eyes were stinging with perspiration salt but I didn't flinch and I didn't blink. My finger began to tighten on the trigger.

The first one walked into my sight ring. The trigger was halfway back when my mind slammed on the brakes. My God! It was an old woman! And there, following close behind her, a young girl of about fourteen. They were gingerly picking their way down the trail like a couple of scared deer. They had probably been hiding when our tanks went past a short while ago and they were trying to get out of the area. They carried no weapons or burdens of any kind.

I watched them walk past, and relief flooded over me like summer rain. They were not a threat to me, or my troopers. I didn't have to kill them after all. I thanked God that I didn't pull that trigger with too much haste.

From my hiding place, I watched them tiptoe down the trail. They were terrified. The old woman kept stooping, bending, and peeking cautiously at the trail ahead, even as she tried to hurry. The young girl kept looking back behind them as if expecting to be jumped by Grizzly Bears. The little one kept one hand out toward the older woman as if trying to maintain bodily contact with her guide and protector. They both kept glancing up at the sky nervously, watching for helicopters, I'm sure.

They were like wild forest creatures, lost and hunted little animals: weak, vulnerable, and totally defenseless. All of my soldierly emotions at that moment: fear, duty, and deadly resolve, melted into pity. Sometimes in combat, discretion and mercy become a part of the equation too.

I watched them disappear down that jungle trail. They hadn't seen the tiger hiding in the tall grass. They would never know how close they came. I watched and waited, but no one else came down the trail.

A few minutes later came a low whistle from the engineer. I gathered up my rifle and trotted over to the ACAV. We saddled up and rode away. A short time later the bomb went off. The ground shook and a big cloud of dust could be seen back through the trees. I smiled. I'll bet that scared the shit out of them. But, I knew they were safe. I had watched them continue on down the ravine and out of harm's way.

I never did tell anyone about those two women. I was afraid that if I did we would have to go back and look for them. Some gung-ho Colonel at headquarters would surely want to take them prisoner for "questioning." And, in the process of being captured, they would probably be killed. It was, after all, a Free Fire Zone and they were "legal" targets. Anyone could take them out, no questions asked.

I do hope that I did the right thing that day when I didn't report them. Better to err on the side of mercy than live with the stain of innocent blood. Incredibly, after sparing the lives of those two women, I felt responsible for their safety. I couldn't let my fellow soldiers or the helicopter gunships kill them after letting them walk by and seeing the terror in their faces. No one ever knew they were there but me.

I hope that young girl is someone's grandma now, and I hope she tells her grandchildren about how she and her grandma sneaked away from those stupid American cavalry soldiers without ever being seen. It would make me proud to hear her tell the story.

Yellow Ribbons:

I was proud to be a cavalry trooper, even if I wasn't technically in the Cavalry. I was "attached" to the unit, a technician borrowed from Division Artillery. Even so, I was an integral part of the unit. I did everything the cavalry troopers did. I rode with them, fought battles with them, lived, slept, and ate with them. I didn't know anyone at Division Artillery. The Fourth Armored Cavalry was my unit. It was home.

But, I was different. My insignia was crossed cannons and not crossed sabers. I couldn't wear the yellow cavalry scarf ... and I mourned. The yellow scarf is an old cavalry tradition, and it was something special in Vietnam.

The cavalry troopers all had yellow scarves, but they never wore them in the field. Yellow scarves made good targets against the dark foliage of the jungle. It was when we approached the gates of a base camp area when the yellow scarves came out.

The yellow scarf was the robe of a king in the rear areas. It was Stephen Crane's Red Badge of Courage, but of golden hue with black crossed sabers embroidered across the back. A young trooper wearing a yellow scarf, especially a dirty and tattered yellow scarf, swaggered before the lowly rabble that was the base camp rear echelon people. That golden badge made a young man someone special. It told the world that he was a combat soldier, an Alpha male, and a veteran warrior. Young soldiers always walked taller when they draped that yellow scarf over their shoulders.

In early April, Captain Daniels conducted an awards ceremony at Bravo Troop headquarters in Dian. We had just come out of the Iron Triangle and had been granted a few days of rest. At the ceremony, several of the troopers were awarded medals. They looked sharp in their clean fatigues and yellow scarves. I was proud of them.

And then, before he dismissed the formation, the Captain ordered me to come forward. I was surprised. I wasn't supposed to be getting any medals that I knew about.

I obediently stepped forward, saluted, and waited to hear what was up. The Captain smiled and made a little speech. He said something like this: "We have a special presentation to make today. I've been keeping track, and Lieutenant McCourt here has shot off more radio antennas with his rifle than any machine-gunner in this troop." (It was true. From where I sat on the ACAV, a couple of radio antennas were right in my line of fire.) The Captain continued: "I have a special award to commemorate his achievement." With that, he stepped forward and pinned a coke bottle cap on the pocket of my uniform. He then grinned wickedly, saluted smartly, and dismissed the formation. Everyone had a good laugh. Including me.

It didn't go down well with a couple of the guys on our track. I don't know if they said anything to the Captain or not, but the next afternoon, Captain Daniels and Sergeant Mobley came to see me. They each had a well-used, yellow cavalry scarf in their hands. They told me they had decided to adopt me into the cavalry.

Without pomp or ceremony, Sergeant Mobley draped his yellow scarf around my shoulders and told me to wear it proudly. He told me I had earned it. To me, it was like winning the Medal of Honor. I have never received an award that meant more to me.

In less than two weeks, my friend, Sergeant Jenies Mobley, was killed in combat. I saw him fall, and a part of me died with him. I have never felt more helpless or experienced a greater sense of loss. His dirt-stained yellow cavalry scarf, the one he gave to me, is draped over my officer's saber on the wall of my study as I write these words. It is one of my most treasured possessions.

Children in the Shadow

The Vietnam War generation has been called the Baby Boom Generation. We are children of a post-World War II population explosion. Millions of us were born in the months and years following the Second World War when soldiers and sailors came home to young wives. We are the sons and daughters of Rosie the Riveter and GI Joe.

We were born citizens of the greatest and most powerful nation the world has ever known. We inherited a proud legacy of world conquest and world liberation. Our birthright was freedom, affluence, and endless opportunity.

We grew up in a world that was highly militarized. Hiroshima and Nagasaki were recent events, and Korea dominated the headlines before most of us started school. War and self-sacrifice had toughened our parents. They were children of the Great Depression, who then fought and won the biggest war in all of human history.

Wars and rumors of wars were a part of our childhood: The Second World War, Korea, the birth of Israel, the Berlin airlift, the Soviet subjugation of Eastern Europe, the Cold War, the Iron Curtain, the Hungarian revolt of 1956, and the Cuban missile crisis. The worry and the stresses of it touched even the little ones. One of my earliest childhood memories is of my uncle Jack telling me that Santa Clause and his reindeer had been shot down over Korea. The news was devastating.

My generation was the first to grow up in the shadow of a mushroom cloud. The threat of nuclear annihilation was ever-present and very real. We lived with the fear of it every day. We were the first to grow up with the knowledge that there might not be a future for any of us. The world could end at any minute in a flash of searing heat.

As children, the worry and the psychological stresses affected some of us deeply. I have sometimes wondered if the whole Baby Boomer generation, that dropped-out, drugged-out, question everything, free love and flower child, hippy generation, wasn't suffering from Post Traumatic Stress Disorder. As teenagers we had all the symptoms: anxiety, fear, guilt, rebellion, a penchant for self-destruction, and a sense of being lost and not fitting in with the world around us.

The roots of the disorder go deep. We Baby Boomers faced the Horsemen of the Apocalypse (Revelation 6) at an early age. War, famine, pestilence and disease were always on our doorstep, thanks to the wonders of modern broadcasting. The plagues of blood and horror were our promised inheritance.

As children, the horsemen never came to carry us away as we expected they would, but our lives and dreams were constantly tortured by the promise of their arrival. "Eat your carrots ... little kids like you are starving in China." I ate my carrots. Somehow, in a way I couldn't understand, throwing carrots in the trash made me guilty of murder. If I wasted food, some other kid would starve. It was a heavy responsibility for a five-year-old.

In first grade we were asked to join the March of Dimes. On the appointed day, we each brought a shiny silver dime to give to a white-uniformed nurse who sat at a desk in the hallway of our school. The dimes were put in a glass jar so we could all see the progress of our contributions. The sacrifice of our allowance and lunch money was going to help fight polio and other childhood diseases.

Behind the nurse was a large poster with the picture of a little girl in an Iron Lung. An Iron Lung was a monstrous mechanical device. It looked like a big steel barrel - a cage that children were put in when the disease came upon them. The little girl looked sad with only her head and blond curls protruding from the barrel. The mechanical beast had swallowed the rest of her. The nurse said the machine helped the little girl breathe, but I knew that couldn't possibly be true. Her mouth and nose were outside of the barrel. It was really just a cage, a place to contain sick children.

We were told that polio could happen to the rest of us at any time, and the way to prevent it was to give dimes to the nurse. Some of us stole dimes from mother's dresser to make offerings of appeasement to the Gods of Disease.

We were also given polio inoculations at school. We were taken classroom at a time, thirty or more at once, and we stood in long lines and waited our turn. As we waited, we watched the uniformed nurses with the big needles as they took each child by the arm. Mother wasn't there. Our schoolteachers walked up and down the line, smiling bravely and telling us to be strong. Some kids cried. Some threw up. A few passed out. Most were strong.

The poster of the little girl in the iron lung stayed in the hallway of our elementary school for a long, long time. It was a constant reminder. That little girl looked down at me every time I walked through that hallway. She had such sad eyes. I always wondered what happened to her. I secretly hoped that the doctors used my dimes to buy her candy instead of medicine.

As six and seven-year-olds, we were taught to dive under our desks at school to save ourselves from an atomic blast. "Duck and cover when you see the flash," was a peppy little jingle from a civil defense film that we reviewed at school often. As an imaginative little boy, the sunshine sparkle of a distant car windshield would scare the hell out of me.

At school assemblies, we watched newsreel footage of atomic bomb tests in Nevada and victims of A-bomb blasts in Japan. On television and in the newspapers at home, the news was constantly filled with the threat and worry of a nuclear holocaust. And, when we turned to the radio for happy music and a means of escape, the programs were routinely interrupted by a hysterical, air-raid-siren tone followed by the somber announcement: "This has been a test of the Emergency Broadcast System. Had this been an actual alert, you would have been told where to tune for emergency broadcast information." The whole thing was God-awful.

Over a period of years, we were conditioned by our government and the news media to actually expect a mushroom cloud on the horizon. Our society was honestly preparing for a nuclear war that would negate the civilizing comforts of civilization and send us back to the age of Neanderthals. We saw the preparations everywhere.

All across the world, America was stockpiling nuclear weapons and shadowboxing with the communists. We were fighting a "Cold War" with our fingers on the trigger. Opposing armies postured, flexed, and sharpened their ballistic spear points. America had Army divisions at the ready all around the world. Fleets of nuclear submarines prowled the oceans like silent, killer whales, while bomb-laden strategic bombers circled the North Pole like flocks of buzzards. Ballistic missiles waited tense and ready in bombproof silos, while military commanders were buried alive deep inside Cheyenne Mountain to protect them from the blast and radiation that would kill us all.

Our parents stockpiled food and water, and converted root cellars and basements into "fallout shelters." Many people stored weapons and ammunition. The whole country was in a state of atomic bomb hysteria. Coalmines near my hometown were converted into "Civil Defense Shelters," and stocked with blankets, water and food. We were told to go there in case of a nuclear attack. We could live in the darkness of the coalmine like rats in a hole until it was safe to venture out into the radioactive nightmare that would be our inheritance.

Even churches poured gasoline on the flames of our fears. Members of my church were expected to have a two-year supply of food, medicine, and clothing stockpiled; enough to get us through the "tough times" that were sure to come. And, all too often, the preaching was about the looming fires of Armageddon. As a teenager, I was told over and over again that my generation would surely see "the end of time" when the wicked would "burn as stubble." At the age of sixteen I stopped going to church. I didn't want to hear about it anymore. I wanted to have a future.

Yes, the gloominess of that mushroom cloud loomed over our childhood like the shadow of the Grim Reaper. I was an observant and an imaginative little boy, and when I saw the grownups around me fretful and afraid, I too was marked with that deep scar of fear and paranoia. I'm sure I'm not the only member of that rebellious, wild and crazy hippie generation who felt that way. Some of us still bear those scars.

1964 was the year my generation began to rebel against it all. The summer of '64 was not like other summers; there was tension in the air. Something was wrong. We could feel it. It wasn't something you could see or put your finger on. It was more like a change in the atmospheric pressure. It registered on the barometers of our consciousness. We didn't know how or why, but things were different.

We had buried our beloved President Kennedy just seven months earlier, in November 1963, and things never quite returned to normal after that. The age of innocence ended with the Kennedy funeral. America lost more than a leader when her president was killed. She lost her self-confidence and sense of well-being. Like the victim of a rape, America had been violated, and for the first time we felt vulnerable and helpless in the face of great evil.

There were wars and rumors of wars in diverse places. There was tension all around the globe. At home, there were endless whispers of conspiracies, charges, counter-charges, inquests, and fact-finding commissions about the Kennedy assassination. Was it a madman, a communist conspiracy, the Mafia, or a political coup? Who knew the truth? For the first time, Americans were suspicious of their government and the information it gave them.

There were other events in 1964 that would change things forever. Silver was taken out of our money and God was ordered out of our schools. Brave Freedom Riders were still challenging the racial policies of segregation. The Beatles did what the British Army had failed to do in two bloody wars when they conquered America with guitars and boyish smiles. And, in a far-off jungle called Vietnam, American pilots were sent to fight and die in hostile skies.

Vietnam was the first war we all got to see on television. The on-the-spot sounds and graphic visuals made it more personal than other wars had been. For the first time, in the comfort of our living rooms, we could see the blood and hear the bombs exploding.

There were many points of contention, but it was the war in Southeast Asia that provided the spark for the youth rebellion of the 1960s. The young natives were restless and the timing was right. The dry tinder of revolt had been collecting for years: dread of the bomb, a new awareness of civil rights, a malaise of affluence, idleness, and boredom in the suburban setting, compounded by fear and anxiety of the future. The war became the unifying focal point, the catalyst for a groundswell of social upheaval and youthful rebellion.

The hippy troubadours told us that the 1960s was the dawning of the Age of Aquarius, a time of universal peace, love, and enlightenment. But, instead of peace and world brotherhood, it was really the beginning of hopelessness, civil strife, long hair, drugs, free love, and dropping out. For the first time, the civilizing traditions that had sustained Western societies since the end of the Dark Ages were openly challenged. Youth, sex, drugs, and rock-n-roll, were worshipped freely, and for many, those things took the place of hope and organized religion. Reverence and respect for hallowed institutions such as church, marriage, civil law, institutions of higher learning, and even basic social civility, were cast aside. Nothing was ever quite the same again.

The Home Front

1968 was also a pivotal year in the fortunes of our country. It was a year of political and racial turmoil like our country has never seen. Bobby Kennedy and Martin Luther King were both assassinated early in the year, and the Tet Offensive in Vietnam blew the lid off the simmering, anti-war sentiments at home. There were anti-war demonstrations on college campuses everywhere, and racial riots in several big cities following the King assassination. The Democrat political convention in Chicago that summer turned into a weeklong riot where the police were as guilty of mayhem as the protesters. For months, America teetered on the edge of anarchy.

The year started with a bang. The Tet Offensive in Vietnam proved to be a decisive battle, the biggest single event of the War. And incredibly, it was a battle that both sides would win.

Tet is a religious holiday for the Vietnamese people, the beginning of the lunar New Year. In 1968, Tet began the last day of January. The Vietnamese communists picked that symbolic day to begin a maximum effort to win the war. For months beforehand, they stockpiled weapons and ammunition while they smuggled thousands of North Vietnamese soldiers into South Vietnam. They hoped that Tet 1968 would be a new beginning, the beginning of their victory over the hated Americans.

It was a well-coordinated surprise attack. The Americans didn't see it coming and the communists held nothing back. The

Viet Cong and NVA attacked in a hundred different places all at once. The battle raged for weeks, even months in some areas.

The communists expected the whole country to join them and rise up in armed revolt against the Americans. When it didn't happen, they turned their venom and their guns on their own people. In places like the city of Hue, would-be communist liberators killed hundreds of innocent civilians in retaliation for their not joining in the fight. Hundreds of others were killed in the crossfire between the opposing armies. In the countryside, many South Vietnamese village officials, seen as traitors by the communists, were also brutally murdered.

The Tet Offensive turned into a two-pronged attack from which our country never fully recovered. We were attacked on two different fronts. The communists attacked the American Army in Vietnam, while anti-war protesters attacked our government and our sacred institutions at home.

We won the fight in Vietnam, but no one seemed to notice. The Tet Offensive was a crushing defeat for the communists. They were beaten everywhere. The ranks of the Viet Cong militia were decimated and the NVA were beaten soundly. The hoped-for peasant revolt to drive the Americans out of Vietnam never happened.

Unfortunately, we lost the battle on the home front. The Tet Offensive sparked an anti-war rebellion that divided our nation forever and toppled an American president. The communists lost on the battlefield, but they would win at the conference table.

In Vietnam, on a tank, in the heat of the battle that was Tet, we received news of riots and demonstrations in cities all across America. We heard radio reports and read newspaper accounts of protest marches, confrontations with police, and young people burning draft cards and American flags. Our friends and neighbors back home were in open revolt against the war. To those of us on the firing line, it was disheartening to say the least.

The hardest part was when kids of our own generation turned their hate and venom on us. We were soldiers, but we still thought of ourselves as being one of them. Those long-haired hippy-types were our friends, classmates, and neighbors. Hell, they were our siblings and our cousins. They were members of our peer group and we identified with them. And, most of us had boundless empathy for their cause. It was, after all, our lives on the line in Vietnam. We soldiers were the ones with the most to loose in this most hated of all wars.

Some people never seemed to realize that soldiers hated the war too. We knew better than anyone how hopeless and evil the thing was, but we had been caught up in it. We knew it should be stopped, but we were powerless to make it happen.

I was shocked when I first realized that many of the hippy-types were blaming me, and people like me, for the war. According to them, it was my service in the military that was causing all of the problems. If I refused to fight, the war couldn't happen, and my shaggy friends at home wouldn't have to be drafted. It was all up to me. Those people decided that I should refuse to fight and go to jail to save them. Some hated me when I didn't do it.

I surely didn't see things that way. I saw myself as a victim of the war. Most soldiers like me were guilty only of being true to the demands of citizenship and honoring the traditions of our fathers. We were the obedient sons. Ours was not to reason why. Let the politicians, and the American people by their votes, sort it all out.

Young people rioting in the streets and burning our flag was a hard thing for me, but when I saw pictures of protesters waving the Viet Cong flag in our nation's capital I became very angry. It was treason. I was facing that flag everyday across that open and deadly space of the battlefield. Men marching under that flag had killed and maimed thousands of my countrymen and were continuing to do so. How could my government allow people to march on my nation's capitol in the shadow of that enemy banner? I truly believe that those people should have been arrested and tried for their citizenship.

Those who marched under that foreign flag dishonored and betrayed all Americans. It is one thing to protest the actions of our government. It is quite another thing to openly support an enemy who is killing our sons and daughters. Free speech is one thing - treason is another.

I was crushed in 1971 when Jane Fonda went to Hanoi to collaborate with my enemy, and then returned home a hero. With a smirk and a haughty air of self-righteousness, she paraded her treason before the TV cameras. She was contemptuous of everything American, and she trampled the noble blood of my friends in the dirt when she wrapped herself in that enemy flag. Incredibly, there was never any formal consequence for her actions. She was the darling of the campus radicals and the politicians were afraid of her.

Jane is the rich and pampered daughter of movie star Henry Fonda. She was a beautiful girl, abounding with wealth, privilege, and high social standing. She used her good looks and her Hollywood connections to become an icon of the anti-war movement. She was the self-made bad girl of the hippy generation, and she basked in the limelight and the notoriety of it all. Jane betrayed her country and those of us in uniform in a way that should have cost her citizenship at the very least. In other wars, in other times, she would have paid with her life. Her actions clearly made her an enemy agent. It was treason by any measure.

I could never understand how someone who professed to hate our country as much as Jane did, would choose to remain here, basking in the bounty and the freedoms she professed to hate. She surely had the means to move to Paris, Hanoi, or any of those other places she told us were so much better than America.

Instead of focusing her efforts on the halls of government, where something might have been accomplished, Jane took her good looks and her camera crew to Hanoi, the capitol of our enemy. It was a great publicity stunt. There, she had her picture taken with North Vietnamese Generals and politicians. She even had her picture taken manning an anti-aircraft gun as if shooting at American bombers. She mocked and shamed American prisoners of war at a photo opportunity in the famous Hanoi Hilton prison.

Jane, and others like her, drove a wedge through the heart of our country. They divided our nation into two camps. You were with the war protesters or against them, there could be no middle ground. The flower children made it an in-your-face confrontation that turned many of us who were sympathizers into their enemies.

The whole thing became a real dilemma for some of us. While truly hating the war and sympathizing with the goals of the anti-war protesters, many of us could not abide the anti-American tone of the protest. We held in contempt those who burned American flags and vandalized our colleges and universities. We would not be a party to that. We loved our country enough to put our lives in her hands; we would not be the instruments of her destruction.

I felt much the same way about the "Vietnam Veterans Against the War" organization. As a veteran, I was very much against the war, but I could not support the likes of John Kerry and his band of rabble. Kerry shared a national spotlight with enemy agents Jane Fonda, Tom Hayden, and others like them, and by doing so, he flushed his credibility as far as I was concerned.

And, I could never stomach the shaggy, unkempt countenance of the Vietnam veterans who protested the war. The military is all about discipline, honor, and pride. Those scruffy, longhaired, dope-smoking, self-pitying veterans in ragged bell-bottomed Levis and faded army jackets filled me with sore contempt. I could never take them seriously. As a soldier and a veteran, that is not who I was.

And yet, I was torn. Had the anti-war veterans been able to put away the drugs, tone down the anti-American rhetoric, distance themselves from Jane Fonda and clean up a little, I might have marched with them.

Overall, the dividing of our culture was a terrible thing, and it gave aid and comfort to our enemy. In spite of suffering a decisive military defeat during Tet, Hanoi was encouraged to press on. The anti-war movement was a second battlefront that ate away at American resolve and self-confidence. I'm convinced that the peaceniks actually prolonged the war and the killing they said they were trying to stop. Why would Hanoi be willing to negotiate in good faith when they were winning on the American home front? Vietnam is the only war in history where the winner lost every battle on the field.

And, from today's perspective, who were those war protesters really, and what were their motivations and true beliefs? Originally, I empathized with them because they were fellow Baby Boomers from the shadow of the bomb. I thought I understood them. In the early years, I saw the anti-war protests as the righteous culmination, the final emotional explosion, of the fear, frustrations, and paranoia of that fretful generation. I saw the protests as a cry for help and a plea for social change and government accountability. As it turned out, I was wrong. The peaceniks were shallower than that.

There had been a shifting mindset among my peers beginning in the late 1950s. It was subtle at first; a quiet and sincere questioning of the direction the world was headed. Originally, it was all about nuclear weapons and doomsday scenarios. My generation wanted to have a future and we were exploring the options.

Music became the language of the rebellion early on. Through music, the goals and the ideals of the movement were communicated to the masses. As early as 1962, there were popular protest songs born from the folk music craze of the late 1950s. "Blowin' in the Wind," and "The Times they are a-Changin'" were both number one hits. Eventually, people like Janis Joplin and Bob Dylan would become the poet/songwriter spokesmen for the Baby Boomer mutineers.

Originally, it was a revolt that centered on survival. We could see that following the same path our parents had trodden was sure to get us all killed. We saw the insanity of the nuclear arms race, and we tried to turn a corner. We were struggling to escape the shadow of the mushroom cloud and the vain traditions of our fathers. Our frustrations would become a primal scream.

To change the world we needed to change ourselves. And so, America's young people set out to make it happen. We had not the power to make changes from the top of society, and so we set out to knock the legs out from under her.

Over the next few years, kids of my generation shocked the world with irreverent, nonconforming, and even aberrant behavior. They changed the way they looked, the way they thought, and the way they did things. They marched in massive protests - civil rights and anti-nuke - and then had love-ins in the park. They burned draft cards, burned brassieres, and wore flowers in their hair. They blocked the steps at city hall and tore-up university campuses. Some called it the tactics of peaceful confrontation.

There was a noble idealism at the heart of the movement, but unfortunately, for many, the ideal became buried in the trappings of the protest. Too often the ideal was overshadowed by the excitement of the rebellion. For many, it became protest for the sake of protest only. Many would-be idealists slid down a spiral of self-centeredness and self-destruction. They lost their way when the movement began to embrace mind-altering drugs and illicit sex.

Real hippies lived for the moment. They expected no future. Some traded promising lives for hashish and LSD. They dropped out of school, smoked pot, and fled to Canada. Most turned their back on tradition and dressed and acted like bums. Many removed themselves from proper and civilized society. Sadly, such actions only hurt their cause.

Many became idle, indigent, and insolent. True believers lived on welfare and handouts. To have a regular job was to be a part of the hated "Establishment." They toiled not; neither did they spin (Matthew 6:28). Some went dumpster diving without shame, or encroached upon the charity of the religious organizations they made fun of.

The hippy-types horrified their indulgent and pampering parents. Young men tied their too-long hair up in ponytails, while Young women sported nippled breasts behind see-through peasant blouses. Each of those acts was an abomination to the World War II mindset. Combined, they represented the end of civilization as we had known it.

By 1967, the transformation of teen culture was almost complete in America. Beaver Cleaver and his big brother Wally had become Cheech and Chong. The language, uniform, and symbols of the rebellion were universal and well choreographed. A kid became a nonconformist by conforming to the standard.

It was sad. In the early 1960s, the peace movement was born with the highest of ideals and the most noble of intentions. But, by the late 1960s, it had lost its way. The clear and thoughtful voices first heard demanding nuclear and social sanity were now slurred by mind-numbing drugs. The bright and eager faces of our future were now sporting unkempt beards and red-rimmed, glassy eyeballs. Who could take them seriously?

There was not enough righteous self-discipline within the hippy generation to carry the ideal of world peace and justice for all into the temple of humanity. The ideal was abandoned at the steps of the temple. A sacrifice was never placed upon the altar. The false Gods of greed and evil were never cast down. It is sad, but the promise and the hope of the 1960s protest movement drowned in a sea of self-indulgence.

History has shown that righteous, meaningful, and beneficial social change requires Godly virtue, temperance, self-sacrifice, and honor. That's the way our founding fathers did it. The hippy generation surrendered to self and completely lost their way. Noble ideals fell by the wayside. The rebellion, born with such promise, died in shame and disgrace.

To prove that point, where are they now? Where are those noble idealists who were out to change the world? Where are those many thousands of righteous peace lovers and colorblind advocates of social justice who marched in the streets and demanded a better world? Where are those longhaired street preachers who told us that money didn't matter and that love and brotherhood would save us in the end? Where are they now, and what have they been doing over the past forty years? Where is Jane Fonda, and what has she done with her money and her life?

I feel betrayed. That love and peace, flower-child generation holds the keys of power now. Instead of the universal brotherhood we were promised, we get scandal after scandal, both from our government and from our business leaders. Things are a mess. We don't trust God, and we can't trust each other. If love and peace were truly rooted in hippy hearts, what happened to it, and where is it now?

Our country was betrayed a second time in 1968, and on a scale seldom seen in world history. On March 31, Lyndon Johnson made a speech to the nation. It was the beginning of the 1968 political season. The country would hold a presidential election in the coming November. Johnson had served as President since Kennedy was assassinated, four and a half years earlier. He was the incumbent, and sure to be the Democrat candidate.

When he addressed the nation that evening, the Tet Offensive was sixty days old and things were still in turmoil across Vietnam. Khe Sanh was under siege and battles were raging all across the country. The Fourth Armored Cavalry was in the Iron Triangle, serving our Commander-in-Chief as tiger bait.

Things were in turmoil across America too. The communist attack had fostered anti-war sentiment like nothing before it. People were marching in the streets and they were mad. It was clear to everyone that our President and our military leaders had been lying to us about the strength and resolve of our enemy in Vietnam. Contrary to what the nation had been told, the war was a long ways from being won. General Westmoreland wanted another 200,000 soldiers for the battlefields, in addition to the 500,000 already serving there. Draft quotas would need to be increased.

Johnson looked into the television cameras that evening with a smug but pouty face, and declared: "I will not seek, and I will not accept, the nomination of my party to be your president." We were stunned. There on national television, in front of the nation and the world, our President tucked his tail and ran. The man was truly without honor or shame. To be voted out would be one thing. To simply quit was quite another.

There are those who say that Johnson's resignation was a peace offering to both the war protesters and the Viet Cong, but

I don't believe it. It was beyond the range of the man's character to be noble. His resignation touched off a period of uncertainty and political instability that only compounded the social unrest in the country. And, what greater gift could a President of the United States give an armed enemy than to resign when that enemy showed true commitment and resolve on the battlefield? Hitler and Hirohito could only have hoped for such an outcome.

In my humble opinion, Johnson's resignation was a shameful disgrace. My President, my Commander-in-Chief, my King, was quitting the field of battle in the face of the enemy. He was the big man who had started the war. The problem was his to fix. He was the man with all the power.

I was incensed. Johnson had started the longest, most expensive, and most controversial war in our nation's history. He had taken us across the Rubicon to the point of total commitment. He was the President who first sent combat soldiers to Vietnam. He had planted the flag of national honor and national obligation on foreign soil and ordered thousands of American soldiers to their deaths to defend it. He had preached the gospel of communist containment while sending other men to fight and die for the cause. He had ordered me and tens of thousands of other young men drafted and sent to the front.

And now, at the very height of the battle, when half-a-million of his soldiers had their lives on the line for him, he was simply going to walk away. We were fighting to defend his policies and his command decisions, and now he was going to abandon us to the fate he had created for us. The ghost of Abraham Lincoln surely wept.

Johnson continued to sit in the big chair in the oval office for another ten months, until Richard Nixon took over in January 1969, but he was only the caretaker of the office. He was done. His heart, mind, and money were all in Texas. The mess he had made would be left for others to clean up. He betrayed every man who ever served him, and especially those who died in his service.

My friends, Jenies Mobley, Howard Williams, and Frank Serio, were all killed in Vietnam three weeks after our Commander-in-Chief made that announcement. Those good men were never given the option to quit and go home. They stayed at their battle stations, where Lyndon Johnson and Robert McNamara had posted them, and died gallantly.

The Battle of Xom Moi (2)

5 May 1968, early afternoon. We are traveling north and returning to the Phu Loi Base Camp. The sun is over my left shoulder. We have been south near Dian and to the west of highway 13, beating the bushes for bad guys. The armored vehicles are spread out in a ragged formation, rumbling through farm fields, banana groves and wooded copses as we approach the base camp. Our day is nearly done and we are almost home. The watchtowers of Phu Loi can be seen clearly above the trees. Home is less than a mile away. The tension of the day is melting away as we eagerly look forward to cool showers, cold beer, and much needed rest.

It is unbearably hot. The Asian sun is a blowtorch. We are riding up-top and the metal skin of the ACAV is too hot to touch with a bare hand. Each rumbling machine has three or four sun-baked soldiers clinging to the top like men riding huge, metal camels. We are all wearing tanker's helmets and flak jackets. We are soaked in sweat and covered with dust. We've been out since before daylight and it's been a long and miserable journey. We ride along silently, enduring the heat and the bone-weary monotony of that last mile of the day.

Suddenly, two enemy soldiers jump up and run like rabbits flushed from cover. I see them, and I am stunned to unresponsiveness. My sun-baked brain struggles to accept it: NVA uniforms, AK-47 rifles, and fully exposed, right out in the open!

The enemy soldiers wouldn't have jumped up and ran, but a tank was about to run over the bush they were hiding in. They are caught out in the open now, and they know they are dead. They make no attempt to surrender or fight. They simply run with heads tucked deep into their shoulders like football players waiting to be tackled. They run across an open field and wait for the bullets.

It seems to take a long time before a single shot is fired, and then comes a spattering of shots like rain hitting a tin roof. The tempo of gunfire quickly increases and finally explodes into thunder as heavy machine-guns take up the chase. Tracer bullets flash through the air and smack into the dry ground around the running men. Dust boils and chunks of dirt and debris are thrown high into the air. One man is clubbed to the ground almost immediately; the other continues to run through the storm, holding his arms high as if trying to shield his face. Finally, he too is slammed to the ground in a tangle of arms and legs. The shooting stops and a cloud of thick, red dust hangs suspended in the air.

I look down in astonishment to see my rifle still lying across my lap. I haven't even picked it up. With complete disbelief, I watch the dust settle over the tragic scene. For a moment I feel pity for that man who ran and waited for the bullets, shielding his face with his arms.

I look over at the Captain. His eyes register shock like someone has just slapped his face. "My God," he said, "that's gotta be a damned OP (observation post). There's an NVA unit here someplace!"

The Colonel is overhead in a helicopter and already on the radio. He and the Captain begin talking it over. In the background comes the deep rattle of a heavy, fifty-caliber machine-gun, an irreverent sound like someone revving up the engine of a motor bike, Brrrt, Brrrt, Brrrt. In front of a tank, the body of one of the men we have just killed is being bumped across the ground by the slugs. The bloody bundle that was once a man is being ripped apart. Bits of meat, bone, and gore are spattering all around.

"Cease-fire!" the Captain screams into the radio. "Cease-fire, damn it! Lieutenant Wilson (not his real name), your people better develop some (expletive deleted) fire discipline and you better get a handle on this or there's going to be hell to pay! You got that, Lieutenant?"

A meek, "Yes sir," is followed by a half-hearted and belated reprimand to the Sergeant who has desecrated the body. The gun falls silent. Everyone reloads and waits.

From over the Phu Loi watchtowers come the first helicopters, drawn to the sound of the guns like vultures to the smell of blood. Inside the camp, air-conditioned command posts and officer's clubs are being emptied as a lot of heavy brass hustles to the helipads.

It was easy to tell when something big was happening in Vietnam. From miles away, the helicopters could be seen like great flocks of circling buzzards over a fight. The helicopters would stack up in tiers over the battlefield, arranged in altitude according to the rank and status of the occupants. The highest-ranking officer would choose to be either the lowest, or the highest helicopter in the stack, depending on the "pucker factor" at the time. If the enemy had recently demonstrated good anti-aircraft capability, the "Big Guy" would always choose to be at the top of the stack. You don't get to be a General by being a dummy, I suppose. We watch the helicopters rise up out of Phu Loi and there are more than a few smiles.

In some ways, the helicopter in Vietnam was a curse to the line units. There was always some guy with an eagle on his collar, in clean fatigues and a helicopter, high overhead in the cool, clean breeze, to give you helpful advice and direct your activities down there in the dirt. Our fight at Xom Moi was so conveniently close to the Phu Loi base camp that we even had a General or two overhead before it was done.

When all the brass stacks up over a fight like that, strange things happen to the men on the ground. They loose control. A confusing situation becomes hopeless. A General in a helicopter can never restrain himself. He makes helpful suggestions to the Colonel about how he thinks the fight should be developed. The Colonel, not wishing to offend the General, passes the helpful suggestions on to the Captain with a few suggestions of his own, of course. The harried and shell-shocked Captain, who has already issued orders to his platoon leaders, must now recant his earlier directives and suspend his own best judgments in order not to disobey his commanders. The platoon leaders who are deeply engaged in a desperate, close-quarters fight, then loose control because they do not have the option to pursue or maneuver as they see the advantage. It happened far too often, and it helped our enemy.

As the Captain discusses tactics with the big brass, the tanks and ACAVS stand still. Heat shimmers from the scorching armor plate and huge diesel engines idle. Sweat drips from my chin onto the acetate map case on my lap and makes a little puddle. The troopers lounge and smoke and sit over their guns, quickly becoming bored. The bodies of the two men we have killed lie scattered in the dust, their pink insides exposed to the tropical sunshine. A couple of soldiers are squeamishly picking through the bloody bundles. They've been ordered to relieve the bodies of any maps, papers, or weapons. The Captain sits with a map spread across his lap, talking into the radio and looking up at the sky as if trying to maintain eye contact with the Big Boss in the helicopter.

Finally, the Captain switches to our radio frequency and tells us to saddle up. We are going to sweep northwest and reconnoiter though a small hamlet marked on our maps as Xom

Moi (2). There is a pottery factory in Xom Moi (2), and just outside the village, an area where clay for the pots is dug out of the ground in a primitive, open-pit mining operation. We know the area. It is marked on our maps as the clay pits.

For clarification, I should point out that the Vietnamese often called a cluster of small villages by the same name. It drove American's crazy. And so, we assigned numbers to each small hamlet in a cluster. That way, we could better pinpoint a location. On our map, there was Xom Moi (1), Xom Moi (2), and Xom Moi (3). The Vietnamese would make no such distinction. To them, all three hamlets were Xom Moi.

We wheel our formation to our left front and assume a full combat attack posture. We know we have NVA regulars some-where very close and we are going to try to flush them out. We have no idea how many there might be. We also know that we have them where they can't run. If we can find them, they will be forced to surrender or fight. It is semi-open farm country around Xom Moi, and the helicopters will nail them if they move in the daylight.

In spite of the heat, we zip our flak jackets up tight and tuck our heads a little deeper into our helmets. Our firing on their OP has surely tipped them off. They might be preparing to meet us. We ride up-top and anxious as we push past the bloody bodies in the field and aim our formation at the clay pits. I tell a gun battery to stand by for a possible fire mission.

We push forward for several hundred yards and enter a big grove of trees that is almost like a park. It is shady and cool there, a welcomed respite from the searing sun. We can see the towers of Phu Loi through the trees less than half-a-mile away. It gives the operation a strange feel. We have never hunted tigers so close to our doorstep before.

Everything is deathly still in the big grove of trees. Huge clumps of bamboo are interspersed among the trees and well-beaten footpaths wander about. There are several water wells and evidence of farming activity, but no people to be seen anywhere. It is a bad sign. The armored vehicles rumble and growl as they pick their way through the shady glen. The tension is very high.

Suddenly, there is a flash and an ear-shattering CRACK from the tank in front of us. At first, I think he has fired his main gun, but in that same moment comes fluttering down around us scraps of C-ration cardboard, seat cushions ... and a man. The tank has taken an RPG hit.

A young soldier comes flying through the air and lands on his hands and knees in the dirt in front of us. He was riding up-top and blown completely free of the tank by the explosion. He is on his feet immediately, but then he just stands there, his face frozen in a silent scream. He stands like he was doused with ice water, shoulders hunched, arms outstretched, and eyes wide with horror. His mouth is open but he makes no sound. He is the very picture of terror and shock: aware that he is being killed, wildly desperate to flee, and yet unable to function. He is unconscious on his feet. There are no obvious, gaping wounds, but blood seeps from his face everywhere as if soaking through paper. A man runs to him, tips him over his shoulder, and runs to the rear with him.

All hell breaks loose. Everyone begins firing at once. The Captain screams into the radio, "Support that tank! Support that tank! Move it up! Move it up!"

The noise is unbelievable. Dozens of heavy machine-guns roar. The flash and bang of cannon fire and exploding rockets is everywhere. The air is suddenly filled with thousands of whistling, popping, screaming projectiles. Tracers flash through the shade of the trees. Falling tree branches and fluttering leaves come raining down like confetti. Dust and smoke boil everywhere.

The disabled tank sits there like a great, wounded animal, not moving, not shooting, and with wisps of smoke rising from the open hatches. To the right of the tank, in the dirt, is the tangled body of another of our men, not moving.

Within seconds we know we are surrounded. We have blundered into an NVA battalion of between five and six hundred men. To complicate matters, we don't have the full troop with us when the lid to that trap comes down on us. We have two platoons and only part of the headquarters section. There are five tanks and no more than fifteen ACAVS in that original formation. We have about seventy men. All the tanks are hit in the first few minutes. It is complete pandemonium.

I can no longer remember that fight as a coherent, step-by-step sequence of events. Everything is scrambled in my mind. What I have is a collection of images buried deep in the shadows of my memory. Some of the images are still frames, single moments in time captured like individual photographs. Others are like home movies, motion pictures that are clear and focused, complete with sound, color, smell, and the rapid beating of my heart as a background chorus. Still others are hazy, black and white images like photo negatives. They are the ghosts of what happened that day, faint and faded renderings without color or sound. They are the dimly remembered images, the peripheral vision that fills in the background information. The dark negatives must be held to the light and scrutinized before the picture becomes clear. It has been many years, but my hands still sweat when I sort through those images.

I remember the heart-stopping noise of it, and the complete shock and terror. We are a well-seasoned team of combat veterans, but none of us has ever witnessed anything like this. The fighting is at close-quarters and unbelievably savage. The North Vietnamese are cornered and they fight like demons. Their only chance is to get right in among us where the artillery and air support can't get to them. They come right at us, determined and desperate, some charging tanks with bayonets fixed.

We fight like we've never fought before. We are surrounded by an enemy who is himself surrounded, and that compounds the desperation and the savagery. For both sides, it is win or die, there is no middle ground. The NVA have us outnumbered by as many as eight or nine to one, but we have the armored vehicles, helicopters, and heavy artillery. It becomes a clash of Titans, a fight to the finish - a cockfight, with blood, guts, and feathers everywhere.

Bullets bounce off armored plate. Machine-gunners stand back-to-back, firing in opposite directions. The smoky trails of RPG rockets crisscross in the air through the middle of our formation. Tank cannons flash and thunder. A tank commander drops hand grenades over the side of his tank into a slit trench that is almost under his track pads and below the traversing range of his guns. A huge projectile makes a hollow pop as it breaks the sound barrier near my face, making me duck and scaring the hell out of me. There is terror in my Captain's eyes when someone screams over the radio that the NVA are shooting at us with big, crew-served, anti-aircraft guns.

I remember complete panic and confusion in the ranks, ACAVS bumping into ACAVS as they try to maneuver and jockey for position. There are shouts, screams, and curses in the radio headset, everyone talking at once. The Captain, and the Colonel in his helicopter, are both trying to take charge of the fight. I'm trying to get artillery in on the bad guys. All the tanks and ACAVS are trying to talk to each other and everyone is screaming for a medic or someone to cover their back. Everyone is trying to get a fix on the anti-aircraft guns. We've got to take them out.

For a while it's a free-for-all, and then the Captain pulls it all together. He boxes the formation. We create an armored phalanx, a defensive formation like a Spartan wedge. The Captain forms the tanks and ACAVS in two parallel rows with the gun shields and gun barrels to the outside, firing in all directions. It's a good move. We can cover each other's backs that way and the NVA troops can't get in among us. But, the tight formation makes it difficult for us to maneuver, attack, or escape.

Our salvation is our firepower, and we hold nothing back. Machine-guns are soon cooking-off. The barrels become so hot the bullets fire as soon as they enter the firing chamber. Our gunners don't need to touch the triggers, just keep feeding belts of ammunition and point the gun. I saw machine-gun barrels glow red-hot and droop with the heat, actually bending out of shape. When troopers poured water over the guns to cool them, the water exploded into steam. When one man ran out of water and foolishly poured a quart of motor oil over a red-hot fifty-caliber barrel, the oil caught fire, cascading down the side of the vehicle and dripping toward the ground.

Without waiting for orders, I quickly had artillery impacting into a rice paddy behind the enemy line. The Captain saw the big shells hit the ground and he grabbed my arm and pointed into the trees. "Right there! Right there! Put it right there!" he screamed over the roar of the guns. We were going for the anti-aircraft guns and the heaviest concentration of enemy soldiers. I had done the right thing. At that point in the fight, artillery was our best defense. The anti-aircraft fire had scattered the helicopters and it would take a while to get close support from fixed-wing aircraft.

I started walking the big shells back into the trees, bringing them toward us and into the enemy positions. There were enemy troops everywhere, and I called for another gun battery, and then another. Before I was done, I was directing five batteries, thirty cannons, into that fight.

A concentration of artillery fire that heavy was an incredible thing to witness up close. It was a wall of fire. The incredible noise, flying debris, and shock wave were terrifying. Big shells screamed through the air. Thundering flashes of light took down the trees, shredding bark and tree trunks, scattering branches and raking tons of dirt high into the air. A boiling cloud of dust and smoke grew taller than the trees. Chunks of wood and ragged shell splinters flew everywhere, raining down over our formation. Red dust filled the air like a fog. The sun was covered by the cloud of dust and became only a bloody spot in the sky.

It was impossible to keep it going. I had to keep track of where each battery's shells were landing so I could make the next correction. And, I had to remember what I had just told each battery to do. The big guns were shooting rapid fire, from different locations, and from two or three different directions. It was impossible to keep up – but I did. I had to. Our backs were to the wall. Time stops in that deadly space between the bullets, but your mind functions in hyper-drive.

I remember artillery impacting so close to our formation that the troopers sitting up-top had their heads bowed into the shell concussions as if they were going into a hailstorm. Tree limbs were somersaulting through the air and spent shrapnel and dirt clods were raining down everywhere. The enemy was danger-close and the artillery was on them.

For a while, I was able to maintain the barrage, but slowly, I started to lose control. I had to focus deeply to coordinate the fire mission and I was losing track of what was happening around me. It was also growing ever more difficult to see the impacting shells through the dust and smoke. And then too, I was struggling to keep my bearings. We were constantly moving and changing direction as we fought and tried to consolidate the formation. An orienting line, a firm compass bearing: north, south, east, or west, is a critical part of directing shellfire. All calculations in the Fire Direction Center at the gun battery are based on the observer-to-target direction. If an FO moves without compensating for the angle, or if he becomes disoriented, the consequences can be severe. What is left and right to you might still be "add" and "drop" to the gun battery.

And, I know it sounds unbelievable, but because of the RPGs, we are still riding on top of the vehicles. It was difficult to keep a map spread across my lap and grease pencils in my fingers while clinging to the track like a monkey to keep from being bucked off. Things were beginning to come unstuck.

And then, Robert Ivie pulled me from the fire. I was sitting up-top, exposed to hostile fire and completely focused on the fire mission. Ivie quit his machine-gun, grabbed me by the flak jacket, and dumped me on my head onto the floor of the track in a shower of maps and grease pencils. I came up swinging and mad as hell. He held a hand up in protest, and pointed with the other to a big tree just behind us (the noise was so terrific we could not talk). Clumps of tree bark were ripped away by the impact of several bullets. Ivie told me later that he looked over just in time to see a couple of slugs zip past my head and hit that tree behind me. Someone had me zeroed in. I was talking to the cannons with radio speakers in my ears and completely unaware.

I was losing control. I started screaming for an AO, an aerial observer in an airplane who could fly overhead and see everything. Luckily, The Colonel had anticipated the need and had already made the arrangements. The AO was already overhead, Drumfire Five-two, in a helicopter. (Actually, I don't remember the man's call sign. Drumfire Five-two is close enough.) He was already monitoring what I was doing. He checked in on my radio frequency and then took over. I was relieved to pass the burden to him. He could see the whole picture from where he was, and he would be better able to focus on the fire mission without the distractions that were plaguing me on the ground.

The AO immediately shut down some of the five batteries I was directing and got the mission down to a more manageable twelve or eighteen guns. I had sought safety in a massed volume of fire; the AO was going for more precision with fewer cannons. He was better able to do that from the air.

With someone else directing the artillery, I was now an extra hand. Both of our machine-guns were manned, and so I opted to help the medics. The medics were being overwhelmed. With rifle in hand, I jumped from the track and sprinted to where the medics were working with a tangle of wounded men at the base of some trees. All of our tanks and several of our ACAVs had been hit by RPGs. Most were still in the fight, but dead and wounded crewmembers were being pulled from the vehicles and dragged back to a low spot by a big clump of bamboo. I did what I could to help. Bullets were smacking into trees around us and artillery was thundering into the enemy positions just a hundred yards away. The noise, dust, panic and confusion were overwhelming.

I looked up through the smoke and the flash of tracer bullets and saw one of the tank commanders running toward us. His tank had taken multiple RPG hits and was beginning to burn. The man came running through the trees, limping terribly, and to my dismay, I saw a big, bloody splinter of bone sticking through his pant leg just above his boot. Incredibly, he stayed on his feet and just kept coming. He was in shock, running wildly in panic and confusion, not knowing where he was going or what he was doing.

I grabbed him as he went by, and tried to wrestle him to the ground. He was a lot bigger than me, and super-charged with fear, panic and pain. I finally convinced him to get down, more than wrestled him. He was a big black man with muscles like a professional boxer.

I went to work on his leg. I ripped his pant leg open and exposed the compound fracture. It was a mess. He had run several yards with the bone broken. The top of his boot was compressed into the raw meat and muscle of his calf. The bone splinter was jutting out like a piece of broken broom handle. Surprisingly, there was very little blood.

The man was thrashing around and beating his head on the ground in pain. He kept screaming, "Mah arm! Mah arm! ... Oh God! Mah arm!" I looked to see. His tattered shirtsleeve was soaked in blood. I cut his shirtsleeve open and saw that his arm was in two pieces, held together by a strap of skin. His upper arm was a big black cannon ball of muscle with a raw, splintered bone protruding into nothing where his elbow should have been. I screamed for the medic.

One of the wounded was just a baby-faced kid who looked to be no more than sixteen or seventeen years old. He was a new guy, and this was probably his first fight. He was lying on the ground, shaking like a leaf and holding his hand over a bloody spot on his thigh. The medic ripped his pant leg open and took a look. There was one small, ragged shrapnel hole in the boy's leg, a mere piece of buckshot. "It's nothing," the medic mouthed above the roar of the guns. He then nodded for me to take over. He had serious wounds to care for. I put a gauze pad over the wound and told the kid to put his hand over it to keep it in place. I put my mouth over his ear and told him to lie low and get on the first medivac helicopter that came in. I then left him there and went back to help the medic.

We never did get a medivac in there. It was too hot. Some time later we had to break out and take the wounded and dead out on the tracks. When the medic went to get that kid with the scrap of buckshot in his leg, the boy was dead. He had hidden there in the grass, in the middle of that battle, and died of shock. His wound was not serious.

Something was happening. The artillery had stopped but the battle was still raging. I ran back to the ACAV and put radio speakers in my ears again. The AO had check-fired the artillery to make room for helicopter gunships. The Cobras were spilling rockets and miniguns into the enemy positions. Things were cool.

Then came a frantic call. "Dragoon Niner-two, this is Drumfire Five-two (the AO)! Your CC track has a couple of gooners in a ditch behind you! We can see them, Dragoon! They're creepin' up on you, man! We got nothing to put on them!"

Our track was stopped in a stationary position for the time being and we were sitting ducks. I grabbed the Captain by the arm and pointed at the ditch behind us (it was impossible to talk above the noise). Daniels was on the radio and very busy. He pushed me back violently and continued to talk into his headset. His eyes were wild and they burned into me like hot coals. His unit was being shot to hell and he was frantic and in shock himself. He had problems of his own. He would not be interrupted – for anything. The man humbled me.

I suddenly became very calm. I was terrified, but resigned. My Captain was busy. I would have to take care of it myself. I was a rifleman now, the only man mobile. And, I was the only man aware of the danger.

I looked it over. It was a big ditch. They could pop up anywhere. I didn't know where they were or what weapons they carried. Our machine-gunners were heavily engaged with other targets. I was on my own. I fought absolute panic rising from deep in my guts.

I couldn't just wait for them to come to us. They might hit us before I could bring my rifle to bear. I had to get grenades into that ditch. But, from where I was, the ditch was a tough target for hand grenades. It was twenty or thirty yards away and it was narrow, twisting, and deep. It was also shielded by brush and clumps of bamboo. I would have to get closer to accurately get hand grenades down on the bad guys. I jammed a fresh magazine into my rifle and stuffed fragmentation grenades into my pockets. In my ears, I could hear my beating heart above the roar of the battle.

I was just starting over the side of the track when a helicopter came screaming overhead, so low that I actually ducked. The prop-wash threw dirt in my face and blinded me for a second or two. It was an old, Korean War vintage, bubble-canopied helicopter with only two seats. From the door of the helicopter, a man was leaning partway out, one foot on the skids while firing a rifle at the ground. It was the AO, the artillery observer who had warned me.

The helicopter came within twenty feet of the ground and hovered unsteadily in the air over the ditch for a few seconds, rising and falling like a great dragonfly caught in the wind. The man on the skids continued to shoot toward the ground. The helicopter then peeled off to one side and clawed for altitude again. I jammed the radio speakers back into my ears just in time to hear the AO scream: "Got 'em, Niner-two! Got 'em both! WAHOO!"

I had been delivered from the mouth of hell. I sat down heavily inside the track, suddenly oblivious to the battle raging all around me. I felt very weak. My hands were shaking uncontrollably.

I keyed the radio switch. "Drumfire Five-two, this is Dragoon Niner-two, I don't know who you are, old buddy, but I'll buy the beer when we hit Phu Loi. I owe you a big one."

There was only static on the radio for a few seconds, and then came a new voice, older, and under great stress. "This is Five-two Papa (the helicopter pilot), Five-two has been hit, Dragoon. We are inbound to Phu Loi for medical assistance. We are leaving your station. Five-two Papa, out."

It wasn't "Wahoo" the man had yelled. He was talking to me on the radio when the bullet struck him. He had screamed. I would learn later that the bullet took him through the leg. He survived, and returned to duty a few weeks later. I wrote him and the helicopter pilot up for medals.

We were going to break out. Our ammunition was running low, the bad guys had been pounded hard, we were shot up pretty bad, and it was time to go. We loaded the dead and wounded aboard the tracks and consolidated the formation. We would pull out and let the Air Force take over for a while.

As we were pulling the formation together, a couple of men came running though the smoke and dust of the battle. They were carrying a man between them, sagging and limp, apparently dead or unconscious. They ran toward our track. I jerked the door at the back of the ACAV open to take their burden. They dumped the man through the open door at my feet and then ran back through the fight without saying anything. I had no idea who the man was, what his condition was, or why he had been brought to me.

I pulled the man inside the ACAV and re-sealed the door. I knelt alongside him in the semi-darkness to check him out. The battle was raging outside and a steady stream of hot machine-gun brass was raining down on us from up-top where Ivie and Poirier were manning the guns. The inside of the track was so filled with gun smoke I could hardly see. Spent machine-gun brass on the floor of the track was deeper than the tops of my boots.

I didn't recognize the man, and I had no idea what had happened to him. I propped him into a sitting position in a corner of the ACAV and was surprised to discover that he was still alive. I looked him over quickly but found no wounds. He wasn't bleeding, and he didn't seem to be hurt anywhere, but he was obviously in bad shape. He was only semi-conscious and his eyes were unfocused, bleary and dreamlike. He seemed to be fading fast.

I shook him, slapped him on the cheek and tried to get his attention to find out what was wrong. He opened his mouth convulsively, like a fish out of water, and grabbed a handful of air with one hand. It was then that I noticed the color of him. He was turning blue.

I froze in horror. He wasn't breathing! Dear God. I was shocked numb. For a moment I hesitated, my mind rebelling against what I knew I had to do.

Ivie screamed at me from the gun mount. "He can't breathe, Lieutenant! He can't breathe!"

My composure and self-control came slowly sneaking back, embarrassed.

I leaned the man forward and slapped him on the back. No response. I stuck my fingers down his throat, fishing for an obstruction, but found nothing. The man gagged and threw up, long streamers of spittle dripping down from his chin. He was sliding towards deep unconsciousness. I tried to lay him down so I could do mouth-to-mouth but there was no place to lay him. I had to do it with him sitting up. The track was moving and there was no chance to take him back outside where I could stretch him out.

I pulled his jaw forward, tipped his head back, put my mouth over his mouth, and blew down his throat. Snot came from his nose and all over the side of my face. Damn! I pinched his nose and tried again. I tipped his head back even more, pulled his tongue forward and held it against his teeth with my thumb. He was struggling and gurgling deep in his throat, and he began to thrash around. I leaned heavily against him to hold him down. I blew into his mouth again and again but he wasn't responding.

The man fought me. He bit my thumb and vomited into my mouth. Gagging and spitting, I turned his head to the side, cleared his mouth with my fingers, and went back to it. I kept trying to get air into him for what seemed like a long, long time, wallowing on my knees in the vomit and spent machine-gun brass, but slowly, I realized that he had stopped fighting and had become very still. His face was a deep, waxy purple and his eyes were cold and distant. The man was dead.

Immediately, the guilt came over me. Because I couldn't save him, I felt responsible for his death. I beat myself up pretty bad. Why did you hesitate, Thomas? Would it have been different had you started sooner? Would it have been different had you not been so squeamish, so reluctant to share bodily fluids with that struggling, dying young man? And, did you remember to do everything they taught you to do in first-aid school? Your efforts were clumsy and unprofessional. You should have done better. What if? And I carry that burden like an anvil around my neck forever. What if, dear God, what if?

Someone told me later that one of our men was pinched between two ACAVS during that fight. He was dismounted and caught when one track backed into another. The soldier I tried to breathe for that day might have been that man. I will never know.

Somehow, we are out in the open again, out in the fields east of the clay pits. We pass the body of that dead soldier to a group of medical people who are loading them onto helicopters. We've been told to button up and prepare for close air support. The Phantom jets are overhead.

We close the hatches and sit in semi-darkness inside the ACAV, Jerry Poirier, Robert Ivie, and me. I don't know where the Captain is. There are only the three of us inside the track. We listen to the shriek of jet engines overhead and the track vibrates with each CRUMP of a five hundred pound bomb.

Clumps of grass, dirt, wood, and spent shrapnel come sprinkling down on us. We are still very close to the enemy and the heart of the target zone.

We sit there, exhausted, looking at each other, and no one says a word. I'll never forget those eyes. There are times when you can communicate with another person to the very depths of your inner-soul without saying anything. This is one of those times. Their eyes speak to me: "My God, what a fight ... and it's not over yet. When the air strike is over, we gotta go back in there."

I look into Ivie's eyes, and Poirier's eyes, and their eyes pose a question that no one speaks: "Maybe one of us this time?" We all knew it might happen. Our friend and track commander, Jenies Mobley, had been killed just two weeks earlier. We were with him, and we all saw him go down. Remembering it haunts me as we sit there in that iron coffin waiting to go back in. "Maybe one of us this time. It's not over yet."

In the excitement of the battle, I had forgotten about the heat. Now I am reminded. It is scorching hot. The track is parked out in the merciless sun and the air in that closed-up metal box is as thick as dirty water. We are suffocating. The air inside that vehicle is liquid with gun smoke, diesel smoke, cigarette smoke, dust, vomit, sweat, scorching metal, hot gun barrels, hot cartridge brass, and hot radio tubes. The sweat is literally pouring from us. Our uniforms are soaked.

I look down at my hands and they are covered with blood from working with the medics. There is blood, dirt, and stinky vomit stains on my uniform. I can still taste another man's vomit in my mouth and we are out of water. At that moment, I would have sold my soul for as humble a price as a cup of water or a bottle of warm beer.

The jets continue their screaming dives for a long time. Bombs burst, the track shudders, and dust filters in through the gaps and cracks of the big vehicle's seams. Again, it's like being depth-charged in a submarine. I'm convinced that we will pass out from lack of air. We are growing light-headed as we bake and dehydrate in that big metal oven.

Finally, it is over. The big jets have nothing left to give. We get an order over the radio to saddle up. We've been reinforced by "C" Troop, and we're going back in.

We blow the hatches, and the cool, hundred and ten degree heat washes over us like spring rain. The stench of napalm is overpowering. We drink in the stinking, dusty air greedily as we stand to the guns. We lock and load, and prepare to go back in. I am so spent: physically, mentally, and spiritually, that I feel almost no emotion. I must dig deep inside myself to find even fear.

The Captain comes back to the track and climbs aboard. He hooks up his radio headset, reloads his rifle and says, "I went back in there and drove a disabled tank out as the air strike was lifting just now." He was proud, and he should have been. I heard later that he was awarded a Silver Star.

It is late afternoon when we make our second penetration of the clay pits near Xom Moi (2). We attack into a glorious setting sun and a blood red Asian sky. We have been reinforced, re-supplied, and we go in with absolute fire superiority this time. We shoot the whole place completely to hell. The NVA have been decimated and we face only weak opposition.

It turns into an orgy of violence and revenge. Nothing escapes. Anything that fights, anything that runs, anything that moves, is gunned down. Grass hootches, farm carts, water wells, gravestones, trees, shadows, and even clay water pots are killed. All of the pent-up fear, hurt, hate, and anger is released in a rampage of destruction.

It stops only after a merciful blanket of darkness desends over the battlefield. A bad moon rises in the eastern sky. We consolidate our forces, pull back, and wait for daylight.

Mid-morning, 6 May, 1968. "B" and "C" Troops have taken possession of the battlefield. Before us is a spectacle that reminds me of the South Pacific islands after the battles of World War II. The cool, shady park of yesterday has been turned into a moonscape. Shattered tree trunks, bomb craters, shell holes, black napalm scars, burnt-out tanks and scattered equipment are everywhere. There are dozens and dozens of bodies.

We are dismounted and "policing up" the battlefield. Our people are stacking captured weapons, searching for documents and collecting souvenirs. We count more than 400 enemy soldiers lying dead on the field. We are told that the commander of the unit, an NVA Colonel, surrendered that morning to a South Vietnamese Army outpost. They said he was afraid to go back up North after loosing his whole command.

We make a temporary CP (command post) near where the enemy anti-aircraft guns have been discovered. There are four of them, but only two were in service during the fight. The other two were never fully assembled. Incredibly, in spite of our best efforts, the big guns still sit defiantly atop their tripods as if waiting to take on more tanks and helicopters. The gun crews are lying dead in tangled, bloody piles all around them. The guns are Chinese made, fifty-one caliber, with long barrels and anti-aircraft sights.

I stand looking at the fallen gunners and I am humbled. Did I do this? This place was one of my primary targets yesterday even though I couldn't see the gunners through the smoke, dust, and trees. I don't know if my shells got them or not, but I tried very hard to kill these men yesterday ... and now they are dead. I can see that they died valiantly, facing our withering fire, defending themselves and their brothers-in-arms. Silently, and almost sadly, I take my helmet off and pay homage with a bowed head. My enemies are tough little bastards. I salute you.

And yet, as I stand there, I allow myself no guilt or pity. It was a fair fight. Those men chose the ground and they got the first shot. Were it in their power, I would be that bloody bundle on the ground. Destiny has brought us all together here, and fate has picked the winner.

As we begin to look around, we are shocked by what we find. The enemy soldiers have been hiding under the towers of our base camp for weeks, maybe months. It was a brilliant strategy. We never looked for them that close to home. We would never have found them if not for that tank running over their observation post.

We discover several tunnel entrances in the area. Some in the clay pits and others cleverly disguised as water wells. Were they attempting to dig tunnels under our base camp defenses? The General sends a special team of tunnel rats to explore the tunnels.

In a ditch near the anti-aircraft guns, we find what we believe to be a couple of Chinese journalists. They are bigger and more robust than most Vietnamese, and their facial features are different. Each has a red star tattooed on his forearm. They are very dead, but still in possession of a damaged movie camera and several reels of film. Our General sends a special helicopter to pick up the film.

I take my rifle and wander away from the CP to look things over. Artillery and bombs have plowed the ground and the litter of war is everywhere. There are broken trees, spent shell casings, ragged fragments of shrapnel, tattered ammo boxes, fragments of uniforms, scattered weapons, web gear, rucksacks, bloody bandages, and dead people lying everywhere. The carnage, and the sheer number of bodies overwhelm me. We have never killed this many before, or lost so many of our own.

I'm exhausted, and my emotional defensive wall has crumbled. My mind is wandering through left field, picking flowers.

As I face the cold realities of yesterday's battle, and my part in it, my mind seeks flights of fancy and armchair philosophizing as a means of escape. I focus on trivial things, avoiding the deeper realities.

I find a couple of enemy soldiers lying in a ditch, very dead, and I'm amused by the fact that they both have new haircuts. The irony of it touches me. What a deal, get a new haircut to get killed in. I actually giggle.

I brood over the two dead soldiers for a while. It does seem like such a waste of time to get a haircut before being killed. In fact, all human endeavors seemed to be a waste of time for people who are just going to be killed anyway. Why does any of it matter? Why bother? We are all going to die anyway. Why eat, sleep, or even get dressed? Why not just stay in bed and die? It's going to happen anyway. Why not make it easy?

The two dead men look like tough, professional soldiers. I look down on them for a while, and I wonder ... could I have beaten them had I met them in that ditch? I thank God that I will never know.

I move on, and find a man killed by napalm, burned black like toast. His limbs are twisted and spidery, fused into unnatural positions by the heat. The flames have consumed his clothing, hair, and all human features. He is a sculpture made of charcoal, a tar baby, partially melted. He is swelling in the heat and beginning to crack open with a pattern like broken glass. The cracks reveal the oozing, inner-pink of him and the smell takes my breath away. I gag, swallow hard, and hurry on my way.

I wander deeper into the shell-plowed battlefield of yesterday, very tired and very humbled. I find dozens of bodies, some full of bullet holes and others blown apart by bombs and artillery with pieces scattered. My God, did I do this? Did I do even some of this?

I find a severed foot lying on the ground. There is no body anywhere close that I can see. The foot is naked and bare, no shoe and no sock, just a man's foot lying in the dust on top of the ground. It is a cold and lifeless object, shocking by what it represents and repulsive in its purple nakedness. I hesitate, and then walk around it. I don't want to be near it.

I'm overwhelmed by what I see and what I feel. My soul is in turmoil. Great joy and great sadness have experienced a head-on collision in my mind, and the result is a tangled wreck of emotions.

On the one hand, I am overjoyed that we won the fight. I revel in the victory. It makes a man feel powerful to win at mortal combat. Winston Churchill said that nothing is more exhilarating than to be shot at and missed. I can tell you that it's true. It's like being reborn. I'm so happy to be alive that I savor every breath of air.

But, there are dark emotions too. I feel deep sadness for the men we lost yesterday, and anger at our enemy for taking their lives. And, to further complicate the issue, in spite of myself, there is pity in me somewhere too, for all of those enemy soldiers lying dead in the dirt. I try to block that emotion with a door of resolution. I can't allow myself to feel pity for the men I helped to kill. There are others of their tribe still out there, and the job is not yet done. We will face them again soon.

And then too, at the very bottom of the dark, emotional swamp, I'm ashamed that I was so afraid when it came time to face those two men in that ditch. And, I feel terrible guilt about the injured man who couldn't breathe, and who died while in my care.

I push all of that aside for now. I don't want to think about it. I shift gears and the emotional roller coaster goes to the top again. I'm proud that I did my job, and did it well. As the artillery observer, I was a key player in our victory. I got the big shells in quickly and put them where they were needed most.

I'm amazed that I actually directed five batteries into that fight simultaneously. It was an impossible job, and I pulled it off, danger-close, without killing me or any of my friends. My old TAC Officers from OCS would be proud.

But then again, the roller coaster drops to the bottom. It is humbling, even embarrassing, to have survived that fight unhurt, and now to witness the full aftermath.

Strong emotions pulling in so many different directions are a form of psychological meltdown. It is mentally and physically exhausting. I feel so very tired.

I walk deeper into what is left of the shady grove of yesterday. There are still a few trees standing along the eastern edge of the park that offer just a little shade. It is cooler there, with less evidence of destruction. There are large clumps of splintered bamboo still standing, and even a few saplings relatively untouched by the shellfire. There are fewer bodies and fewer of our troops snooping through that area too. I go there, attracted by the promise of shade and the hope of fleeting solitude. I want to be alone for a while. I need to collect my thoughts, gather my wits, and put my emotional self back together. Who knows, I might even thank God that I am still alive. I walk along slowly, ambling, going nowhere really, just looking it over and feeling very tired.

And then, I hear a very distinct "Ka-click," and my heart stops cold. I know that sound! From somewhere very close to me, someone has just pushed a rifle bolt closed.

I stand very still, looking down at the ground, my breath sucked-up tight and my mind stunned numb. My God, was that really what I think it was? If so, I'm in big trouble!

My mind reaches out and holds my head down while I think about it. "Don't look for him," my mind said to me. "If you make eye contact he will know that you have seen him and he will kill you. He might not know that you heard him lock the rifle."

I'm caught in a trap, alone and exposed. I stand there, looking down at the toes of my dusty boots. My mind is racing. It starts to make sense. Of course, stupid, it is probably a wounded Gook who couldn't get out last night when all of his friends slipped away. He is hiding in a spider hole, or maybe in one of the many clumps of shredded bamboo. He must be hidden pretty well too, or I would have seen him already.

"He doesn't want to shoot," my mind said, trying to be calm and practical. "He knows that if he shoots, he's dead too. My guys will get him."

My mind is having this very reasoned, intellectual discussion with my body that is frozen in fear and waiting to be killed. My guts are tied in knots. I'm breathing very shallow like someone already in great pain.

I quickly look up at the sky. It is deep Asian blue and filled with great, billowing white clouds. Everything is clean, cool, and beautiful up there. It looks peaceful and inviting. Is this the day, and is this the time? I try to be brave, but I mourn. Dear God, I don't want to die!

I take a deep breath, turn on my heel, and walk away. I walk slowly back the way I came, trying to act as if nothing has happened. I'm holding my breath and my mind is braced for the impact. My back is as taut as a bowstring. I fully expect, at any moment, to feel hot metal sever my spine. The irony of it catches me. My God, I'm the one waiting for the bullet this time!

It doesn't happen. I simply walk away.

Back at the CP, I sit down heavily on the ground in the shade of the ACAV. Everyone is busy and no one speaks or pays any attention. A helicopter has landed and our guys are passing captured weapons and other booty to the eager crewmembers. Men are talking, laughing, and joking with one another. They are flush with victory and happy to be alive.

The world is filled with different realities. I'm trembling, and completely spent. I light a cigarette with shaky hands and look up at the clean, blue sky. What now?

I think about it as I struggle to put my emotions back on the tracks. What are the options? Do I go back with a squad of soldiers and kill him now ... or what? I wonder; can I watch him die, and be responsible for his death, knowing that he let me live? Can I ever look myself in the eye again if I do that? Do I owe that man something now, or is he really just a snake to be killed wantonly, in spite of his foreign humanity?

And then another thought. Is that man now looking up at the clean, white clouds too, and praying to God that he did the right thing by letting me walk away? I smoke my cigarette and kick it around in my mind for a while. I have a big decision to make.

Slowly, I begin to talk myself out of it. I remind myself that I really didn't see an enemy soldier. I don't know that he is there for sure. I only suspect it. In fact, I might have imagined the whole thing. Maybe I didn't hear that rifle bold snap closed after all. Maybe it was something else. Maybe it was nothing at all. Maybe I'm beginning to see and hear things that aren't really happening. Maybe I'm shell-shocked and getting Froggy. Maybe I'm sliding off the tracks of reality like that old war veteran from my childhood, Leonard Allred.

I decide that it would be embarrassing to sound the alarm, gather a fire team, and charge in there to kill an enemy who isn't there. The troopers would all think I'd gone nuts, and maybe they would be right. Just a few days before, during a brief firefight, I had reported seeing an enemy soldier go down, but when we swept in to count the body, we could find no trace that he had ever been there. I was shocked, and humiliated too. It was scary. Maybe I was going crazy. I couldn't let something like that happen ever again. My Captain might have me sent back to the States in a straight jacket.

I decide to let it lie. I will do nothing and hope that it didn't really happen. But then, if you really are there, wounded enemy soldier, I hope you make it. Thank you, for my life.

While I'm sitting there in the shade, brooding about it all, Captain Daniels yells at me to come over to where he is standing. He has wandered away from the CP a few yards and is standing over a fighting hole dug into the side of a deep ravine. I find him standing over the body of an enemy soldier who is still sitting in the hole. The man is dead over a rifle that still points at a burned-out tank just a few yards away. The flies have found the dead man, and they climb in and out of his ears and happily buzz around his head and shoulders. The buttons on the man's shirt are drawing tight as his body swells in the tropical heat. Soon they will pop off.

The enormity of what we did yesterday is soaking into the Captain too, and like me, he seems to be philosophizing and seeking a path for his mind to escape. "Look at this," he says, as he sweeps his arm in a wide arc, as if to introduce me for the first time to the world of shattered trees and shattered bodies. "Look at this, Mac ... this is unbelievable!" And then he looks down at the dead enemy soldier and says, "My God, Lieutenant, what's it like for their side?" His voice trails off into space as he ponders it.

And then he looks back at me with deep, brooding eyes, and he says, "What's this doing to my troopers, Niner-two? My troopers are just kids."

The irony of what he said settled over me immediately, but I saw no reason to smile. I knew what he meant.

Many times in the years that followed, I would think back to what he said, where we were, and what we were doing when he said it. I was twenty-one that summer, my Captain just a few years older. We were not kids ... not anymore. We were old soldiers.

Thunder III

About a week after the big fight at Xom Moi (2), I was promoted to First Lieutenant. It was a standard, time-in-rank promotion and not a reward of any kind. Rank was easy to acquire in the expanding Army of 1968.

In early June, we went back into the Iron Triangle for the third time since the beginning of the Tet offensive. It was the monsoon season now, the season of wet and hot. It rained the whole time we were there.

I had never imagined anything like the monsoon rains of the jungle. The rain fell as hot water and it was like being in a Sauna all the time. The air temperature and the humidity were both over 100. We were always soaked clear through, and half of the wet was perspiration and not rainwater.

There was a mist that went up out of the jungle, so thick and dense with warm moisture that it was hard to breathe. Warm water fell as rain, dripped down from the overhanging foliage, and then immediately evaporated back into the air as hot steam while it was still raining. It was like living and working in a pressure cooker. The mist cut visibility in the thick foliage to a distance of only a few yards, and we never knew what might be hiding in the vapors.

It was a tough environment for tanks. The red mud was slippery, a thick, greasy slime of jungle clay mixed with hot water. Our tanks and tracks were almost helpless. We were not very effective as tiger hunters during that trip.

The warm water ruined most of our personal gear and we couldn't keep our weapons dry and free from rust. My cigarettes got wet through the cellophane wrapper while sealed inside a plastic box in my shirt pocket under my flak jacket. We got raw, open sores on our shoulders from the wet chafing of the heavy flak jackets, and I found maggots in my toothbrush holder. The inside of the tanks and tracks, where we lived, ate and slept, were covered with greasy red mud, tracked in by army boots.

I spent five days and nights in the hot rain without being able to get dry or change clothes, and like a fool, I didn't take my boots off the whole time. Because of the Tet Offensive in early February, I had missed my in-country orientation where they cautioned soldiers about such things, and I didn't know that I had made a big mistake until it was time to change clothes. When I finally did get a chance to change my wet clothes, the skin on my inner-arms, inner-legs, and feet came off with the clothing. Big slabs of wrinkled, waterlogged, bathtub-skin came off like huge, peeling, second-degree burn blisters. The Army had a name for it. They called it "Jungle Rot." It was a painful condition, the raw soreness compounded by the chafing of any type of clothing.

I didn't make a big deal about it. I didn't want to leave the unit to spend time in a stinking hospital or infirmary when I wasn't wounded. A fighting man should have some pride. It would be embarrassing to be sidelined with anything less than an honorable wound. Luckily, I had a place on an armored vehicle and I didn't have to walk much. I was sure I could tough it out, and I did. I'm probably lucky that I didn't get a serious infection, maggots, or even worse. I bummed a variety of salves, ointments, and disinfectants from the local medics, but most of it I couldn't use. Anything alcohol-based caused excruciating pain. To use Calamine lotion was like being boiled in oil.

On the fifteenth of June, as we came back out of the Triangle all covered with mud and raw sores, I was informed that I was being sent back to Division Artillery. The Colonel was nice about it, and he thanked me for my service, but he said he thought I had used up all of my second chances. I was the senior FO in the Fourth Cavalry by then, the only one not wounded or killed after serving through the Tet Offensive and the chaotic months immediately following.

In Vietnam, the standard combat assignment for an officer and a Forward Observer was six months in the field. I was pulled off the line after serving only four. No one ever said it, but I think part of the reason I was reassigned early was because I was getting shaky. I had been in constant combat for four months, with heavy responsibilities and under great stress. I desperately needed a rest and a chance to re-charge my batteries.

But, I felt like a traitor when the time came to leave that unit. I had traveled through the valley of the shadow with those men and they needed me. The troopers had faith in me, and they looked to me to lay down that magic carpet of fire and steel that turned the tide of battles. And then, who would look after Robert Ivie and Jerry Poirier now that Sergeant Mobley and I wouldn't be there to do it?

Who would know to start a fire mission before the Captain knew he needed it? Who would put the big shells where they were needed most? Who would know to use Willie Peter in the dark to panic and scatter the barbarian hordes, or to shoot the back azimuth to clobber the enemy mortar crew? Who would know to borrow a shirt with sergeant stripes so he could buy the guys a beer in the NCO Club when the snooty Officer's Club wouldn't let them in? Who could possibly replace me?

I felt terribly guilty leaving that unit. Those good men who drove the tanks and fired the machine-guns had to stay on the line for a whole year. And, I felt guilty that I had not been wounded. It was embarrassing to leave that unit without a Purple Heart. Few men got to pack their bags and walk away from "B" Troop while I was there. Most were carried out on stretchers. To walk away with my duffle bag over my shoulder made me feel like somehow I hadn't done my job. Had I been a good trooper, I would have been carried out like the rest of them.

I was disappointed too, when I met my replacement. He was a brand new Second Lieutenant, fresh from the States. He was as green as grass, scared to death, and completely overwhelmed by his new assignment. He was everything I had been just seventeen weeks before.

There was a great void between us now, this new guy and me. He was the picture of anxious innocence - I was the old combat veteran. I was experienced, knowledgeable, and skilled. I had kicked the devil in the ass ... and touched the face of God. This new man could never replace me.

This new man could sit in my place, use my radio, and take my job, but he didn't know what I knew, and he would never measure up. And, I tried to be compassionate, but I couldn't feel pity for him knowing that his perfect incompetence might put my cavalry troopers in danger. For the first time, I began to understand how the First Sergeant had felt about me when I first showed up as the new replacement: "Good God, not another one!"

I was assigned to a self-propelled, 155mm gun battery at a fire support base called Thunder III. The First Division had a whole string of fire support bases along Highway 13 between Saigon and the Cambodian border. Thunder III was one of many. It was between Chaun Thaun and An Loc.

As an experienced First Lieutenant, I was given the job of Fire Direction Officer. The guy I replaced had been relieved of duty. He was in the process of being court-martialed for making a mathematical error and killing a couple of friendly troops. Remember, there were no computers or hand-held calculators in those days. Everything was done with slide rules and long division. When you were tired and under stress, it was easy to make a mistake.

At first, I was afraid of my new job. Fire Direction is a very safety sensitive and mathematically intense occupation. And, the Army is unforgiving when mistakes are made. I also had to train a whole new FDC (Fire Direction Center) crew because the old bunch had been reassigned after the "friendly fire" incident when their officer was court-martialed. It was a tough job. I had to bury myself in the books and learn all over again what they had taught me in OCS. Somehow, and with the help of some good people working for me, I managed to pull it off.

There were about 200 men serving at that lonely jungle outpost: one artillery battery, a rifle platoon of infantry, and a platoon of four "Dusters," twin-barreled, forty-millimeter anti-aircraft guns mounted on tank chassis, to help with perimeter defense. We also had overlapping artillery support from other nearby firebases if we needed it. Our mission was to provide that same artillery support to other units, and to help keep the road open.

There were some good men at Thunder III, but the attitude and the "feel" of the place was creepy after what I had come to know with the cavalry. Those men were not aggressive, frontline combat soldiers, and to me, it was like being demoted to the second string - the junior varsity team.

And, those innocent artillery soldiers didn't know it, but they were all on the short list to die. The only reason they were still alive was because the NVA had willed it. I saw the perimeter defense as inadequate, and the soldiers who guarded the wire were laid-back amateurs ... at least the artillery troops who held part of that responsibility. On my first inspection of the perimeter defenses, I found a man on guard duty without a bolt in his rifle. He had lost it weeks ago and didn't report it because he was afraid of "getting into trouble." He had stood guard for weeks in a combat zone with a non-functioning rifle. No officer or NCO had ever checked his weapon. It was a bad sign of how the unit functioned. I wanted to have the guy court-martialed, but the Captain gave him an Article 15 (in-unit disciplinary action) instead. It was just as well. It was the Captain who should have been court-martialed.

And, I noticed immediately, that while there were wooden sidewalks everywhere to keep the soldiers up and out of the mud, there was no overhead cover on many of the hooches (sandbagged cabins). The Mess Hall and several of the sleeping/living quarters were only sandbagged walls with canvas tents for overhead cover. An artillery air bust or a few well-placed mortar rounds in the middle of the night could have wreaked havoc on that outfit. I couldn't believe that those men were fighting the same war that my cavalry squadron had been fighting. Had the line troops been that lax, they would have all been dead. I decided that the NVA didn't want Thunder III, and neither did I.

And then, to make matters even worse, my new commander was a charlatan who spent most of his time sucking-up to the Colonel. Everything he did at that base was done for show. The place had to look good from the air so that when the Colonel flew over, everything looked tidy, clean, and ready for inspection. It didn't seem to matter to him that we couldn't hold the perimeter. He had never seen real combat and he didn't expect that it would ever happen.

Our Captain actually held formations in that jungle outpost in the early morning hours. He lined his soldiers up in long, neat rows and had a head-count. He stood in front of the assembled ranks and dictated his orders for the day as if he were at an army base in the States. I was outraged. In a jungle outpost in a combat zone, it was a criminal act that endangered his men.

I pointed out to him that one enterprising VC with a machine-gun could simply wait for our morning formation, position himself to have good enfilading fire down our lines, and with one belt of ammunition he could take out most of our unit before we could react. The Captain only laughed and told me I had a great imagination. I became very creative at finding excuses to dodge his morning formations. I really expected it to happen.

In many ways, I was more afraid while serving at Thunder III than I was when attacking fortified positions on an ACAV. It is a curse to be a combat soldier with an imagination. I could see all the ways we were vulnerable. Having met the devil with the cavalry, I worried about it constantly.

The VC did throw a few mortar rounds into our perimeter late one night, and our fearless leader got a chance to show his stuff. As we braced to defend our weak perimeter, our Captain was nowhere to be found. He told one of his junior officers later that he had been "pinned down" by the mortar fire and unable to make it to the CP. He came slinking in ten or fifteen minutes later, in full combat gear, when it was apparent that the shelling had stopped and the bad guys were not coming through the wire.

I didn't get to read his after-action report to his superiors, and I can only guess what it had to say. I didn't know until a few weeks later that he had turned himself in for a Bronze Star and a Purple Heart.

I didn't see the recommendations, but I'm sure our Captain gave himself a Bronze Star for being the big man in charge who, by his heroic leadership, repelled the enemy attack and saved us all. In reality, there was no attempt by the VC to even probe our perimeter – thank God. And then, the man had scraped his elbow diving for cover. He felt that qualified him for the same decoration Sergeant Mobley and Jimmy McBroon were awarded for giving their lives. He shamelessly turned it in for a Purple Heart.

His "concern for his personal safety" under fire, and his shameless exploitation of his command position and a few drops of mistakenly spilled blood to win medals, only added to my reasons to have contempt for the man.

It is sad, but in Vietnam, a lot of medals were awarded in that same shameful way. Medals are good for a soldier's career, and some officers were prone to give them to themselves or to each other. Senior staff officers were often tolerant of the shameless self-promotion. Medals are good for troop morale ... and they don't cost much.

By the time my Captain's shiny new Bronze Star arrived at the unit, a month or so later, I was serving as his Executive Officer. He ordered me to pin the medal on him at a special awards ceremony to be held in front of all his troops. Thankfully, someone at division had turned down his request for a counterfeit Purple Heart.

Pinning a medal on that man was the most distasteful thing I was ever ordered to do as an officer. It was hard for me not to show complete disdain. The Captain knew how I felt, but he didn't care. His assembled soldiers all knew that he didn't deserve the decoration, and they too were filled with sore contempt. I could never understand how a man could wear a badge of honor after winning it with dishonesty.

In late August, I went to Hawaii to meet Jeannie for five days of R&R (rest and relaxation). It was the halfway point in my tour of duty. She flew in from California and I flew in from Saigon. We met in Honolulu. It was good to see her again.

Each soldier in Vietnam was given a five day R&R sometime during his yearlong tour. The Army paid the soldier's transportation to some exotic place like Thailand, Singapore, Australia, the Philippines, or Hawaii. They would not let soldiers go back to the continental United States for R&R. They were worried that too many would go AWOL.

Those of us who were married always chose Hawaii. And, each soldier had to pay the full cost to get his wife there. The Army wouldn't cover it. We also had to pay all expenses while we were there. The Army did maintain a few "R&R centers," but the facilities were very limited in space and services for the large number of troops who wanted to use them. Most of us didn't bother.

For Jeannie and me, it was our second honeymoon. It was beautiful Hawaii, and it should have been a delightful, fun-filled and exciting time, but it wasn't. The shadow of the war followed us everywhere. And, I was exhausted. I spent most of the time sleeping. I slept in the hotel room and on the sandy beaches of Waikiki. We didn't go to a Luau or to see the Polynesian dancers and I didn't care. It was wonderful just to be with her again, able to sleep all I wanted, and not be responsible whether people lived or died.

Instead of going with big groups of tourists, we spent most of our time alone, watching the sunset over the ocean from the veranda of our 22nd floor hotel room, or lying half-asleep on the warm ocean sand while the breakers roared and foamy water tickled at our bare feet.

Jeannie caught a lot of flak from her co-workers, friends, and family when she got home because she didn't "go anywhere or see anything" while she was there. People just didn't understand. We were not on vacation. We were holding hands across a battlefield. We knew that those five days might be the last days we would ever have together. Who cared about roasted pigs,

Polynesian dancers, and some sleepy-eyed crooner named Don
Ho? It was hard to laugh and have a good time while counting
down the hours until we would be separated again. Sightseeing
and crowded tourist destinations were not high on our agenda.

Jeannie was beautiful in Hawaii, and just the way I always
saw her at night in the jungle. She came to me often during
those long, scary nights. Whenever I closed my eyes, I could
always imagine her smiling face and feel her presence near. In
my dreams she was a Goddess with long, flowing hair, silk lace
and perfume. Now, for a few short days in Hawaii, it was real.

But, in Hawaii, I was hesitant to be intimate with her. We
were still newlyweds and still getting used to the intimacy and
the physical sharing of the relationship. The nasty skin condition from the jungle followed me to Hawaii and I was terribly
embarrassed about it. It had been eight weeks, but the raw ugliness of it was still only partially healed. Had I been able to do so,
I would have postponed my R&R for another month or more to
give myself more time to heal.

Jeannie was wonderful about it all. She was understanding,
thoughtful, compassionate, and reassuring. As I struggled to
apologize and explain, she put a finger to my lips and told me to
be still, and then she came to me as the fulfillment of all my
dreams. In the days that followed, we were delighted to discover
that the jungle rash was not contagious.

Luckily, while in Hawaii, we found that warm sunshine
helped to take the rash away. I laid out on the clean ocean sand
in my swimming trunks and let the warm sunshine work its
magic on my arms and legs.

We rented a car one morning and toured the island. I
bought her a pink bikini and she actually wore it. She was a
sweet and modest little farm girl, and a bikini was an embarrassing thing for her to wear, even though she looked wonderful
wearing it. In perfect modesty, she wore a short, nightgown-

type swimsuit cover until we were all alone. She shared the beauty of her surfer-girl, bikinied self only with me, and it made me feel wonderful to be treated so special. We found a secluded little cove with a small patch of uninhabited beach, and we spent the afternoon there all by ourselves. It was great.

I took her to a fancy restaurant and we had a good laugh. The menu was in French and we didn't have a clue. And then, lurking in the shadows of the potted plants, some guy in a tuxedo was standing by with a towel over his arm like he was waiting to wash our dirty little paws or wipe caviar from our greasy little chins. We giggled, and Jeannie said he was standing by in case we were clumsy and spilled something.

I did spill something when the guy in the potted plants leaned over my shoulder unannounced and struck a cigarette lighter in my face to light my smoke. I was only a few hours out of the jungle, and the sudden, unexpected flash made me duck and cover. I kicked the table hard, spilling water glasses and scattering silverware across the floor. All over the restaurant, highbrow people in proper evening attire stared at us in upper-crust disgust, and we fled the place like the out-of-place hillbillies that we were.

We did have a good laugh about it, and then found an eatery that was more in tune with our social class. What that snooty personnel clerk in basic training had told me was true after all. I certainly wasn't upper class when it came to high-brow restaurants.

All too soon, our five-day second honeymoon was over and we had to catch airplanes that were pointed in different directions. It was hard to leave her again. She was brave and held her tears until I couldn't see. I hope I did the same. She flew east and I flew west, and our married life was put on hold for a second time. In six months we would have a third honeymoon, if God willed it, and the bad guys continued to miss.

Thunder III

I watched the blue Pacific roll past beneath the wings of the big 707 as I headed back toward the valley of the shadow. I was very much afraid this time ... more so than I had been the first time. I had met the devil, and I knew what to expect this time. I asked God to take care of my Jeannie, and I asked him to help me be brave.

It was terrible going back to Thunder III. I hated the place and I had no respect for the man I was working for. I was afraid to go back there too. I knew how vulnerable the place was, and how easily a good NVA unit could take it. As a self-defense measure, I started looking for a way out.

On the first day of September, I was moved out of FDC and made Executive Officer of the gun battery. I was now the #2 artilleryman at Thunder III, just one step below my war hero Captain. To celebrate, I called Division Artillery and volunteered to be a full-time AO. I was turned down. It was a popular job and there was a waiting list.

I spent the next month and five days at Thunder III, shooting 155s in support of infantry and cavalry FOs in the field, planning, plotting, and shooting H&I (harassment and interdiction) fires at night, and running ammunition convoys between our lonely outpost and the big ammo dump in Bien Hoa. It rained all the time. My spirits were as soggy as my boots.

Staff Officer

In September, I got word through the grapevine that my old unit, the Quarter Cavalry, was in need of an Artillery Liaison Officer. The man who replaced Captain Rice had been killed in a mid-air collision between two helicopters. The job called for a Captain.

I was but a humble First Lieutenant, but I figured what the hell, I had nothing to loose and everything to gain by asking. I called the unit commander on the telephone and volunteered for the job. I told the new cavalry Colonel about my prior service with the unit, and asked him to talk to his staff for references. I had been gone only three months and some of my old friends were still there. The Colonel seemed to be impressed, and he said he would get back to me.

A few days later, the cavalry Colonel called me back and told me he was fixing it up with Division Artillery. As soon as the orders were cut and the artillery people found a replacement for me at Thunder III, I would be back in the cavalry. I danced an Irish Jig all around the commo shack.

I wrote Jeannie a letter and told her what was up, but I twisted the truth just a little. I told her the Colonel had offered me the job. (Actually, he did, after I had asked him, if I could have it.) I hoped Jeannie wouldn't be disappointed that I was going back to a line unit. I had promised her that I wouldn't volunteer for anything.

On October 6, I joined the Fourth Armored Cavalry at Quan Loi as the newest member of the squadron headquarters staff. I was the new Artillery Liaison Officer. I had Captain Rice's old job ... and I was thrilled.

As a member of the headquarters staff, I attended all the briefings and planning sessions. I was a Combat Section Leader, and I directed the actions of the Forward Observers on the ground (three of them, one for each troop). I also had three staff people working for me who monitored radios, manned our headquarters track, and took turns at all-night vigils keeping an eye on things. I pre-planned and coordinated artillery support for all of the cavalry operations, and served as an aerial artillery spotter when needed. I flew with the Colonel on his Command and Control Helicopter where we could share maps and communicate face-to-face. I was a key player in the organization. It was a great assignment.

On my very first day back with the cavalry, we had a big fight near Quan Loi. I recorded that we fired 2,612 artillery rounds that day, and our body count number was only 43. But, it was okay. We did the best we could. In the jungle, bad guys on foot are tough targets. For my first time in Vietnam, I directed some of the artillery fire from a helicopter. In my new job, I would be flying often.

To fly over that country was an incredible experience. Vietnam was a moonscape. There were bomb craters and shell holes everywhere. America dropped more bombs on that poor, third world country than were dropped by all sides on all fronts during World War II. I don't know if anyone ever figured up the total number of artillery rounds expended during that conflict. As mentioned earlier, my small unit fired over twenty-six hundred in a single day.

There were no industrial targets, railroads, cities, or bridges to flatten in South Vietnam. All of that ordinance went into the countryside, aimed at shadows and trees where the bad guys might be hiding. I thought it was a terrible waste of munitions and treasure. The cost of it must have been staggering. Each shell crater cost hundreds of American dollars to dig, and the whole land was pockmarked as if scarred by disease. From the air, much of the countryside north and west of Saigon looked like those bombed-out tropical islands from the South Pacific battlefields of World War II.

Great swaths of forest, fields, and jungle were battered, torn, and disfigured terribly by the incredible destruction. It looked as if a great hailstorm of meteorites had rained down over the land, impacting into the soft dirt below. The holes were everywhere and they were numberless. There were big craters, little craters, and middle-sized craters. Some were old and eroded by rain with weeds and bushes growing around the edges. Others were new with clean, fresh dirt recently exposed. Most of the holes were filled with stagnant, dirty water, a breeding place for mosquitoes, leeches, and disease. Nearby trees were broken, dead, and mangled.

Great swaths of jungle along all the major roadways had been "Rome Plowed." A Rome Plow was a bulldozer mounted with a special blade to cut down trees. The Rome plows cleared a "safety zone" along the roads to protect American convoys. In many places, the safety zones were two or three hundred yards wide on each side of the road.

In other places, whole sections of the country were defoliated with Agent Orange. The toxic chemical killed everything green and left whole forests dead and dying. The ugly gray and brown of it screamed at the heavens in agony. It was a terrible thing to witness. The residue of the chemicals washed into the rivers that provided sustenance for millions of humble people. The forests were defoliated so American and South Vietnamese soldiers could see into the trees to better aim our bombs and shells.

On October 16, the Cavalry surrounded and sealed off the little village of Thu Duc, northeast of Saigon. The intelligence wizards suspected that some of the villagers were VC militia. As an officer on the Colonel's staff, I was assigned to lead one of several "teams" of soldiers and Vietnamese Policemen to search the village. My team had about ten American soldiers, a Vietnamese interpreter, and a couple of South Vietnamese policemen. We were assigned one small section of the village. We worked our way from house to house, searching for weapons and any clues of VC involvement. I remember one house in particular. The people knew we were coming, and they were all huddled inside.

We walked in without knocking, irreverent, and without respect. The family was grouped tightly in a corner, clinging to one another: young man, young woman, and three little kids. They were terrified, and the children were crying. I pointed my rifle at the young man's navel and ordered my soldiers to search the house.

My people went to work, sorting through bedding, digging through boxes, poking into corners, and probing the grass ceiling with fixed bayonets. While they worked, one of the Vietnamese policemen talked to the young father. I didn't understand the words, but I understood the tone and the body language. The cop was rude and condescending. He was feeling cocky, being backed-up by my rifle and the ring of tanks around the hamlet.

I stood there for a long time with my rifle pointed at that little family while my people sorted through the intimate corners of their lives, and while I did, something died inside of me. I was so ashamed. I looked into that young man's face and I saw fear and utter humiliation in his countenance. I was violating his home, his family, and his manhood - and he was helpless. I was shaming him in front of his wife and little children. "My God," I thought to myself. "No wonder they hate us."

I thought of how I would feel, and what I would do, if the situation was reversed and that young man was the one holding the rifle. I decided that some things are surely more painful than dying. I knew that if it were my home and family being violated, I would do anything to get revenge and redeem my self-respect. I realized for the first time that we were the best recruiters the Viet Cong had. By our callousness, we were chasing our friends into the ranks of our enemy. There was no way we could win this war.

I looked into that young man's eyes as his little family clung to him for comfort and protection. He was trying hard to be brave and to put up a good front for his wife and children. He was also struggling to hide his hatred for me, so as not to provoke me, but I could clearly see the rage behind the terror in his eyes.

I was deeply embarrassed, and I mourned, deep down inside where no one would ever see. But, I held the rifle firm, aimed surely at his brooding heart. I stood my ground in spite of my misgivings, and waited for my soldiers to do their duty. I was an Officer and a Gentleman, following orders. I had been given a mission to fulfill and I was ever faithful.

We found nothing of interest in that humble, little home. We moved on to the next house, and then the next adventure. I never saw him again, but that young man's eyes have haunted me for almost forty years.

I often directed artillery fire from the air during those months I flew with the Cavalry Colonel, sometimes from the command and control Huey and at other times from an Oh-6 "loach" from the cavalry air wing. The term "loach" stemmed from the military acronym LOH that stood for "Light Observation Helicopter." As an experienced veteran, I often provided AO support for my FOs on the ground instead of calling the guy from Division Artillery.

In my file of Vietnam memories, one of those AO missions stands head and shoulders above all the others, and I didn't even get to shoot. I was with the headquarters section at the Dian Base camp when I got a call that one of our small units was in a fight and needed an AO as soon as possible. I volunteered to go. Dark Horse, our air wing, sent a loach to pick me up. They radioed ahead that the observer's radio was on the blink and I would need to bring my own. I commandeered a backpack, PRC-25 radio and caught a ride to the helipad.

The LOH touched down and I jumped into the rumble seat. We were airborne immediately. The "rumble seat" on the early model OH-6 was built into the side of the helicopter. There was no door, just a single seat tucked tightly into the side of the ship. The seat faced out the side of the helicopter and the space was shallow and cramped. The observer in the rumble seat had no direct, physical contact with the two pilots who were in another compartment and facing forward.

As we zoomed off into the wild blue yonder, I tucked my backpack radio and map case under my arm and fumbled for the seatbelt. There was none. My God! I was winging my way into the clouds, sitting sidesaddle on a thin strap of nylon webbing and I didn't have a seatbelt! I flipped the switch on the headset to intercom and talked to the pilots. They said they knew there was no seatbelt back there, but not to worry, centrifugal force would keep me in. I asked if that were true, why were they all buckled up. No one answered.

The pilots had much more room than I did. They were facing forward and they each had a closed door and a Plexiglas bubble wrapped around them. I had no door, and the toes of my boots were sticking out over nothing. The wind was making my eyes water. My whole seat compartment was pressed into smooth, polished aluminum, and I had nothing to hold on to.

My guts sucked up tight enough to take my breath away as the full realization of what was happening soaked into me. I locked my elbows against the metal sides of the seat compartment and tried to still my thundering heart. I had flown in the rumble seats of OH-6s before, with a belt, and never had any problems. I told myself that if I were calm and reasonable, it would be all right. I closed my eyes and breathed deeply, trying to gain control of my panic.

Some people have phobias. A phobia is an unreasonable fear. Some people are afraid of water; others fear spiders, rats, or snakes. My unreasonable fear is a fear of heights. I can fly in airplanes and helicopters and usually do all right, but when on tall buildings, ladders, and vertical walls, my knees and my heart fail me. The one thing I could never do in my military training was to rappel down the face of a cliff. I was not cut out to be an Airborne Ranger.

And now, I found myself at two thousand feet, sitting in the rumble seat of a frisky little helicopter, looking down at the fast-moving ground with nothing between me and the jungle floor but air. I was perfectly panicked. I was suffering vertigo, a light-headed dizzy feeling brought on by panic and fear. I was afraid I would pass out.

We got over the battle area and it was time for me to hook up the radio and coordinate with the troops on the ground. The portable radio was wedged under my right arm and against the back of the seat. I was terrified, and I couldn't let go with my elbows to tune the channels or fish for the hand-held radio mike. There was no way I was going to be able to use a map.

And then, the pilot went into a tight, slanted orbit so I could better see the ground. When he did, the floor of the helicopter moved out from under me and I was left still sitting on the seat, but looking down at the jungle from an inverted, 45 degree angle.

The pilots were right, centrifugal force was keeping me in the helicopter, but my fingernails were leaving scratchy marks on the aluminum fuselage and my heart was so high in my throat I couldn't swallow. I felt as weak as a canary and the world was framed in inky blackness. I was going into shock. I fought to retain consciousness.

In panic, I keyed the intercom mike and told the pilots to take me home. They were incredulous. What the hell were we doing there if I wasn't going to direct the artillery? I told them I couldn't do it, and they had better get me down damn fast or I was going to pass out.

We peeled out of orbit and headed back to Dian. The pilot radioed the helipad to have a medic standing by, his AO was sick. He told the truth.

We touched down on the tarmac and I stepped out onto solid ground. My whole body was trembling and I was so weak I could hardly stand. The pilot took off immediately, without even speaking to me, and went winging back toward Dark Horse headquarters and the Officer's Club. The medic wasn't there.

I went back to the headquarters section and got on the radio to see if my failure to respond had resulted in any friendly casualties. I was happy to discover that close air support from helicopter gunships had accomplished what I had failed to do. It all turned out okay and I was happy.

From then on, whenever I got in a helicopter, I checked the seatbelt before I ever sat down.

I spent a lot of time in November and December in the base camp areas of Phu Loi, Dian, and Lai Khe, coordinating the activities of individual Forward Observers in small unit actions. Things were fairly quiet as far as the war went, and our cavalry units were being sent out in small, platoon-sized detachments to guard convoys and bridges or to support various small unit operations. The headquarters section didn't go out very often. The Paris Peace Talks were in the early stages and we were not involved in any big task force operations or major, full-squadron offensive sweeps like we had been doing following the Tet Offensive earlier in the year. It was a different kind of war now.

I spent a lot of time on "radio watch," monitoring other people who were out in the bushes and standing by in case they needed help. It was good duty. Often, we were on radio watch at night, and quite frequently, we stayed up all night. Nothing sums-up the experience better than a letter I wrote to Jeannie during one of those long and boring nights.

November 10, 1968

Sweet Regina,

It's two o'clock A.M. and I've got my bayonet propped under my chin to keep my head up. If things get any worse, I'll have to scotch tape my eyelids open. We have some people out on an ambush patrol tonight and I'm sitting here on radio watch waiting for something to happen.

Things are hunky-dory here. No rain for a while. It's been hot as hell. I spent the day lying in a big mud puddle with a couple of stray dogs. Too damn hot to get up and do much.

I think I told you I got the powder and stuff you sent. My feet and other interesting parts of me have all cleared up now. Now if I can just get rid of the fungus in my bellybutton and the spider web cracks in my ears, I'll be all right.

Do you remember the can of powder that belonged to you that I dragged back here from Hawaii? I never did tell you about that, did I? Well ... I never really noticed how perfumed the stuff was until I got back to Thunder III. Yep, nine guys living in a three by five room, underground with a constant temperature of around 210 degrees. You know the scene, just a tangle of sweaty feet and armpits. So I go out one mosquito infested evening and take my monthly shower, and without much forethought, commences to spray my tender bod with that cute little pink powder can, and the wind comes up a little, and there's a scream from the bunker, and out tumbles a couple of wild-eyed GI's screaming "women! They're here, I can smell 'em." An they commences to come my way, guided by their noses, and nearly mob me, and I grab an ax handle, and begins to recon with 'em, an I lays a few heads open and more of 'em just keeps coming, an I climb up in the radar tower, naked, just me and the ax handle, and kicks 'em off the ladder as they come scratching and clawing to the top. And I sit there for three days and four nights before the rain washed me down a little and they lost the scent. It was terrible, terrible.

Well, my faithful chronometer says it's now three A.M., and nothing has happened yet. Guess maybe the gooks stayed home tonight. I sure would if I had the chance. I was telling Happy Dunlop, one of the guys here, the other day. Yessir, I says to Happy, I says, "Hap, you know when I get home I ain't never going nowhere, ever again. I'm just going to stay at home. Yvonir, I says, I'm gonna booby-trap the front gate, plant mines in the driveway, put punji pits all over the lawn, build a bunker in the basement, sandbag the living room, board up the windows, break all the lights, and sit wild-eyed in a corner with a grenade in each hand and just get used to being a civilian again."

It's 0335 now, and I just finished taping my eyelids back. The tape is pretty stout. I hope you like guys without eyebrows. I'm afraid mine will come off with the tape. Oh well ...

Did I tell you I'm composing my own songs to play on my guitar now? Yep, I wrote a real pretty one yesterday. I'm real proud of it. It's called "Stay out of the Wheat Field Grandma, you're going against the Grain." It's bound to be a best seller.

Well sweetheart, I guess I had better wake up one of my

guys to take over for a while before I fall off this chair and hurt myself. I've already smashed my nose and broke my lip by dozing off and hitting my face on the table. I'm so tired I've even quit swatting at the mosquitoes. I just sit here and growl at them. Guess I'll go pour some hot coffee over my head.

Take care honey, I love you.

Christmas was an adventure too. Bob Hope came to Lai Khe that year while we were there. We were looking forward to seeing the show, but they sent us out to protect the base while Bob Hope and the pretty women entertained the rear-echelon folks.

Our guys were angry. We lived in the field, and we had been promised a "stand down" for the holidays. The Bob Hope Show put us back in the jungle. There would be thousands of Remington's Rangers (typewriter soldiers), gathered into one great, juicy target, and they needed protecting. I was disappointed, but I understood it.

Most people in the States, who watched Bob Hope entertain the troops on TV, never realized that the combat soldiers were the ones who seldom got to see the shows. The line units were always sent out into the boondocks to provide "cover" for the event. Most of the "Grunts" who got to see the show at Lai Khe that year were flown in from units that were out of our area of operations.

The whole Quarter Cavalry went to the field, including the headquarters section, to protect Bob Hope. We spent most of a week patrolling the jungle, baiting the tiger, and sleeping on the ground. We heard about the show later, and were shown a few fuzzy, long-range photographs.

Another thing bothered me about that Christmas. We were supposed to have a truce between Christmas and New Years without any combat operations. It was a deal our government had made with the communists in Paris. But, as Christmas came and went, we continued to send out ambush patrols each night. I asked the Colonel about it, and he said it was easy to figure out. Before Christmas, we were sending out "offensive" ambush patrols. Now, for the Christmas truce, we were sending out "defensive" ambush patrols. He chuckled, as if it were a practical joke.

I didn't catch the humor. It was a clever play on words, but I was embarrassed to be a part of it. I always felt that men, armies, and nations, should be able to keep their word.

The Colonel was invited to a Christmas party given by one of the South Vietnamese Army units stationed nearby. He exercised his prerogative as Commander and sent me as his proxy. It was an adventure. I couldn't speak the language, had no idea what was on the menu, and could only smile and nod during polite conversation time. Luckily, there were a few other American officers there, and one of them was a Special Forces Captain who was fluent in the language. He acted as interpreter. He talked the rest of us through the menu and the protocols. The Vietnamese did show that they had a sense of humor. They made the Americans eat with chopsticks while their guys used knives and forks. It was a good move that helped to break the tension. Laughter is a universal language.

I was on radio watch on New Year's Eve. I was sitting at a radio table in a big armored vehicle parked outside the cavalry barracks at the Lai Khe Base Camp. At the stroke of midnight, there was a magnificent display of fireworks to welcome in the New Year.

From all around the base, people just started shooting. It seemed to be spontaneous, and it grew and grew into an explosive crescendo that rocked the Asian sky. Long ribbons of tracer bullets arched high into the air and winked out as they approached the stars. Parachute flares popped open and drifted down lazily, lighting up the New Year with a pale, yellow glow that shimmered over the buildings and the trees. There was the crack of rifle fire, the pop of pistols, and the happy CRUMP of grenades exploding beyond the wire. Everyone spilled out of the buildings and bunkers to watch it happen. No one tried to stop it.

From our vantage point atop the armored vehicle, we could see the same thing happening at other American camps all around us. The distant horizons were dotted with the faint glow of flares and the reaching, arching streamers of tracer bullets.

It was an appropriate celebration. 1968 was finally over. It had been a year like no other year. It had been a year of blood, turmoil, and contention that tore our nation apart. We had won the biggest battle of the Vietnam War, and yet, '68 was the year we lost the war on the streets of our own hometowns.

Bobby Kennedy and Martin Luther King had both been assassinated that year, and Lyndon Johnson had resigned in disgrace. Americans had fought Americans on the streets of our nation's cities and on the lawns of our college campuses. I had spent the whole year in the valley of the shadow where several of my friends had given their lives for their country. My beautiful young wife had spent three hundred and thirty dark nights all alone that year, watching the war on television while hoping to see or hear news of her far-away soldier husband.

Yes, I was glad to see 1968 come to an end. She was a blood-stained, ugly old witch, evil, hateful, and scarred by sore tribulations. It was good to see her die. As a nation and a people, we couldn't take much more of her.

It was good to change the calendar and make a new start. Things could only get better in 1969. If I could hang on until Saint Valentine's Day, I could go home to my sweetheart and put 1968 behind me.

The Freedom Bird

I extended my time in Vietnam by ten days so I could get out of the army at the end of my combat tour. It was Army policy that soldiers returning from the combat zone be processed out, instead of reassigned, if they had less than ninety days remaining on their enlistment. By extending my tour ten days, I qualified.

I left the cavalry at Dian on the ninth day of February 1969, and caught a ride on a supply convoy to Lai Khe to process out at Division Artillery. I was there for about three days. The last thing I had to do was have the commander of 8/6 Artillery sign my exit papers, stating that I had turned in all my gear, passed my medical exam, and was all squared away with payroll and travel orders. The man was a Lieutenant Colonel, and I went to his office with my papers in hand.

I had never met the guy, even though, on paper, he was my boss. When I went to see him, he was all business. He looked over my paperwork, and then he told me that he wouldn't sign until I had thrown a going-away party for him and his staff.

I was confused, and just a little angry. I was the one going away, and he was telling me that he wouldn't clear my departure until I had thrown a farewell party for him and his pals. I thought he had it backwards, and, the whole thing sounded like extortion to me. He smiled smugly and told me it was the "customary" thing to do.

I reminded him that I had spent my whole tour with the cavalry, and I didn't know him or any of his staff people. If I was

279

required to throw a party, he could surely understand that I would like to throw it for the people I knew and had served with. The Colonel was brusque and condescending. He reminded me that "technically," I was a member of "his" unit, and because of that fact, I owed him and his whole staff a big drunk.

I left the Colonel's office with my papers unsigned. I was furious. I couldn't get on an airplane for home without an authorizing signature. I was embarrassed too, and didn't know what to do. I didn't have the money to throw a staff party. Nearly everything I made was sent home for Jeannie to put in the bank. The Army provided everything overseas, and my self-imposed monthly spending allowance was very meager. I didn't have the means to throw a staff party if I had wanted to.

I was walking down the hallway from the Colonel's office, angry and completely distraught, when I passed the office of the Executive Officer. The Executive Officer was a Major, and he was sitting at his desk reading some papers. I slammed on the brakes and skidded to a stop on the freshly waxed floor. Hell yes, what did I have to loose? I turned on my heel and walked into the Major's office. I handed him my papers.

As the Major looked over my papers, I told him that if it was okay with him, with his permission, I would leave immediately and return to my old unit to say goodbye before catching my plane. The Major said sure, he understood, and then he signed my papers. I saluted, shook the man's hand, and then ran like hell. I went straight to the airfield and bummed a ride back to Dian on a Chinook helicopter. I looked over my shoulder for the next two days, waiting for the Colonel's goons to come for me with handcuffs and blackjacks. Lucky for me, it didn't happen.

Back at the Fourth Cavalry, I was able to have a small, farewell party with the staff. I did buy a round of drinks or two, but I was given much more than I gave. The cavalry soldiers were real people and I was proud to have a place among them.

The Freedom Bird

As I gathered my things to depart, I discovered that someone had broken into my footlocker in a storage room at cavalry headquarters. All of my wartime souvenirs were gone. I had collected a pair of Ho Chi Minh sandals made from truck tires and inner tubes, a couple of NVA officer's belts with brass buckles, a Chicom bayonet, a hand-forged VC belt knife, and a Russian artillery compass. Everything was gone, including some of my clothes, books, and photographs. They were never recovered.

On February 15, 1969, I caught the Freedom Bird for home. As I topped the ramp to enter the plane, a young stewardess in a mini-skirt was there to greet me. I remember she was a pretty girl, and she smelled like an escapee from a French Cathouse. All the stewardesses on that freedom flight were overplaying the girl thing, and it made the soldiers smile.

There were four or five mini-skirted stewardesses on that flight, and as we took our seats, they were all running around and trying to drum up some revelry. The stewardesses were wearing party hats and blowing those stupid noisemakers that people use on New Years Eve. The girls wanted everyone to smile and be happy. We were going home, and we should be celebrating.

But, we were a somber bunch. Most of us smiled tolerantly at the playful banter, but we weren't in the mood to celebrate yet. I don't know about the other guys, but getting on that airplane was bittersweet for me. I was highly emotional.

I was thrilled that my combat tour was over. I could go home now, to a beautiful young wife and a boundless future. But, I was suffering survivor's guilt. I couldn't stop thinking about Mobley, Glowacky, Yamashita, Greendyke, Captain Serio, Sergeant Williams, and dozens of others whose names I didn't even know. Those good men would never catch a Freedom Bird ... and I felt guilty. Their blood would forever stain that dark and forbidding land, and the shadow of their lost lives took the sparkle out of my going home celebration. All the way home I was moody and glum.

The American Army committed a terrible mistake by sending us home like that. There was no decompression, no debriefing, no counseling, and no further contact with anyone from the military. In World War II and Korea, American soldiers went home on troop ships that took most of a month to cross the ocean. The soldiers were with people they knew, and they had time to wind down and sort out the experience with others who had been there to share their burdens. There was a transitional period between combat and homecoming. In Vietnam, we went from the combat zone to California within the space of 26 hours.

And, we went alone. There was no one to share our experiences or anxieties with. We went to Vietnam alone, and we flew out of there alone, even though the airplane was filled with other soldiers. We went as individuals and not as units. The people sitting next to you were strangers who had served with different outfits, doing something else, at a place you never heard of. They didn't know the things you knew. They hadn't seen the things you had seen. They didn't know the people you knew.

There was no one to talk to who could properly relate to your personal experiences. There was no one to share your joy, triumphs, guilt, misgivings, or anxieties with. There was no one to offer a different perspective or a second opinion as to why or how certain things had happened. On that airplane we were isolated, each one of us. The emotions and anxieties of war were buried deep in every heart, and we dealt with it in our own private ways.

Most of us were still shell-shocked and highly charged when turned out on the streets as civilians. It was dangerous, and damaging to our psychological selves. We suddenly found ourselves in a world where we didn't fit. We were openly criticized, and often ostracized, for having served in Vietnam. And, many of our civilian friends and neighbors let us know that we should be ashamed.

It has always been tough for soldiers to deal with the aftermath of war. Most societies have rituals they perform to exorcise the ghosts of anxiety and guilt from those they send to be warriors. Some cultures have homecoming parades. Others have scalp dances around the campfire where those who have carried the burdens of the conflict can be welcomed home and honored by the tribe. The public show of acceptance and honor does more than make a soldier proud. It validates his sacrifice and puts the societal stamp of approval on the things he was called to do. It restores his self-respect and his sense of worth within the society.

When the people you were fighting for, and who sent you there, now ignore you, or worse yet, now tell you that you did the wrong thing and you should be ashamed, the effects can be psychologically devastating.

And, a lot of us were emotionally scarred by the Vietnam experience itself. For a long time after I came home, I was incapable of feeling strong emotion. Nothing reached the heights or depths of where my emotional triggers were set. I couldn't feel deep happiness, anger, sorrow, or pity. I was numb in the civilian world.

I was accustomed to such a wide range of highs and lows in my emotional life that nothing in the civilian world could touch me. Nothing reached the high emotion of mortal combat, and nothing sank to the spiritual lows of helplessly holding a friend as his blood soaked into the dirt and the light went out of his eyes. I was numb to everything in the emotional middle range of civilian life. The flames of war had cauterized my emotional connectors. I couldn't cry at funerals and I couldn't laugh at jokes. I was incapable of showing deep love, deep sadness, or even deep anger. I couldn't be goaded into a fistfight, and yet I worried that I might kill someone if properly provoked. I kept a loaded gun close at hand everywhere I went. To Jeannie I was a stranger. I didn't understand what had happened to me for a long time.

As our Freedom Bird lifted off the runway and escaped into the clean, blue sky, a lusty cheer went up from the soldiers on that plane. For a few moments there was a backslapping celebration, and then everyone settled down into the boring routine of flying home. There were no books or in-flight movies, just a set of headphones that played the same pop-music tape over, and over, and over again. Even today, when I hear Otis Redding sing, "Dock of the Bay," it takes me back to the blue Pacific, white billowing clouds, and silver wings out the window. Most of us retreated deep inside ourselves and semi-hibernated during that long flight home.

I never closed my eyes during that twenty-six hour flight. I watched day turn to night and night turn to day again over the ocean. I watched silver wings glide over distant blue water, and replayed the whole Vietnam experience over and over again in my mind. God had been good to me. I could have been killed, many times.

We finally touched down in California. We landed at the Army's Oakland Air Terminal and taxied up to the terminal gate. The runway was close to the perimeter fence. We had to leave the airplane and walk fifty yards or so to enter the buildings. When we did, there was a group of protesters lined up along the fence, shouting obscenities at us.

I had heard stories of such things, but this was my first encounter with the peace-lovers. It wouldn't be my last. I would meet them many times on college campuses. There were at least forty unwashed hippy-types, carrying signs and giving us the finger as we left the airplane. They were far enough away that we couldn't hear everything they were shouting, but we certainly got the message. I still can't believe the Army let it happen.

I processed out of the Army the next day. As we were going through the routines, another First Lieutenant and I were taken into an office by ourselves, and there, an Army Major with a big patronizing smile offered us our Captain's bars if we would reenlist for just one more year. The Army was still hard-up for junior officers. We both smiled knowingly, and told the guy thanks, but no thanks.

My time to be a soldier was done. I had marched through the valley of the shadow and returned. I had charged the cannons and won a medal (Bronze Star – for the Xom Moi fight) to make my grandpa proud. I had passed through the mouth of hell and cheated the jaws of death. Now, I was ready to retire the tattered colors of the regiment and go home. Screw the King.

I caught a taxi to the Oakland Airport and bought a ticket for Salt Lake City. I had a couple of hours to kill before my flight took off, and for a while I just sat in the air terminal and watched. It was culture shock.

It was amazing to see people dressed in bright colors. In Vietnam, everyone dressed in olive green or black pajamas. In fact, everything in Vietnam was a varying shade of earth tone: green, gray, black, or brown. One seldom saw bright colors on anything.

Now, in California, fire engine red and canary yellow shocked my sensibilities. Bold, bright colors were everywhere, and somehow it seemed almost sinful to see people decorated with such colorful flamboyance. It would take a while to get used to it.

And, to a soldier boy just home from the war, the girls in the airport were a delight to behold. I had been around guys for way too long. Many of the women were wearing mini-skirts, makeup, and big, bouffant hairdos. They were beautiful creatures, and I sat for a long time and just watched them parade by. I hadn't seen anything like it for a long, long time.

Finally, I decided to go to the lounge and buy myself a welcome home drink. I didn't want to get drunk before going home, but a little buzz wouldn't hurt anything. I was officially off duty, a civilian still in uniform, and besides, I deserved it. I found the lounge to be dimly lit and almost empty. I sat down at the bar and ordered a drink.

The bartender was watching TV and polishing glasses with a towel. He gave me a patronizing sneer, and then he asked to see my ID card, "Sir."

I was shocked, both by his question, and by the manner in which he presented it. He was rude and condescending. And ... his disdainful use of the term "Sir," got my blood up.

I was embarrassed too. I was an Army Officer in full uniform, just off the plane from Vietnam. I had led men in mortal combat and served my country well. My ribbons and badges were there, on my chest, for all the world to see. And now, this snooty bartender was mocking me by requiring me to prove that I was an adult. The disrespect for me, as a person, and for the uniform I was wearing, made my heart hurt. But ... what the hell, I told myself, trying to find an excuse to give the man the benefit of the doubt: rules are rules. I swallowed my pride, painted on a placid face, and dug for my wallet. I had turned twenty-two just a couple of months earlier. I might have been baby-faced, but I was legal.

And then, a couple of guys started giggling behind me. The sound of it made the hair on the back of my neck stand up. I slowly turned to see, and discovered a couple of businessmen-types seated at a table just a few feet away. They were both young men, early thirties, in white shirts and ties. They were soft and fluffy individuals, mildly overweight with pink cheeks and potbellies - desk people obviously. They were grinning, winking, and nodding at each other, enjoying the show as the bartender gave the soldier a bad time. Neither had the courage to look me in the face. When I turned to them, they both quickly looked away. The valve on my adrenaline tank cracked open and my bloodstream started preparing for fight or flight.

I sat there and sipped at my drink for a while, listening to the giggles and muffled whispers behind me. I fanaticized about killing them both. I looked around and decided that the best weapon available would be a chair. If I moved fast, and caught them by surprise, I could probably break both of their heads before the cops got there.

But then, I wouldn't get home for a long time if I went to jail for aggravated assault in California. Jeannie was waiting for me in Salt Lake. This was not the hill to die on. I downed my drink and went back to the terminal. I could hear snickers and giggles as I walked away.

I was first in line to board the plane for Salt Lake. I picked a seat by the window with a good view. It was growing dark, but what the hell? And then, I noticed that no one wanted to sit next to me. People would walk up, pause, look me over, and then move on to somewhere else. It slowly dawned on me that it was the uniform they didn't like. My God, how things had changed while I was away. That plane was stuffed clear full of people, but the two seats next to me remained empty. It made me feel like an outcast.

As soon as the plane was airborne, I asked the stewardess for a drink. She brought me a mini-bottle filled with bourbon and a coke. I drank three or four or six of them between Oakland and Salt Lake. My sensibilities and my senses were numbed by the time the plane landed in Utah.

As I sat in the half-dark cabin of that airliner and watched city lights pass far below, I was only fifty hours out of the jungle. And, as I sat there, I discovered that I still had the red dirt of Lai Khe under my fingernails. I was embarrassed. Officers should be better groomed than that. In California, I had tried to scour the stink and the dirt of Vietnam from me, but soap and water was not enough. The stain of Vietnam was following me home.

Jeannie met me at the airport with my parents and we had a fine reunion. She was beautiful, and when I held her to me I couldn't hold the tears. I had made it. I had come back to her whole, alive, and with all of my moving parts. The nightmare was over. We could start our lives together.

We got home to our apartment about one o'clock in the morning. Jeannie got up at five and went to work. She was responsible for the payroll at the Green River Missile Base and she couldn't miss work on Mondays. As fate would have it, I got home on a Monday.

It was okay with me that she went to work. I didn't like it, but I understood. I too, was loyal to a fault. Maybe that's the reason we have had such a good marriage over all these many years. We both take our promises, and our commitments, very seriously.

I got up that first morning and ate breakfast alone. Later in the afternoon, I drove the sixty miles to the missile base and picked Jeannie up from work. She took the rest of the week off.

I ran into one of my old high school classmates on the steps of the Post Office that same morning. He told me all about his adventures at college, and about the good job he was trying to get. He never asked me about where I had been or what I had been doing. I started trying to tell him, but he had to go. He said maybe we could get together and talk some other time. I ran into that attitude a lot in the weeks, months, and years that followed.

Veterans of Foreign Wars

I had been home from Vietnam for only a few months when I received a card in the mail inviting me to join the Veterans of Foreign Wars. I was thrilled. If anyone understood the way I felt about the war, it would be other combat veterans. I needed the camaraderie and the sense of belonging.

I remembered back to the summer when I was fourteen and had played "Taps" on my trumpet while the VFW men fired a rifle salute to fallen comrades. I remembered how proud I had been to be a part of that ceremony. I remembered too, about watching those old soldiers march in parades under the billowing flags when I was a kid. It was something that had always made me proud to watch. I would be honored to be a part of it now. I had surely earned a place among those old soldiers.

On the appointed day, I went to the VFW hall to sign up. I was eager, and arrived a little early. There were three guys already there, all from my father's generation. They were sitting at a bar, drinking beer.

They turned to look at me as I entered the room, and one of them asked what it was I wanted. I told them I had come to join. They all just sat there for a moment, and then the guy who did the talking said, "You must be one of those Vietnam kids?" They all smiled. I was stunned.

There was an awkward pause. They didn't introduce themselves and no one asked my name. I wasn't invited to sit down, or to join them. And then, with a self-satisfied and patronizing air, the man said, "Everyone here was in The Big One - World War II."

The roof caved in on me. I couldn't believe it. I had come to expect that holier-than-thou attitude from the longhaired peaceniks out on the street, but to be ambushed and gut shot by my brothers-in-arms was beyond anything I could have imagined. I didn't see it coming. I would never have guessed.

I have wished in the years since, that I would have told them where to put "The Big One," but I was so taken by surprise that I reacted poorly. I stood there in stunned disbelief for a second or two, and then stammered something like, "Well ... maybe I'll come back another time." I turned and walked out of there, and never went back.

On March 29, 1973, the last American ground forces were pulled out of Vietnam. We had been there for eight long years. The fighting continued, but the full burden of the war was turned over to the South Vietnamese military. Richard Nixon called it the "Vietnamization" of the war.

As the last American soldiers withdrew, dark clouds gathered in a fretful Asian sky, a portent of storm and disaster. The King had given up the Holy Crusade and withdrawn his Knights to the shelter of his castle on the far side of the sea. Native stable boys and courtesans were left to face the wrath of the infidels alone.

We left the South Vietnamese with mountains of guns and military hardware, but their third-world economy could not maintain it without massive infusions of American aid. A grudging congress began to tighten the money spigots.

And, without the strong arm of the American military to lean on, the South Vietnamese were adrift without firm resolve or conviction. Their government and military were corrupt and in many ways incompetent. Years of following American soldiers into battle had not made them stronger. When they were called to lead the charge, they broke ranks and ran.

It was all over on April 30, 1975. Tanks flying the Viet Cong flag knocked down the gates of the American Embassy as Saigon became Ho Chi Minh City. I watched it happen on TV ... and I wept. I couldn't go to work that day. I went for a long walk in the Pinion and Juniper trees of Eastern Utah instead.

And then, in 1977, newly elected President Jimmy Carter kept a campaign promise and issued a blanket pardon to all of those who had dodged the draft during the Vietnam War. He also set in motion a policy where those who had deserted the armed forces during the war could have their dishonorable discharges expunged. He said it was time to put it all behind us and to "heal" the wounds of Vietnam.

By his actions, Jimmy Carter validated everything the anti-war protesters had said and done. By his measure, we who had answered our nation's call had been only fools. His decree told the world that Jane Fonda was right and I was wrong. In the eyes of Jimmy Carter and the majority of Americans who had elected him, the draft dodgers who ran and hid from the war were the heroes in the end. On TV, the haughty smirks of those returning from Canada told the whole story. They were welcomed home with cheers. It was a tough thing for those of us who had walked the Valley of the Shadow.

And so, ... a lingering question. Did my friends die in vain in Vietnam? I don't think so. Fighting for another man's freedom is noble, and that's what we were there to do - I heard Lyndon Johnson say it himself in a training film. As soldiers, we had no choice but to hope that it was true. We went to the jungle with faith in our country and with trust that we were involved in something that was honorable, even if we didn't fully understand it. We were there to oppose slavery and oppression, and at our moral core, I believe we were like the Grand Army of the Republic that fought for Abraham Lincoln.

It is true that our leaders were less than honest with us. The man who sent us there, and more than one of his successors, were unworthy to be Kings. But, as soldiers in the ranks, the vast majority of us served with honor and we are not stained by guilt or shame. We answered our nation's call. It was our duty and our moral obligation as citizens. If American involvement in Vietnam was misguided, the sin is not ours. Our hearts and our hands are clean. Those men of high rank and power will answer to God for the betrayal of our faith. And then too, there is satisfaction in knowing that we won every battle. It was others who lost our war ... not the soldiers who fought it.

And, in the big scheme of things, to die is something we are all destined to do. Most of us will die of disease, or in some tragic accident, or by simply wasting away with old age. Our death will be a matter of biological routine, something that doesn't matter to the rest of the world and in the end accomplishes nothing but to release us from this prison of earthly clay. My friends in Vietnam died differently. They died gallantly.

Like the police and EMS workers who charged up the stairs at the World Trade Center during 9-11, my friends in Vietnam gave their lives with courage and commitment. "Greater love hath no man than this, that a man lay down his life for his friends" (John 15:13). My friends died for each other, and they gave their lives to you and to me. They died serving their nation and their "friends and neighbors" who had sent them there. They went to God as brave and noble young soldiers, and I'm sure that God is proud of most of them. If their deaths are without merit, it is only because we do not honor their sacrifice.

Until July 1986, I felt an obligation to remember everything about Vietnam. I couldn't forget my friends who had died, I would betray them if I did. It is called survivor's guilt, and it was a burden to carry. I relived the war every month of every year. Every Memorial Day, Veteran's Day, and the somber anniversaries of battles and ambushes, I paid homage to the memory of those fallen soldiers.

Jeannie carried that burden with me, and she carried it for years. She supported me in my efforts and she was wonderful. She came to know those dark anniversaries too, and every year she gave me a special hug on the third of April and the fifth of May. She was kind and understanding when I needed to be alone on Veterans Day. I don't know what I would have done without her.

It all changed in July 1986 when something incredible happened. Jeannie, our four little boys and I, went camping on Elk Ridge in Southern Utah. The high desert forest was beautiful, and we camped out in the open air with no tent and no trailer. It was a clear moonlit night. Stars hung like diamonds in the clean, desert sky and the Milky Way was a shining mist of diamond dust that spanned the heavens. The whole world was quiet and peaceful as we slept out under the stars.

I lay awake for a long time that night looking up into the vastness of space and into God's eternity. Things were beautiful there. I drifted into sleep in perfect peace and contentment. My sweetheart and my sons were snuggled all around me. Life was good.

Sometime during that night, I had the most remarkable dream. I found myself in full military uniform: buttons, brass, and ribbons, and sitting at a great, rectangular table. The table was beautifully set with white linen, candles, crystal, and silver. The table and the chairs were made of beautiful, ornately carved wood, and a magnificent chandelier hung on golden chains above the table. I was sitting at the head of the table, in the place of honor.

All the other people seated around that table were American soldiers in full dress uniform. I couldn't make out their faces clearly, but I slowly came to realize that every man at that table was a soldier I had known to be killed in Vietnam. I was amazed, but I wasn't afraid. Those men were my friends.

A young soldier on my left stood and held his crystal goblet to propose a toast. We all stood and waited for his salutation. And then, the young man turned to me, and I recognized him as Sergeant Mobley, my track commander, and the man who had given me the yellow cavalry scarf. He held his crystal chalice out to me in a gentleman's salute. All the others at the table did the same. And then he said: "It's over now. You don't have to remember it anymore."

I awoke with a start. I found myself lying in the silver moonlight, looking up at the twinkling stars. It was the early hours of the morning and the world was dark and still. Jeannie and the boys were sleeping peacefully by my side.

I lay awake for a long time thinking about it. Was it a dream, or was it real? I wasn't sure. But then I decided that it really didn't matter what it was. It was real to me. What are dreams anyway? Are not some dreams as real as this fragile, mortal existence? Who knows where reality ends and the world of dreams begins? Perhaps life is just a dream. Life's experiences are different for each one of us. Life is full of different realities.

And, as I lay there looking up into God's forever, I realized that I had been given a gift. Real or not, I could put it all behind me now. I had been relieved of the burden of remembering all the details about Vietnam.

That amazing dream, that fallen soldier's salute, was a cleansing ritual for me. It was a formal release from active duty. From that night on, I didn't have to feel guilty about living while other soldiers had died. It was okay to live, and laugh, and love, and enjoy my life. Those good men had understood, and they let me know that it was okay.

I still honor those fallen soldiers, when and how I can, but it is not a burden to carry any longer. In the years since that dream, I have worn a little American flag on my lapel. That little flag represents Jenies Mobley, Howard Williams, Frank Serio, Jimmy McBroon, and all the others who gave that last full measure of devotion to their country in Vietnam. I wear that little flag to honor them.

I wear it too, to honor men like Captain Daniels, Jerry Poirier, Robert Ivie, Chester Housekeeper, Smokey Clark, and all the others who put everything on the line for their country in Vietnam ... and then came home again to lead good, decent, and productive lives.

Welcome home guys, and thank you for your service.

TM

Other works by the Author

The Split Sky:
A Journey of Discovery in Utah's Nine Mile Canyon.

The delightfully amusing tale of an innocent, sixteen-year-old boy (the author) who finagles a summer job as a cowboy on a large cattle ranch in 1963. It's a true story about open spaces, unexplored canyons and Indian ruins, a mountain lion chained to a barrel and an ocean of hay. It's about horses, dogs, wild animals, ghosts, snakes, grumpy old men and pretty girls. It's about growing up, overcoming adversity, and learning to walk tall. It's a powerful story, told with delectable humor, sharp wit, and deep emotion.

"...Written with a fine taste of sharp-lined humor, The Split Sky is one memoir that reads from cover to cover like a Hollywood adventure film come true."

- Midwest Book Review

ISBN: 0974156817 Southpaw Publications. Copyright 2002. 308 pages. Retail: $17.95
Available postage paid through Southpaw Publications for $17.95. 435-637-4544

White Canyon:
Remembering the Little Town at the Bottom of Lake Powell

An eyewitness account of things that were, and things that were lost. A true story about the author's family and others who were willing to gamble everything on a chance to find radioactive treasure in the red rock canyons of Southern Utah in the 1950s. It's a story about the background, mindset, aspirations, and heartbreaks of people who played a part in America's last "gold rush," the frantic search for yellow uranium. It is also a story about childhood, a dam, a lake, and a beautiful river canyon. White Canyon is written with deep feeling, thoughtful insights, subtle humor, and historic perspectives.

"... A fascinating book ... a treasure, a priceless cultural study of life and childhood in the 1950s, in a town and landscape now gone."

- The Times Independent

ISBN: 0874156809 Southpaw Publications. Copyright 2003. 225 pages. Retail: $14.95
Available postage paid through Southpaw Publications for $14.95. 435-637-4544

www.southpawpublications.net • tom@southpawpublications.net